NO LIFE JACKETS

TALKING HEADS TALKING ARMS

*Conversations about Canada's Armed Forces at the
Beginning of the 21st Century*

Volume 1

NO LIFE JACKETS

EDITED BY

JOHN WOOD

Benson & Hedges

BREAKOUT EDUCATIONAL NETWORK
IN ASSOCIATION WITH
DUNDURN PRESS
TORONTO ∞ OXFORD

Copyright © Breakout Educational Network, 2003

www.breakout-ed.net

Publisher: Inta D. Erwin
Copy-editor: Amanda Stewart, First Folio Resource Group
Designer: Bruna Brunelli, Brunelli Designs
Printer:Webcom

National Library of Canada Cataloguing in Publication Data

Talking heads talking arms/edited by John Wood.

Three of the 16vols. and 14 hours of video which make up the
    underground royal commission report
Includes bibliographical references and index.
Complete contents: v. 1. No life jackets—v. 2. Whistling past the
    graveyard—v.3. Playing the ostrich.
ISBN 1-55002-427-2 (v. 1).—ISBN 1-55002-428-0 (v. 2).—
ISBN 1-55002-429-9 (v. 3)

    1. Canada—Armed Forces 2. Canada—Military policy. 3. Canada—
Foreign relations. I. Wood, John. II. Title: Whistling past the
graveyard. III. Title: underground royal commission report.
IV. Title: No life jackets. V. Title: Playing the ostrich.

FC603.T34 2002   355'.033071   C2002-902307-6
F1028.T34 2002

1   2   3   4   5   07   06   05   04   03

Printed and bound in Canada.
Printed on recycled paper. ✿
www.dundurn.com

Exclusive Canadian broadcast rights for the *underground royal commission* report

intelligent television

Check your cable or satellite listings for telecast times

Visit the *urc* Web site link at:
www.ichanneltv.com

About the *underground royal commission* Report

Since September 11, 2001, there has been an uneasy dialogue among Canadians as we ponder our position in the world, especially vis à vis the United States. Critically and painfully, we are re-examining ourselves and our government. We are even questioning our nation's ability to retain its sovereignty.

The questions we are asking ourselves are not new. Over the last 30 years, and especially in the dreadful period of the early 1990s, leading up to the Quebec referendum of 1995, inquiries and Royal commissions, one after another, studied the state of the country. What *is* new is that eight years ago, a group of citizens looked at this parade of inquiries and commissions and said, "These don't deal with the real issues." They wondered how it was possible for a nation that was so promising and prosperous in the early 60s to end up so confused, divided, and troubled. And they decided that what was needed was a different kind of investigation — driven from the grassroots 'bottom,' and not from the top. Almost as a provocation, this group of people, most of whom were affiliated with the award winning documentary-maker, Stornoway Productions, decided to do it themselves — and so was born the *underground royal commission*!

What began as a television documentary soon evolved into much more. Seven young, novice researchers, hired right out of university, along with a television crew and producer, conducted interviews with people in government, business, the military and in all walks of life, across the country. What they discovered went beyond anything they had expected. The more they learned, the larger the implications grew. The project continued to evolve and has expanded to include a total of 23 researchers over the last several years. The results are the 14 hours of video and 16 books that make up the first interim report of the *underground royal commission*.

So what *are* the issues? The report of the *underground royal commission* clearly shows us that regardless of region, level of government, or political party, we are operating under a wasteful system ubiquitously lacking in accountability. An ever-weakening connection between the electors and the elected means that we are slowly and irrevocably losing our right to know our government. The researchers' experiences demonstrate that it is almost impossible for a member of the public, or in most cases, even for a member of Parliament, to actually trace how our tax dollars are spent. Most disturbing is the fact that our young people have been stuck with a crippling IOU that has effectively hamstrung their future. No wonder, then, that Canada is not poised for reaching its potential in the 21st century.

The *underground royal commission* report, prepared in large part by and for the youth of Canada, provides the hard evidence of the problems you and I may long have suspected. Some of that evidence makes it clear that, as ordinary Canadians, we are every bit as culpable as our politicians — for our failure to demand accountability, for our easy acceptance of government subsidies and services established without proper funding in place, and for the disservice we have done to our young people through the debt we have so blithely passed on to them. But the real purpose of the *underground royal commission* is to ensure that we better understand how government processes work and what role we play in them. Public policy issues must be understandable and accessible to the public if they are ever to be truly addressed and resolved. The *underground royal commission* intends to continue pointing the way for bringing about constructive change in Canada.

— Stornoway Productions

Books in the *underground royal commission* Report

14 hours of videos also available with the *underground royal commission* report.
Visit Stornoway Productions at www.stornoway.com for a list of titles.

TABLE OF CONTENTS

FOREWORD

"I'm feelin' blue 'cause they've turned my navy green."
Lyric from a mid-1960s cabaret song

The conversations in *Talking Heads Talking Arms* originated as interviews collected for a documentary television series, *A Question of Honour*, which is currently being prepared for broadcast by the Breakout Educational Network and Stornoway Productions. The interviews were recorded periodically between 1994 and early 2002 and focus on the Canadian military since World War II, with an emphasis on the period following the cold war and the collapse of the Berlin Wall. The year of the interview is noted at the beginning of each conversation.

Because our soldiers are currently front and centre in Afghanistan, the media, and therefore the public, is at the moment more aware of the activities of our Armed Forces than usual, or at least some of our Forces. We forget, or we don't even know, that we have soldiers stationed in many other parts of the world as well. These troops are working hard, living in difficult environments, and are often caught up in situations just as dangerous as those our troops are facing near the Afghanistan–Pakistan border. We have not really heard much about most Canadian soldiers in similar circumstances over the past 10 years; unless, of course, they have been involved in some kind of trouble, scandal or other public relations disaster.

My earliest memories of war, or rather the talk of war, come from the radio. About the time that I began to differentiate between *Fibber McGee and Molly* and the CBC news, I knew something very serious was going on somewhere "over there."

I clearly recall a Sunday lunchtime in our kitchen when I heard that something shocking and quite terrifying had happened. My father pulled down the atlas from the bookcase to show me that Hawaii was far away and that I needn't worry.

Fifteen years later, when I started university, I joined the University Naval Training Divisions (UNTD) at HMCS Donnacona in Montreal. This was 1956 and the Suez crisis was smouldering in the Middle East. Now, the Suez crisis didn't particularly bother or even interest me. I didn't join the military because I wanted to go off to war; I joined because I wanted to see the world. And it had to be the navy rather than army or air force because my family members were maritimers and I was enchanted by the sea.

The UNTD was the reserve version of the ROTP, the Regular Officer Training Program, both of which disappeared in the early 1970s. We trained one evening a week during the winter, spent our summers at HMCS Stadacona in Halifax or HMCS Naden in Victoria, and early each summer we were assigned to a ship. We were sort of reserve midshipmen, officers in the making, but we were also the lowest of the low and required to do many of the unofficer-like chores of an ordinary seaman, like scrub out the "head" during a north Atlantic gale.

We were commonly referred to by more tolerant full-time sailors as "Untidies."

On the West Coast, if we were lucky, we'd head for Hawaii. If not, it would be the Queen Charlotte Islands. I was lucky. I went to Hawaii.

As we sailed into Pearl Harbor, we passed the USS *Arizona* sticking out of the water, still lying where she had been sunk on December 7, 1941.

I suddenly remembered where I had been sitting on that distant Sunday morning, looking at a map when I was three. I was now 19 and I knew where Hawaii was, and it wasn't very far away at all. After that, being in the Royal Canadian Navy was no longer just a summer job and a chance to see the world.

When I left the navy and graduated from university my life, for a while, took me away from Canada. When I got home the Canadian military was turning green. I began to lose faith in the government as the military I had known disappeared.

As an adult I have devoured books about war, directed plays and films about war and written a play and a screenplay about British soldiers in Egypt during World War II. But I had not kept up, until this project came along, with what had been happening to the military in Canada. When I was asked to screen these interviews for the series, I realized that I had almost lost touch with the military world in the last 30 years. These new conversations, with a broad range of people, revealed a military I had little knowledge of. I had heard about cover-ups and scandals and watched some of the Somalia inquiry, but beyond the headlines I didn't know much about what the military was doing, and more importantly what the government wasn't doing. These conversations gave me an extraordinary insight into the workings not just of our Armed Forces, but of our country.

What we have in these three volumes is a relatively complete record of many of these conversations. The interview questions have been cut out and, as interviews can often wander from topic to topic and back again, repetitions, false starts and stutters have been excised and the conversations have generally been tightened. I have tried to keep the "voice" of the speaker intact, and I suggest that the reader "listen to" rather than simply "look at" the text.

Although there is a logic to their order, these conversations needn't be read one after the other in succession. Finding a sequence was a long and difficult process, but an order eventually seemed to emerge on its own. The conversations in *No Life Jackets* are all with serving or retired soldiers, sailors or airmen; those in *Whistling Past the Graveyard* deal mainly, but not exclusively, with our activities in the 1990s in Somalia and Rwanda; *Playing the Ostrich* takes a broader look at the Canadian

Forces and government policies from the widely differing views of people within the political, academic, military and diplomatic worlds.

After I had completed work on these pieces and was preparing the glossary and appendices, I asked an interested and worldly friend to have a look at them. He said that reading the conversations alternately enraged and humiliated him and asked, "Why didn't I know about this?" I am not assuming that other members of the Canadian public have remained as ignorant as we have over the years about the topics covered here, but I am sure that a lot of the facts and opinions expressed in these conversations will come as a surprise to many.

There is a fourth book in this series of conversations about the Canadian military called *The Chance of War*, in which soldiers talk about their experiences in Bosnia and Croatia and the homecoming after their tours. They know first hand the consequences of some of the decisions that are examined in these books, decisions taken by their government, acting for the Canadian people. I hope that these discussions will enlighten those who read them and contribute something to the growing need to discard our bunker mentality and bring everything into the open.

John Wood
Stratford, Ontario
March 2002

"I figured, if I'm going to be in the army, the infantry's where it's at. The 'No Life Like It' campaign didn't really influence us that much. We used to say there are 'No Life Jackets.'"

Howard Michitsch

PART ONE

NICK STETHEM
Captain (Retired)
1994

As a young officer Nick Stethem served in Germany in the early 1960s when 4 Brigade was at the height of its capabilities as the "most professional component of the British Army of the Rhine." Later, as an army captain with the 4 CMBG in Germany, he felt that the government's policies were putting the lives of the soldiers under his command at risk. In 1974 he resigned. In private life, as a strategic advisor and military counsellor to business, Nick continued to speak out publicly, often as a military analyst on television, and participated in the process that led to the defence white papers in 1987 and 1994. He was president of the Royal Canadian Military Institute when he died in 1998.

My father was in the military. My grandfather was in the military. My great-grandfather. And so on. As far back as we're able to go, certainly as far back as Cromwell, we were military men in one form or another. I joined the army in 1964. I went to Collège militaire royal de St-Jean and then on to RMC, graduating in 1969.

My first real work with the army, as opposed to training, was three months with the Royal 22nd Regiment in Germany in 1968. Then after graduation in 1969 I was posted to 2 Commando of the Canadian Airborne Regiment. I spent three years with the Airborne Regiment in Edmonton and was then posted to 3 Mechanized Commando in Germany in 1972, where I remained until 1974 when I resigned from the Armed Forces and went into civilian life.

The reason my career, or the career that I had planned, was cut short was because I disagreed profoundly with the defence policy of the day. At the time I wrote a long memorandum of resignation explaining why, and then spent several months speaking to senior officers explaining the basis of the memorandum. But fundamentally defence policy had become a fraud and I found it extremely difficult to tell my troops that tomorrow it was going to get better, that should anything happen we would be able to do the job when I knew for a fact that we couldn't do the job and that tomorrow things were not at all likely to get better.

The response to my memo of resignation was most interesting because as I went up the line to a more and more senior level in order to explain what I was saying, I found a general agreement. In other words, no one actually disagreed with what I was saying. Some tried to convince me to stay in but most said that in fact they themselves might follow the same course or might have followed the same course were it not for the fact that they were married and had children or had X number of years in. Or still had something that I did not, which was a faint hope of being able to change things.

I think I hoped in some small way, perhaps vainly, that my resignation would make a small point. It seemed to me at the time, and I was very young then, that the generals weren't resigning in protest, so I, as a young captain, would resign in protest, and as I say, I had the vain hope that that might actually mean something. When I left the army I had absolutely no intention of being involved in things military or questions of defence policy. I had absolutely no intention of taking the argument public. I simply wanted to be done with it because I was extremely angry.

In 1968 I spent three months in northern Germany with 4 Brigade (with the Royal 22nd Regiment) at a time when that brigade was a fully equipped mechanized brigade holding a part of the frontline on the north German plain as a part of the British Army of the Rhine. There was absolutely no question of the capability of the brigade. There was no question of its role, of its critical role in the defence of Germany. And it was a highly respected unit.

When I went back in 1972 for a two-year posting, the brigade had been moved to southern Germany. It had been reduced to the point that it could not survive on the battlefield, sitting in a reserve position on the French border about as far away from the battlefront as you could get and still be in Germany, wondering on a day-to-day basis how many men it would lose in the next cut, what equipment it would have, what its role would be in the event of war. It was a unit that, despite the good intentions of all those within it, could not be taken seriously. It was a sad shadow. All of this was done as a result of the changes that took place during unification in the late 1960s and the defence review that took place at that time, probably predicated on the idea that there wasn't going to be a war anyway. And we wanted to save money.

Mind you, we wanted to remain members of NATO, that's why we left this shadow of a brigade there. That was necessary if we wanted to keep a place at NATO's table.

Our allies harboured no illusions about the reality of Canada's commitment and its capability. They were sympathetic on a military level because they recognized that Canada's soldiers, sailors and airmen were having to live in difficult times. But on a political level, beyond the niceties of diplomacy, it was a joke.

Very little has changed since 1974. I'm still angry, although perhaps that anger is tempered by a little experience, and I hope a little wisdom. I understand now why Canadian defence policy has been such a persistent failure since the mid-1960s. When I resigned from the army I didn't understand that and it took quite a few years of battling away over questions of defence and foreign policy in Canada before I began to understand where we'd originally gone off the rails.

Post-War and After
Essentially what Canada did in the late 1940s was build a position based upon what it had done in the Second World War. Canada was then a powerful state. You could argue perhaps the third or fourth most

19

powerful state then standing up after World War II, and we managed to get ourselves at the high table of NATO in a very powerful position. And we sustained that in fairly reasonable form until the mid-1960s.

About that time we tried to have it both ways. We decided that we would keep our place at the high table of NATO while steadily reducing the armed force on the argument that really there wasn't going to be another war, so what did it matter what was really there. So long as we kept up appearances, it really didn't matter if we had the real capability because a war wasn't going to happen. The world was nuclear daggers drawn and the idea of soldiers clashing on a battlefield was seen to be out of date. The unfortunate thing is that just after the time that we had come to that conclusion, the theories of grand strategy changed, and suddenly conventional forces became important again and we began a process of trying to cover up our deficiencies. And that went on for the next 20 years.

There was some rebuilding under the Liberal and Conservative governments beginning in the late 1970s, early 1980s, but that was an attempt at a stopgap. What was missing was a sense of what defence was all about, what Canadian foreign policy was all about, and I suppose that connects to the national confusion of what Canada is all about and where we fit in the world. It's really when you go back that far, behind the arguments, that you begin to understand why you cannot generate what would seem to be a logical and reasonable foreign and defence policy.

If you looked to the exercise in Germany, you'd see the armoured personnel carriers roll across the field behind the tanks. What you wouldn't see is the slow erosion of the troops inside the armoured personnel carriers. The slow wearing away of the equipment itself, the armoured personnel carriers and the tanks with them. What you wouldn't see is the fact that the artillery on an exercise would be limited in the number of rounds. In the mid-1970s we ran out of ammunition for training the Armed Forces. There wasn't any at one point.

It was attempting to maintain a position without paying the freight, attempting to maintain the power without making the effort that power demands. It's rather like trying to hide the signs of age and decline behind makeup. What we tried to do was to maintain a façade of ability without the substance.

I suppose when you really get down to it, one of the fundamental flaws that we have to deal with is a feeling on the part of some Canadians that Canada has power for some reason other than the effort it makes in the world — as though Canadian power stems from a native niceness and from a natural fount of good ideas found among Canadian civil servants, or somewhere in the national identity. And these ideas can be given to the United Nations or to NATO and put to good use in the world.

Has this pretence fooled anybody? No. Not at all. Well, yes, it has fooled some people — Canadians. Canadians actually have come to believe a myth about their own position in the world. The unfortunate thing is that politically the myth can be quite useful. You can convince the Canadian populace that Canada's government is actually deploying power in the world based upon this niceness when in fact the power of Canada in the world has eroded consistently since the late 1960s. I suppose the irony is that the foreign policy review undertaken by Pierre Trudeau was a tremendously ambitious attempt to build a better position for Canada in the world, even though in the end you could argue, historically, that it failed. In fact, it is at that point that Canada's position in the world began to grow weaker.

Analyzing Foreign Policy

The apparent aversion to an understanding of the utility of force and the realities of international power that seems to exist in large parts of the Canadian foreign policy debate comes from a number of sources. The first is perhaps the fact that Canada tried to reinvent itself in the 1960s. We tried to move away from imperial history and a position in the world in which force was an accepted matter of fact into a world which, if not a product of the age of Aquarius, certainly offered new approaches to power, new avenues to power. Now, you can see why this might be important with the decline of empire and the growth of the power of the United States. Here we are sitting next to the fellow who absolutely dominates in terms of traditional power, whether you measure it in economic or military or in terms of political elbowing out there in the world. Cultural power as well.

So what we were perhaps looking for were new ways to define power, new avenues to develop influence. That process — combined with the philosophical baggage that came along at the time at which we were reinventing ourselves, changing the ministry of this and the ministry of that into this or that, with a new logo and a new flag — was being undertaken at a time when people were assuming that the world had changed. A not unfamiliar sort of thought. Again today we're assuming the world has changed. It's unfortunate that those ideas eroded what was something that is fundamental to any understanding of Canadian power or the requirement for power on the part of Canada.

The difficulty for Canada is that military power is not historically central to the Canadian identity in the way that it is in the United States. The military was a part of the creation of the United States. For Canada the military was something that was a product of empire. In fact, as much as we could we wanted someone else to do it for us and the British did for a long time and some would argue that the Americans have been doing it for us since the British stopped. So military power was not central to the Canadian identity.

Second, there was no real threat. Once the United States had become an ally we did not have a threat. The idea of the Russians coming over the Pole is simply too remote for words. The idea of anybody sailing across a major ocean and dropping an armoured column on the Canadian coast is nonsense. So there's no immediate threat. What in fact you end up having to do in order to understand, on a street level in Canada, why defence is required is to go through a fairly sophisticated argument about one's position in the world, about the need for influence to support questions of trade and to support questions of diplomacy. You have to have people understand that all of the dimensions of a nation's international character are all part of a single spectrum. It's not simply a question of defence here, foreign policy here, trade there. All of these things happen, if you like, in the same room.

When I was in Brussels once, years ago, we were trying to withdraw from NATO and at the same time to get a special arrangement with the European Community for trade. An old friend of the family, a senior British Army officer, said to me in a corridor, "Don't your people understand that Brussels is a small town?" NATO headquarters and the European Community headquarters are both in Brussels, and here we were trying to withdraw from one, cut them loose, and going up to the other and grovelling for a better position. It simply did not make sense.

For someone to understand that interrelationship requires a fairly sophisticated understanding of the way the world works. For a European the question of the requirement for defence, the requirement for the use of power in foreign policy, comes with all of the history that surrounds Europeans. The questions are not remote. They're as close as walking across a battlefield at Waterloo or seeing the damage to the cathedral in Cologne. For Canadians, though, those things are remote. That element of history is distant from our own shores. What is required for Canadians is the development of a fairly sophisticated public argument that brings the ideas out, that allows people to develop an understanding of why we have defence in the first place, before we get down to debating whether or not we need ships or tanks or airplanes. In the mid-1980s the government accepted that this sort of a discussion was required and decided to produce a green paper on national defence that would create this kind of public argument. We would develop the sophistication upon which you could then develop the white paper arguments.

In 1984, 1985, I wrote a green paper for the Department of National Defence which was designed to develop a public argument. It was simply designed to get the argument to a stage where one could then discuss what was required politically for a white paper. In other words, bring the public along so that we could really get a sense of what sort of support there was for defence policy and for specific directions in policy. At the time the government accepted the argument that this would be a good thing.

But as the government encountered more and more political problems, I suspect that the idea of developing a defence argument on top of various scandals that were going on at the time seemed rather like political overload. The argument was also made by the new defence minister, Erik Nielsen, that defence was the prerogative of the government and that public argument was inappropriate and that we should go straight to a white paper.

Unfortunately the white paper did not appear until three years later and the response to that white paper made it obvious that an educational argument was absolutely necessary for Canadians to be able to understand why the government was making these various moves. Without a process of argument from the fundamentals, from the basic understanding of why we need defence in the first place and what it's all about, without that argument building up to a fairly sophisticated level, you could not approach the questions of defence in Canada.

One of the things that has always concerned me is the question of whether or not such an argument is really in the interests of politicians, senior civil servants and perhaps even the generals who are concerned with the defence debate. You could make an argument that a sophisticated under-standing of defence in Canada would be incredibly counterproductive because that would then create a demand for a realistic policy, which would then create a need for real defence spending, something that the government simply is not prepared to deal with. If you have a sophisti-cated understanding of defence in Canada, you are faced with a require-ment to meet the real demands of Canada's position in the world, to in fact get out there and spend, to create the kind of force that Canada requires to develop the influence that it should have and that it needs to survive.

To a large degree Canada's bluff has been called. Unfortunately it's been called out there in the real world and the fact that it's been called is not visible to most Canadians. Most Canadians assume that we've been out there doing a good job. Canadians believe that we've been doing our bit. There we are in the Balkans. There we were in the Gulf.

The Gulf
The worst example of politically trying to manipulate the situation is found in the Gulf War. We sent ships to the Gulf with the intent of not allowing them anywhere near the actual potential naval combat. We sent two squadrons of fighters to the Gulf, and then held them back from operational commitment at any level where they were at risk or at risk of doing any damage themselves until the very last few days of the war. We failed to send ground troops based on the argument that we didn't have the troops in Canada or they had other commitments or we couldn't get them there from Canada, when in fact we had a brigade group sit-ting in Germany that was capable of going, that was ready to go and would have gone riding the coattails of the American forces, which were also deployed out of Germany.

Of course, had we sent that brigade, we would not then have been able to finesse the situation because that brigade would have probably been a part of the British division and would not have been able to avoid fighting. We sent people to the Gulf with the definite intention of sending people to war but ensuring that they didn't fight. We sent forces to the Gulf in order to take part, but then made sure that they were never at risk either of being shot themselves or of killing anyone else.

The Gulf War was an attempt to have it both ways. I suppose it really typifies Canadian defence policy. We wanted to be there but we didn't want to pay the freight. We wanted to be part, but we didn't want the pain; therefore we sent forces to the Gulf to take part but not to fight. We sent ships to the Gulf and then made sure that, instead of turning north to take a turn on the picket up in the northern end of the Gulf, they turned south to run the warehouse, where there was no threat. We sent fighter planes to the Gulf, and then we made sure that the fighter planes were always one stage of operations back from the action. As soon as there was no threat to the fleet, we put our fighter planes over the fleet protecting them. As soon as there was no high-level air defence left, we put our fighters in as high-level air defence, high-level defence for the fighter-bombers that were going in low.

The political aim, so far as I could understand it, of sending the Forces to the Gulf was to show Canadians that we were out there and willing to participate with our allies but to avoid Canadians having to see our troops being injured or our troops doing any killing. It was all upside. Not only did we go to war in the Gulf and participate with everybody else, at least according to the word from Ottawa, but at the same time there weren't going to be any body bags coming home, we weren't going to lose any equipment and there wouldn't be any pictures of Canadians killing anybody. Just perfect. An absolutely perfect military operation from government's point of view. Now, mind you, for our allies it was a totally transparent fraud. So the only people who were fooled by this were Canadians.

The fall after the War I was in Zurich at a meeting of the International Institute for Strategic Studies, and I ended up drinking in a café with a group of Royal Air Force officers and some other senior allied officers. We were talking and suddenly someone yelled out a joke: "How many awards for valour did Canada give out in the Gulf War?" And the punch line was general laughter. That was one of the most unpleasant moments of my life, but it sums up what we really did in the Persian Gulf.

Canada lost a lot of mileage in the Gulf War. It was an attempt at a political finesse that failed. Our allies saw straight through it. The unfortunate thing is the Canadians didn't.

I don't think what really happened in the Gulf is understood by the Canadian people, in part because there is a general lack of understanding of what defence means. You don't have the sort of sophistication of defence columnists in the local paper. You don't even have correspondents on a normal basis covering the Canadian Forces in the field. I get my news out of Bosnia, my television news from the BBC, and I watch British troops doing their bit, or French troops doing their bit. I don't know whether the CBC even bothers to send people up with the Canadian troops. I suppose because so little information comes back to the Canadian people about what is actually going on, it is then possible for the government to stand, as it did during the Gulf War, and say, "Look, we've got two ships out there and a couple of squadrons of fighters, and we're right in there."

Now, the fact that the two ships are counting socks down in the south end of the Gulf and doing a good job, that's a valuable job, but it's not the same as taking a turn up at the front end, up in the north end of the Gulf. And we have two squadrons of fighters there. Doing backup for everybody else who's actually fighting. Again, a useful job but it brings you no kudos. If we had simply taken one of the ships and put it up in the frontline to do, let's say, a week's duty and then gone back to counting socks, that might have made the point that we were willing to share the risk. But the simple fact was, in the Gulf we didn't want to risk. The government, or someone advising the government, came up with this brilliant strategy of being able to go to war and avoid war in exactly the same moment.

When people raise internal security problems like Oka and the difficulty of shipping troops from Canada and whether or not we should have sent a brigade group to the Gulf, they're in fact talking nonsense because the brigade group we would have sent to the Gulf was the European-based brigade group, which would probably have been fit into a British division. That brigade group would have ridden on the coattails of the massive American redeployment from Europe to the Gulf, with support available from people like the Germans and even the Japanese, who could not actually partake in the conflict but were looking for ways to contribute. There were ways to do it and with troops that were in fact not available in Canada.

Therefore, the kinds of arguments one might make about the inability to transport, lack of availability, are arguments that I would question strongly. At the time I believe that the recommendations that went forward to the war Cabinet of the day were, from the military side, that the brigade group could be sent, and from the External Affairs side, that it would be a good idea for the brigade group to go. In talking to friends I found out, though, that when recommendations came back to Defence, they were that External Affairs had said it wasn't a good idea to send the brigade group, and back to External that Defence had said it wasn't capable of sending the brigade group.

So you had, based on the information that I was privy to at the time, a decision to try to avoid sending the one element that would actually have had to go into battle, that would have generated risk of a bad outcome in the Gulf, but which was also the one element that would have given Canada a major play in the Gulf conflict. As it turns out, since the Gulf conflict was over so quickly and with such a low level of casualties, it would have been for Canada a very cheap exercise.

Peacekeeping
Canada continues to have a vision of peacekeeping that in fact died some time between the Congolese operation at the beginning of the 1960s and the Nigerian civil war at the end of the 1960s, when the international community was unable to sort itself out and insert peacekeeping troops. Peacekeeping changed into something else entirely once the Berlin Wall had fallen and Glasnost had occurred in the Soviet Union. It became possible to deploy forces on peace operations that involved the whole spectrum of problems that we simply weren't prepared to deal with in our vision of peacekeeping.

We had this vision of troops who would stand between two enemies, convince them to be reasonable, pat them on the head and send them on their way, giving both sides a degree of security knowing that the fellows in the blue berets were in the middle. One such operation went on for a long time and that was Cyprus. Well, there aren't any operations going on at the moment that I can think of that are like that. Now they're bloody and violent ... an attack on a UN convoy in Mogadishu that was repelled by armour and four helicopter gunships ... a French armoured vehicle attacked by four rocket-propelled grenades in Bosnia, responded to by NATO aircraft. In Bosnia the British are dealing with plans for a fighting withdrawal from Bosnia that involves between 10,000 and 14,000 troops with armour and artillery. The secretary-general of the UN told the Security Council that it might be necessary to have a fighting withdrawal from Bosnia that would involve forces other than UN forces, presumably NATO in large numbers and with heavy equipment. I look at all of this and at the Canadian troops in Bosnia and wonder what our plans are for a fighting withdrawal. I wonder which tanks we're going to use.

But we don't have tanks. There is the problem.

Canada no longer has the kind of army that is designed to do precisely what everyone is going to have to do if a fighting withdrawal takes place from Bosnia. We don't have the tanks. We do still have the artillery, but we don't have infantry fighting vehicles. We've allowed that sort of equipment to decay and rather than replace it, we have created visions of a future that allows us to have progressively lighter armed forces. It's rather like being a trucker, and you drive a big 18-wheeler, and as that starts to break down you realize you're gonna have to get a new truck. So you get a slightly smaller truck and you convince yourself that trucking has changed as a business. Eventually you work yourself down to carrying parcels in a Volkswagen while 18-wheelers are passing you on the 401.

The fact that we put our soldiers at risk is fair enough. Soldiers are paid to be at risk. Where we break faith with the soldiers is when we pretend that we don't need to give them a particular piece of equipment because the world has changed. When we pretend they are not under the degree of threat that they are under, if we decide to make a policy decision for the soldier to go into Bosnia armed with a broom handle and that's what Canada wants, then that's the soldier's job. But if we say that the soldier can go into Bosnia with a broom handle and be perfectly safe, that is profoundly dishonest and a betrayal of the soldier.

I would say that we are sitting on the edge of a major betrayal of the soldier in the field. We can perhaps find excuses for the pretence that has gone on for the past 30 years, all sorts of political and historic excuses.

But now with people actually at risk in the field, the time for those excuses is gone. We could argue in, say, 1970 that there never was going to be a conflict, so really, did it matter whether the soldiers had X amount of armour or Y amount of armour? We could argue in the 1980s that it was really all academic if we bought this or that piece of new capital equipment. For all sorts of extremely good reasons, at least in the eyes of those making the excuses, things were put off because nothing was going to happen tomorrow. "We'll re-equip the navy and we'll re-equip the air force, but the army can wait." Well, those excuses aren't there anymore. The problem is real. The army is out there in the field and it can't wait.

The Defence Debate

In the past 20 years I think I've been before between eight and a dozen committees. I've consulted for two different political parties, each of which took its turn in government. I have consulted for several different governments on the issues involved in understanding why Canada needs to develop a realistic defence policy to deal with the world out there.

We have several different defence processes going on at the moment. We've got a Commons/Senate committee attempting to look at defence policy and a defence white paper being prepared by the deputy minister from National Defence and his staff, in parallel with the parliamentary committee. The parliamentary committee is going around the country to solicit ideas and consult with the people, but officials in the Department of National Defence are writing the defence white paper. This is the actual document that will present the government's idea of where we should go in the future.

If you look at the calendar for delivery dates of the committee report and the defence white paper and allow for such things as translation, printing and all the sort of bureaucratic elements that go into the production of a white paper, it becomes highly dubious whether or not the parliamentary committee will have any input into the white paper since the white paper will be effectively complete before the parliamentary committee begins to draw its conclusions and write its report. I believe that the minister, David Collenette, is sincere when he says he wants to go out and consult. And that is exactly what he's doing. He is speaking to those involved in the defence debate across this country.

Unfortunately that intent is insufficient to overcome the bureaucratic machine which will produce a white paper, whatever the committee finds out and whatever the minister finds out. I am not suggesting the minister doesn't have power over the white paper, but what I am suggesting is that he will have far less influence than the strategies of the senior civil servants who are actually producing it.

A Nice or a Niche Role for Canada

One of the elements in the debate over Canada's involvement in the world and in peacekeeping is the search, on the part of those who would simply like to see a niche role for Canada, for something that allows for a very low price to get maximum influence. There are also those who, philosophically, would like to see the world as a more peaceful place than it really is and therefore create a vision of the world and an armed force to suit that vision, which is totally unrelated to reality. In other words, those who would have a constabulary force, lightly armed, to whip out there to save the day for the UN secretary-general. They really have no knowledge of what is happening in Bosnia or Somalia or Haiti or in any of the UN operations in recent years. Those operations demand backup of heavy forces.

Perhaps the people that upset me the most are those who suggest that Canada should not only be the idea man coming up with all the good ideas that everyone else will then carry the freight for, but that Canada should be the one who provides the brains behind the operation, that Canada should be out there providing the computers and the communications and the good thought that will allow all those nations that are well stocked with happy peasants to go out there and bleed on the United Nations battlefields. I find that profoundly immoral. And not simply immoral, but also highly conceited.

This vision of a niche role, of providing brains rather than guns, is an attempt to find a high-impact, low-cost contribution to international security, to United Nations operations and to any alliances we belong to. If we can find a niche role that we can fill that is inexpensive but vitally important, then that is the perfect solution for Canada. The problem is that in all of these operations, the single most important niche, the one that is the ultimate leveller, is that of the foot soldier out in front. If you aren't taking part in that role, then the rest simply does not matter. You're not sharing the risk. It is the risk that is the highest contribution that you make. That counts more than dollars and that counts more than brains.

The vision of Canadians having a unique role in the world, being uniquely nice, uniquely acceptable, is a vision that is apparent only to Canadians. Internationally it is simply not there. It is true that we are a relatively harmless people. We don't carry a lot of political or ideological baggage and therefore we're acceptable in most places. We really aren't out to hurt anybody, politically, economically, socially or philosophically. That makes us safe, but that does not give us a positive benefit. That's a negative. We are not offensive.

But you can't build an international position around the fact that you're not offensive. We have to get out there and do something positive. We're judged, not by our niceness, but by our actions; not by the fact that we're willing to stand there, but by what we're willing to do; not by the fact that we're willing to wear the blue beret of the UN or stand up and make speeches in the General Assembly, but what we're willing to actually put at risk and put on the ground. And that's what counts in measuring us.

There was a time when the statement "Canada has a small but good army" figured in nearly every discussion of the NATO alliance. That reaches back into the 1960s, but it died very quickly in the 1970s and 1980s. Yes, we have well-trained people, but the value of that training becomes moot if the tools aren't there to use the training. Being able to say, "My gosh, the Canadian Forces are extremely good individually," becomes a backhanded compliment when you can't put those individuals together into formations that are actually useful in undertaking a job in the field.

So all of the compliments and fine words about individual Canadian soldiers, sailors and airmen are so much hot air if the sum of all of those soldiers, sailors and airmen really comes to naught because the equipment is not there, because the structure is not there, because the support is not there and because the money is not there. It doesn't matter how good the individuals are if the sum of the individuals does not produce some real effect out in the world. Who cares how good the individuals are if their sum means nothing?

When I try to understand how it must be for those who sit on a defence committee, for those who wear generals' uniforms, or for those who are senior civil servants responsible for the development of this kind of policy, I suppose I'm biased. Years ago I resigned because the policy was a failure. But I cannot understand how one can go on for year after year, for committee of inquiry after committee of inquiry, for failed defence white paper after failed defence white paper, and still carry on with some sort of rationalization that eventually it's going to get better, that we'll just go through this exercise one more time and perhaps the next time we'll be able to fix it. Perhaps at some point in the future, if this committee doesn't do it, we'll still fight the good fight and the next committee will do it.

Now, a parliamentarian can carry on and say, "Well, by staying in the system, that gives me the opportunity to change it next time." For a general: "If I stay on then perhaps in my next job I'll be able to turn it around." As a senior civil servant, one can somehow juggle one's priorities so that you can ignore soldiers at risk in the Balkans, or helicopters that you were going to use for medevac but are now probably more dangerous than leaving the patient lying on the ground. How it's possible to just allow that situation to go on and go on is an enormous question. You begin to wonder after a while just how long it goes on before someone stands up and says, "This is a load!"

As someone who sits on the outside but is occasionally involved, I've reached a point where I want to chuck it all and say, "Done with it, finished!" I want nothing further to do with the issue because I've failed. For 20 years I have failed to change defence policy, to influence it such that the position of those soldiers that I talked to on the day that I resigned, and explained why I was resigning, hasn't improved a jot. And that's my failure.

The failure of those sitting on parliamentary committees is sitting still when the ideas of parliamentary committees are not implemented or overridden by other priorities. The failure of the generals is that they continue to wear the uniform when they recognize in their heart of hearts that the position of their soldiers is reaching a point of absurdity, in terms of risk. And the failure of senior civil servants, who have developed an influence over areas of foreign and defence policy is, I suppose, the foul conscience of allowing other career imperatives to influence decisions that will put human beings, who must be to them faceless, at risk.

CHARLES "CHUCK" THOMAS
Vice-Admiral (Retired)
1994

*J*oining the RCN as an engineering cadet in 1954, Vice-Admiral
(Ret) Chuck Thomas rose to command Canada's navy in the
late 1980s. He then became vice-chief of the defence staff, a position he held during the Gulf War. In 1992 he resigned, publicly
declaring that the defence budget was unrealistic for the demands
the government was making of the Canadian Forces. He now lives
in Victoria where he remains active in the defence debate through
the Defence Associations National Network, a policy and educational interest group.

There was a change in attitude amongst the people as time passed during my career. Mostly it was not a difference in morale, not a difference
in enthusiasm, but a concern for the equipment they had to work with
when they contrasted that with the jobs they were being asked to do.
Clearly, over the period of my service, we got smaller, we got less capable
and our equipment got ever older.

Equipment

The Armed Forces are a very technological business. You can't survive in the world that they're being asked to live in with simple spears and enthusiasm when the other guy has capable modern equipment. Certainly in the last 20 years we've seen the relative level of our techno-logical capability decline, and very little will to do much about it. When I speak of will, I'm talking about political will. You have to invest 30 percent of your budget in order to keep the equipment the Armed Forces own technologically up to date.

I spent about 10 years of my career involved, in a central way, in the naval re-equipment program and, relatively, we were successful. The new ships are now coming on-line. But you've got to remember that they were taken to Cabinet for decision in 1977 and they are just now arriving in service. Seventeen years from when the government made the decision to go ahead with the program till the ships are being delivered, and there were five or six years of work preparatory to that decision, before 1977.

The corvettes of World War II were sufficient unto the task they had then — maybe just. But they aren't any use in today's world. The frigates that have been delivered are world-class general-purpose vessels. But if you're going to do in Canada what we did in the production of those frigates, you start by setting up the industries to produce them. They didn't exist before the frigate decision was made. It takes a long time, the way the Canadian government is structured, to reach a decision to spend $8 billion.

The decision was reached and the frigates are being delivered. Before that the air force had their F-18s delivered, but with the time span those F-18s are more than half worn out. We never did get around to buying any of the smart weapons for the F-18 so that they could deliver air-to-ground munitions. In that period of time the army had a delivery of tanks. They're worn out and they haven't had much since. We're left with a situation today where we've got a small, effective navy, an air force with a decent transport capability and some half-worn-out, under-equipped F-18s and an army that's generally under-equipped. And where it is equipped, its equipment is old.

The world has changed and we're not doing peacekeeping as invented by Lester Pearson, where you and I have a dispute, we're both liable to lose something, so we invite a third party in to let us get out of this dispute without total loss of face. Now we're dealing with banditry where the bandits are well equipped, better equipped than our people. And our people go in as peacekeepers, but in fact what they're involved in is a war and they're not equipped to be in that war if it turns ugly. And sooner or later it's going to.

They're all at risk. If we continue to follow the Canadian tradition of walking softly and carrying a big microphone, involving ourselves politically in the difficult places because that's a part of having influence, then we better be prepared to pay the price. You don't get anything for free. And we've been getting defence for free for quite a while. If we want to continue, we better buy those people the equipment they need for the places we're going to send them.

We certainly perceive ourselves to be a voice amongst the big guys, but we have had a free ride, and the free ride is over. If we're going to continue to be there at the big table, we have to pay the bill and buy the equipment. If the Canadian citizenry has believed that we have been involved effectively, and that we can continue to be involved effectively without paying the price, then they're being misled.

But from today forward, given it takes five to 10 years to produce that new equipment, if we want to continue to play a part in those ugly places in the world for the good of mankind, then we better buy the equipment. And if we don't, the parliamentarians will bear that responsibility, individually and directly, for what happens to our kids when they're in that ugly place.

The reality is that the defence issue in Canada boils down to "How much are you prepared to spend on the capital equipment?" You can have just as much defence as you're prepared to pay for. Everything else is make-believe. It's words written in water. And they'll disappear in the hard light of day, quicker than dew.

When I left the Defence Department the budget was about $12.4 billion. That's a hell of a lot of money. Half of it was going into the supporting of bases and sewers and overhead and all the people it takes to run all those things, and I never saw a sewer yet that could fight worth a damn. The equipment portion of the budget was being starved.

The two major expenses are overhead and people. Equipment is 20 percent and falling. In the Trudeau years it got as low as nine percent and the best we ever got was about 25 percent of the budget. That, in a technologically dependent business, is a recipe for bankruptcy. And that's where the Armed Forces have been headed.

The problem is, when you spend $12 billion a year, the politician expects to get something for it. He doesn't want to hear about the decision somebody made 12 years ago that didn't produce the equipment today. And of course all the decisions that you might take today will affect something after the mandate of the current government. Now, there's one way around that equipment problem: you go and buy whole sets of equipment from the Americans or somebody. But that has a political price in Canada because the whole defence procurement is tied to Canadian jobs, and that's as big an issue as what capability you get for the money.

Defence is subsumed by interests other than pure defence. The reality of the state of equipment of the army is they shouldn't be in these places they are in the world. That's a hard nut for the people who are serving and who are the head of the army to deal with. Because if they aren't ready to go, what's the reason for having an army?

There are a whole set of internal pressures and debates that affect the people who are serving and affect their ability to say, "No, we can't go." But any objective analysis of the equipment versus the situations they're in tells you that they're right on the margins. And five years from now it's going to be worse. And 10 years from now it's *Alice in Wonderland*. Unless you invest, you're dealing in one of the finest moving museums in the world. But it's not an army.

The Gulf

In the Gulf, by happy chance, we had on the shelf, waiting to be fitted into the new frigates, a great deal of equipment which we could lash on to the old ships and make them safe to go and do an effective job of work. They weren't what they should have been, but they were good enough. The air force was asked to send the F-18s in the interceptor role. They're outfitted for the interceptor role and they're good at it, and they went and did that. It got more difficult when they were asked to go to the air-to-ground bombing role because expensive $40-million airplanes and highly trained pilots delivering stupid iron bombs is a good way to get them shot down. Anybody with a rifle can have a go at them in that low-altitude environment.

We sent hospital and security people but we didn't send the land force. I'm not sure we could have got them there because we don't have our own transport. I'm not sure we could have supported them there because we don't have our own communication and supply. In Europe we existed on the backs of our allies, the American and British and German lines of supply, and we simply have never paid for that extended logistic capability. So I don't think we could have got them there or could have supported them if we had decided to send them. Fortunately, in my view, we didn't.

The navy takes its logistics with it. It has the support ships and it is a package. It can go. The air force has very good air-to-air refuelling capability providing there is airplane gas at the other end, and in a place like the Gulf there's a lot of it. Supporting them on the ground when they get there takes a great many airplanes flying in the support role. But the air force has a pretty good transport capability.

Crunch time comes when you deal with the large volumes that go to supporting a deployed land force. Despite the massive capability that the U.S. possesses, 90 percent of the stuff that's required to support that army in the Gulf went by sea, in big ships. You can't take ammunition and large-volume things by airplanes. There just aren't enough airplanes in the world. We don't have that capability. And the deployment, therefore, of a large army group from Canada to someplace is something we simply can't do and haven't paid for.

Choices

We are at the mercy of our allies. We have always been. We're not going to go and do anything significant in the world on our own. And the people who envisage light peacekeeping, they're talking about really light, what the guy can carry on his back as he gets off the airplane, in which case it better be a pretty benign situation. Now, I don't see many of those benign situations in the world we live in. It is not ordered structures that invite the peacekeepers in. It's the bandits I talked about before, and they all want to win. They think they can win. The idea of sending lightly armed peacekeepers, a sort of cross between boy scouts and a police force, is fallacious. It may even be immoral.

It is a legitimate choice for Canada to decide not to be involved in the evolving world in an attempt to keep it orderly, but we should understand that there is a price to be paid for that. That price has something to do with influence. I'm not sure how welcome we're going to be at the Group of Seven when we're a non-participant in keeping the world orderly for the world's commerce. If we decide we're going to be in the field and be effective, there is a price to be paid for equipment that we're not paying. We either pay the price or we don't go.

There are two issues here. The parliamentary committee on defence, I think, are well-meaning, honourable people, and members of Parliament are mostly pretty ordinary Canadians. They can come to a recommendation and make that recommendation to government, but that's not what's going to happen. What is decided within government, within the policy branch and by the collective hierarchy of DND, and by the minister, is all influenced, in a very major way, by the troubles of the minister of finance. It may well be that the financial crisis in this country is such that further defence cuts are going to occur. I understand that. I pay taxes like every other Canadian.

But somewhere between the difficulties with money and the expectations of policy there is a reality. Whatever it is we're going to spend on defence, we ought to be spending it on defence, not on supporting bureaucracy on bases, an infrastructure which just gets people elected. The bases don't fight.

When we finally get down to Canadian Forces that we can afford, we commit them to do only the things that they are going to be equipped for. No more. Playing Alice in Wonderland in the world we live in, unstructured and undisciplined and dangerous, is a luxury we got away with in the past. I don't think we can get away with it in the future. Whether the politicians of the day are prepared to bell the cat, to call it like it is, and to limit their expectations to that which the country is prepared to pay for, I just don't know.

But I think the fact that they are faced with that choice ought to be clear to every Canadian, to understand that we're not going to get anything for free. And our sons and daughters who are going to join the army, the navy and the air force will be at risk because we Canadians have chosen that risk for them. If we don't buy the equipment they need for the places we are going to send them to in five and 10 years from now, they're at even greater risk.

Being Responsible

We have a long tradition in this country of civil control of the military. It is the civil authority which sets the priorities. It is the minister who decides where we're going to go. He gets advice from the military, and in the end it is the government that decides what money is going to be spent on capital equipment so that future governments have defence options. It's always an issue of the future, it's never an issue of today.

Politics always creeps into every decision that is made by government, but the minister has the right to expect unfettered, hard-nosed advice from his military advisors. The minister better make sure he gets it, that it isn't filtered through people who are more conscious of the political realities than are his military advisors. He has the right to ask face to face, "Is this the thing we ought to do?"

I liked being asked hard questions by politicians when I was serving. The Defence Department had been wrestling with writing a new defence policy for two years, my entire tenure as the vice-chief. In the end, as the sort of general manager of the firm, which the vice-chief is, I did the sums. I came to the conclusion that what was being promised didn't match the money that was going to be spent, and most particularly the money to be spent in the capital account. I said it wouldn't fly, that the policy advanced by me and my colleagues was invalid. My advice wasn't listened to.

The policy went forward to the government anyway and I said no. I resigned on the issue. It was a public action. Didn't have much effect. I was never called before the parliamentary committee on defence to explain myself. Never.

That wouldn't have happened in the United States. If the vice-chief of the joint staff in the United States had resigned in protest, he'd have been called before a lot of public bodies to explain himself. *Front Page Challenge* took more interest in why I'd resigned than did the parliamentary committee. I'm not sure that any of the parties in Parliament wanted to open up the defence debate to an intense public scrutiny because it's damn awkward for them.

The differences between Canada and the United States are profound. There is a public interest and debate on defence issues in the United States and there is not in Canada. There is a structure in the United States where, when military officers are called before congressional committees, they're expected to testify on their own expertise, in their own right. In Canada you are expected to speak within the policy that is stated by the minister. It needn't be like that. There are rules for parliamentary committees that could cause them to be closer to the American model, but they haven't been exercised.

There simply is not a very big constituency in Canada for the defence issue, and the bureaucracy and politicians are probably comfortable with the fact that there isn't a big constituency. It makes the absence of decision easier. And that's what we've seen, a lot of absence of decision.

But the chickens have come home to roost.

JIM ALLEN
Colonel (Retired)
1994

Jim Allen had a 37-year career with the Canadian army in the infantry. He served on five peacekeeping missions, including the Golan Heights mission and the UN Truce Supervision Organization in the Middle East. In 1992 he was the commanding officer of the 2 PPCLI in Cyprus. His service with NATO included three years with the Canadian Brigade in northern Germany and five years as a senior logistics war planner with HQ Central Army Group in Heidelberg. He was also the chief of staff of the United Nations observer group on the Iran–Iraq border in 1989. He retired to Kingston, Ontario, but remains outspoken on defence issues, particularly when senior officials exaggerate Canadian capabilities.

Peacekeeping
We used to say that peacemaking was diplomats playing the normal diplomatic game, while peacekeepers kept the peace and enabled them to reach a lasting solution. Not much has changed, but people have gotten the terminology all mixed up. Now we have all kinds of people in the UN, in Canada and in other countries using peacemaking in the sense

of war or peace enforcement, in Somalia and in Haiti for example. If you look at peacekeeping in the traditional UN sense of interposition forces and peacemaking as diplomatic activity to back it up and to lead to a lasting solution, not much has changed. But a lot of people now seem to be thinking in terms of putting military forces in to force solutions upon the combatants instead of getting them to agree diplomatically.

In Yugoslavia you have a very large UN presence and I'm not quite sure what it is. It's certainly not traditional peacekeeping, despite the fact that the parties in the conflict, to a greater or lesser degree, want them there. But they're not doing traditional peacekeeping. They're getting shot at. They're getting killed. It's closer to war than it is to peacekeeping. I don't think that the Canadian public understands that the Canadian peacekeeping missions of the past 50 years have been changed dramatically, as in the case of Bosnia and Somalia.

Peacekeeping has only been one of many roles that the military should be called upon to perform, and it's usually been fairly low down on the priority list. Our primary obligation as a nation and as an army is to ensure the protection and security of Canada. That requires, to use the jargon of DND, combat-capable forces, general-purpose forces. What it requires, basically, is that we have to be able to fight a war if necessary to protect Canadian interests. And don't ask me to identify the threat because it could come from anywhere, as it has in the past.

The reason Canadians have been successful in traditional peacekeeping is because we were trained for war. We were well trained for a role in NATO, a role in Western Europe or a role in the defence of Canada, and those qualities of a well-trained military force stood us in good stead in putting well-trained officers and men into all kinds of UN peacekeeping and observer situations.

We are not the only peacekeepers. There are all kinds of other competent nations in traditional peacekeeping, as well as in peace enforcement. You can point to Lester Pearson in 1956 in Suez and so on, but there are many other nations that I've served with that have very competent men, officers and troop forces that can carry out peacekeeping. In the last mission I was in we had 25 nations in Iran–Iraq providing 350 observers. Canada provided, at the maximum, 20 of those. The rest were provided by other nations.

During the cold war we were able to get away with a lot of commitments to our allies without really having our bluff called. We had 45 years in NATO and we did originally, in the first years of NATO, have credible forces over there in the British Army of the Rhine. But after the decimation of our forces by the Trudeau regime, we were getting free security from the rest of NATO and making only a token contribution.

I'm a cynic and a skeptic about any defence reviews that I've seen in Canada because they always talk a good fight and then the implementation leaves a lot to be desired. Usually the government that comes out with the white paper on defence is out of power or has changed its policy a few years later. We had a classic example with the Mulroney Conservatives, who in 1987 gave the Defence Department all kinds of reasons for hope. They were going to do some equipment purchases, and three years later they were doing severe reductions. So I'm a cynic.

Speaking Out
The voices of the serving soldiers, the military professionals, are a key part of the defence equation and they have been silenced. It wasn't until a few years ago that a serving officer could write a professional article in a magazine without getting it approved, nickel-and-dimed, by his superior officers or overridden by his bosses.

There was an officer recently, a veteran in the force, who wanted to speak out on stuff that he'd had experience with. He said he was called up before his superior officer and the head of the public relations in National Defence and told if he wanted to do this interview, he would have to do it as a civilian and would have to submit his resignation. If he had something worthwhile to say, I suppose I would say to him, "Get up and say it and be prepared to put your career on the line." But when the man threatens you with firing for doing that, there could be a very interesting court case. We are Canadians, with all the rights and privileges that entails under the law. He should be encouraged to speak out and if he does speak out, he shouldn't be threatened with dismissal, unless he's doing something totally against the wishes of the nation.

The Canadian public is generally ignorant or, as the historians have said, they're unmilitary. But that's nothing new, that's the way we've been throughout our history. Many countries share that with us. The difference is that in Canada the politicians were able to literally get away with policies that in most other countries they would have been thrown out of office for.

The Canadian military and the Canadian strategic community are a tiny part of Canada and they're not a credible lobby in Ottawa. They don't have a voice. The MPs don't care, many of them, or don't know. When you mention defence to the local MP, even though he's got a base in his riding, all he's concerned about is the base. The larger issues of national security and defence are not bottom-dollar issues for him.

If you don't allow the military to speak out when they're serving, how is the public to know what the military really thinks about the defence policy? That's the situation you have. The press coverage of defence issues, if I may say so, has been abysmal.

The Gulf

I said, in an article on defence policy after the Gulf, that one of the greatest embarrassments to me as a serving officer was to hear the commander of Mobile Command of the Canadian military promising a contingency plan which would look at putting 12,000 Canadian soldiers in the Gulf when we had nowhere near that capability, nowhere near it. We would have been threatening Canadian lives if we'd even attempted to put that sort of a force in the Gulf without months of training and re-equipping.

Many of our senior officers have adopted sycophantic attitudes. They have become more servants of the political masters, and I'm not suggesting that they don't have to follow political guidance and leadership, but if an officer makes an outrageous statement, such as the one above, he has an obligation to resign, in my view, if he is challenged on that. He shouldn't have been in the high position he was. He was too stupid to be the commander of Mobile Command if he didn't know the incapability of Canada at that moment in time to produce that force. Some of the politicians may have known, but they didn't care because they wanted us to sound like we were warlike because the Gulf War was about to break out. The Americans certainly knew it. The British knew it. The French knew it. The major allies knew that we were producing a token force in the Gulf.

So it was an embarrassment to many of us.

The 1987 white paper was, as white papers go, one of the better documents because it clearly stated that we had a significant commitment-capability gap. In other words, we had too many commitments and too little in the way of forces to carry them out. It said that the commitment-capability gap could lead to Canadians getting killed if we were ever forced to put troops into a combat situation. That was in 1987. The Gulf War comes along and we have a senior officer talking about putting 12,000 troops into the Gulf. Nonsense.

Leadership

Our ratio of senior officers to troops is a national embarrassment. We are worse than most "banana republics," and I use the term "banana republics" in quotes to apply to all smaller powers around the world. We have far too many generals, and not only generals, senior officers, and I say that as a colonel. When I was in, there were way too many of us. There are way too many lieutenant-colonels and majors and captains. I won't go into the ratios, but they're probably the worst in the Western world, and maybe in the world. Now some reductions have got to be made. Aim for 20 generals total instead of 120 or whatever we've got now.

We have a standard rule, a brigade is a force of approximately 5,000 soldiers. If you've only got 70,000 people or 75,000 people in your forces, and if you add in the reserves, let's say we have 100,000 people in the Canadian force. Divide that by 5,000 and you get 20 generals. Add five for UN appointments and whatever, and you can easily run the thing.

The DND military leadership under the chief of defence staff has no credibility left with most of the serving officers that I know and nearly all of the retired officers that I know, and not only officers, but soldiers. You've got to change the team at the top. You've got to put somebody new in there, somebody with a few new ideas who is not a captive of his political masters, yet is responsive to them and is prepared to speak out as Admiral Thomas did, who could take it no longer and resigned as the number-two man because he wasn't prepared to accept what the chief of the defence staff and the official hierarchy were presenting for defence policy.

In order for the Canadian public to be aware, if the serving people aren't allowed to speak out and to freely criticize, then how is the public to understand what's going on in defence, unless we've got reporters burrowing into national defence policy and into National Defence Headquarters and being present on foreign missions, getting the true story of how defence policy is being developed and implemented? It's not being done except in rare instances now. Allan Fotheringham is no great defence analyst, but he did say in one of his *Maclean's* columns that our naval contribution amounted to, I think it was, a "rust frigate brigade." How he got the terms mixed up I don't know, but his message was clear.

What was the DND reaction? In the next issue of *Maclean's* they had a naval officer write in and pounce on Fotheringham for making a mockery of these gallant Canadian sailors in the Gulf, instead of dealing with the reality of his comment, that we had outdated, obsolete ships there which were put well out of harm's way to not embarrass us.

A national trait in Canada, let's say since the Second World War, has been for government to shoot their mouth off and not be prepared to back it up with either fiscal or military measures. It was embarrassing to me as a Canadian during the Gulf War and the lead-up to the actual six or seven weeks of conflict, to have our minister of external affairs and our prime minister going around the world issuing bombastic, jingoistic statements, when they knew that we had little or nothing to contribute to winning when it actually came to the shooting war.

The Gulf War went off very smoothly with little input from us. No Canadian body bags were brought home and everybody said, "Look what we can do with our Canadian Forces." Now, I know this is a harsh thing to say, but it would in many senses have been better if we'd had some Canadians killed because then the Canadian public might have started asking questions. Why were they killed? Why did we have them there without the proper means? Of course, none of that happened so everybody says the Gulf War was a great success. We avoided a national embarrassment very narrowly.

I'm astounded that questions about the casualties we've had in Bosnia, for example, the mine incidents and the other woundings and fatalities, weren't being raised by the politicians with the government and by the citizens with the government and the military. When Mulroney sent 2,000-plus soldiers to Bosnia, there was almost no national debate. The chief of the defence staff caved in and said we'd got the troops to do it.

We didn't have the troops to do it, and our training and operations base here at home has suffered badly since that decision. But I've heard little or no public debate about why we are having Canadians getting killed in a no-win situation in Bosnia.

It's not peacekeeping. It's not peacemaking. It's not even peace enforcement. It's a muddle.

Defence Policy

The Canadian military policy has got to be an extension of our foreign policy and the two of them have to work hand in glove. What we need is a clear definition of what Canadian vital interests are, and following from that you end up with your detailed policy recommendations and actions.

A United States secretary of state back in the 1800s said that the United States should not go abroad in search of monsters to destroy. It would support liberty wherever it wants to fight for itself, but it was not going to send troops abroad to support them. I think his policy, 160 years later, is still valid for Canada. Because somebody is starving somewhere in the world, unless there's a vital national interest involved, doesn't mean that you send Canadian troops there.

Many Canadians would say that there is a higher reason to send forces abroad in cases like Somalia, and they would quote humanitarian and human rights issues. I sympathize and I understand that, but when you're putting soldiers lives at risk, the reason has to be of vital national interest or very close to it, and feeding starving civilians in Somalia or anywhere else in the world is not necessarily of vital national interest. If we were feeding starving civilians in Greenland or somewhere closer to Canada where there was a direct link to our own territory and our own interests, maybe I would see it.

I would say to the Canadian people, "Just think how lucky we've been." The Americans had over 40 soldiers killed in that so-called humanitarian mission in Somalia. No Canadians were killed. We got very little out of Somalia except national embarrassment. We're lucky we didn't have a bunch of body bags coming back like the Americans did. You've got to remember that the only reason Canada was in Somalia was because the U.S. was taking the lead. The only reason we were in Haiti was because the U.S. was taking the lead. Unless the U.S. is there, Canada would not have the means or the capability of organizing a humanitarian protection operation.

I'm not suggesting we have to build up in any significant degree, but we've got to rationalize what we've got. We have to go back to the fundamental idea that nobody can predict the future despite what some people will tell you, and that war is part of the human condition and will continue to be part of the human condition.

When I was at NDHQ people were forbidden to use the word "war." They were talking about general-purpose combat and near combat. All of this is nonsense. Absolute nonsense. Let's recognize war for what it is: part of the human condition. Let's do our best to stop it. Let's do our best to contribute to peacekeeping and peacemaking and, if necessary, peace enforcement. But let's also recognize that our bottom obligation is to the Canadian citizen, to have a force available here.

There's no end to history. Wars are going to continue. We have to be prepared to defend our country in that kind of anarchic, international situation. That means having capable military forces. Unless we've got them, we can't do any peacekeeping because our success in peacekeeping has been due to the fact that we've had reasonably capable military forces, which have steadily deteriorated over the last two or three decades.

PETER HAYDON

Commander (Retired)
1994

A former career officer in the Royal Canadian Navy, Peter Haydon retired in 1988 after 30 years of service in submarines destroyers and as a staff strategic planner. From 1979 to 1986 he served as a member of the Canada–United States Military Co-ordination Committee and of the Strategic Planning Staff of the NATO Supreme Allied Commander Atlantic. He is now a senior research fellow with the Centre for Foreign Policy Studies and an adjunct professor in the department of political science at Dalhousie University in Halifax. His current interests focus on emerging concepts of sea power and maritime strategy and their function in diplomacy and international crisis management.

Every state needs a military. The question is how much military. The state is never absolved of the obligation to defend its borders, defend its people and defend its sovereignty. We've got to determine what threat level you are prepared to deal with. What levels of risk are you prepared to accept? The secondary function of the military is to act as an instrument of foreign policy so that you can operate in conjunction with other people on a broader basis to maintain a more stable world order.

The capabilities must be based foremost on the national requirement. In Canada's case a vast ocean, enormous landmass and a huge air space that goes with both of those determines that you have to have forces that can stay aloft, stay at sea for extended periods of time, and must be able to cover great distances.

You must also have a concept of mobility whereby you can move soldiers, for instance, from their base in Ontario to northern Canada if there is a crisis or a security threat that needs to be addressed. So the first function you must have is mobility. The second function you must have is flexibility because you must operate at great distances. You can't come home to pick up the piece of kit you left behind. You hear it called a multipurpose force in some cases, but what you're looking for is a versatile force that is inherently flexible.

The view that you do not require any territorial defence forces seems to have come into the debate and that, I think, is naive. You cannot predict what the future is going to be like five years from now, 10 years from now, 15 years from now. Military capabilities take 10 to 15 years to build up from scratch. You can't just take a military capability off the shelf.

The people who are advocating getting rid of major military components and specialization have no true eye on the future. You must retain some versatility so that you're not going to be caught by surprise, as the country was as the result of disarmament in the 1920s and 1930s when the Second World War came and the Canadian military was totally unable to meet the demands placed on it by its politicians, going into the European war.

Some people are suggesting that perhaps Canada's military does not need offensive military capabilities like heavy tanks, artillery, fighter-jet squadrons, anti-submarine warfare and so on. But to believe that fighter aircraft, tanks, heavy armour, heavy artillery are offensive weapons is a totally naive concept, lacking any knowledge of the basic fundamentals of the use of military force, particularly as we go into the 21st century.

The tank, for instance, is a defensive weapon more than it is an offensive weapon. It is there to protect the troops on the ground. Anti-submarine warfare is for self-protection as much as it is for offence. It's a skill and is related to the weapons package that goes with a ship (and very often an airplane) and it's used to protect other ships and the parent ship itself. Looking at these capabilities as offensive and therefore redundant is to essentially deny the basic operating procedures of the military systems.

These are things that are going to be needed more and more as international operations get more complex as a result of the level of armament that is coming into some areas of turmoil and trouble. The level of armament, for instance, in Bosnia today is quite sophisticated and that means that if you have 30-year-old technology trying to protect Canadians, the risk to life and limb is very much higher. The Danes, for instance, when they went into Bosnia, took tanks with them as a protective measure. Those people that are advocating this massive disarmament — and it is massive disarmament — of basic capabilities are in fact advocating putting Canadian military people at risk to a much higher level than before.

Professionalism and Equipment

I would have to say that in my view the Canadian army is no longer an effective fighting force.

Professionalism is on a slow downward spiral at the moment. The events in Somalia begin to make one thing clear, that perhaps the professionalism that used to exist in Canada's very fine military is eroding. There are other situations where morale and discipline, and therefore professionalism, are not to the high standard that we once expected of our people in uniform, and this is cause for considerable concern. In fact, they are used just as a job market for government to do jobs around the world regardless of the consequences and the risks that may be inherent in some of those jobs.

As this slow erosion takes place, you begin to see that the "pride of service" is beginning to go. The pride of being a loyal soldier to your country is less dominant than it was. More and more you see the army and the navy and the air force being used as a job force, and people joining to get a job rather than joining for honour and for something they believe in.

When a government ceases to spend wisely on its military, it ceases to maintain its investment in professionalism, training, equipment and the ability to respond quickly, and you go through a process that is the same as disarmament. In jargon terms that is known as structural disarmament. It's an involuntary disarmament that happens bit by bit, and you will find then that the professionalism and the ability of the military to do difficult things becomes less and less, as more and more of each defence dollar is burned up in the administrative system rather than in the operational system.

A modern military must spend about 25 to 30 percent of its capital budget on equipment to give you the necessary replacement of equipment at the right time. Through the 1970s the government was only spending six and a half to eight percent on capital equipment. So equipment was being pushed longer and longer into service without the necessary modernization or replacement. The result now is that you've got a backlog of equipment that needs desperately to be overhauled and replaced and there's just not enough money there to do it. So now you've got a priority problem as well as a funding problem.

The average frontline soldier is quite convinced his government is not giving him the right equipment to protect himself and to do his job at the same time. It'll vary from service to service. The navy is in better shape because it has new ships. They've got good equipment and they're fine. But Sea King helicopters are not fine; the APCs in the army are far from fine. The F-18 fighters are OK for now, but the time's going to come very shortly when they're going to need some work and some money.

Our NATO Responsibilities
Let's have a look at NATO spending. There's been a lot of accusation that Canada has not carried its fair share in the alliance. Anybody who's served in NATO over the years will tell you that one of the constant concerns of the NATO bureaucracy and the NATO administration was to get the Canadians to pay a realistic share of collective defence, and it was collective defence against a common threat. The Canadians were always lowest amongst those nations able to pay well. If you compare Canada to the Netherlands, to Norway, and to some extent to Denmark, those three countries paid more per capita than we did. We were not giving to NATO what we said we would give. This is the backsliding.

The brigade to relieve Norway in case of a Soviet attack on the northern flank was promised but everybody knew it was just simply a paper tiger. With the Norwegian brigade, the CAST Brigade Group as they called it, one of the greatest concerns of those of us who worked in NATO was attempting to get the Canadian government to change the timing at which it would be able to deliver that brigade to Norway. The concern within NATO simply was that by the time the Canadian brigade got there it would be too late, the Russians would have come through. Successive Canadian staffs attempted to push the government to shorten the delivery time of that fighting unit to Norway, all to no avail.

To reduce the delivery time, a number of things would have had to have happened. One, the CAST Brigade Group would have needed to be assembled in one place with all its equipment. That didn't happen. Two, there had to be a better system of embarking that brigade onto ships in Canadian ports, taking it across the Norwegian Sea and dropping it off in north Norway. Those ships never got there. In fact, they did a spot check of the Norwegian ships that we had the contracts with, and one ship that was supposed to be doing the sea lift was in the North Pacific. That commitment was a sham.

The constant refusal in the Canadian government to honour its commitments was nothing short of an embarrassment to those of us that were trying to work in the NATO staff to carry our fair share of collective defence. There was nothing you could do about it. The politicians would be given good military advice but they would ignore it. The decisions they made were made for political purposes.

Economics
For a number of years one of the major problems of Canadian defence economics has been the integration of regional economic requirements with defence contracting and defence spending. Now you see this in several places. One good example is shipyards. A major shipbuilding contract has potential political leverage in the region and would therefore have potential to buy votes or to make the government look good in certain areas. Aircraft repair, aircraft construction — again, the same thing. You can make a choice as to which region of the country that contract goes to.

Where we have a narrow ribbon of population, the military in many places has become the driving force in the economy and bases have been established first and foremost as a means of pumping money into a local region rather than being in the area where it is most operationally sound to spend that money. If you want to close a base, it's not a question of "Do you need the base? Is the base redundant?" It's a question of what is the political fallout going to be of closing that base, particularly if you've got a base that is a major contributor to the local economy. What you've got is essentially a systematic politicization of the defence budget, so that it becomes part of the overall national political structure.

You see the systematic politicization of the military in civil-military relations. You see it in the implementation of social policies into the military without taking sufficient care to make sure that military capability is not eroded by the heavy implementation of a social policy. For example, the recent requirements for disabled people to have equal access to military jobs is completely at odds with the other requirement that the military be mobile and able to move quickly into a combat situation. That's just one side of it. Basically what is happening is that the military advice being given to politicians is being made for political reasons rather than on the pure grounds of military requirements.

Arguing Policy
I've appeared before the parliamentary defence committee twice. I was naive enough to believe that the committee process would lead to significant change. But I see the old issues being thrashed over and over again. I see a reluctance to embark on the necessary structural changes, reorganization and modernization to provide this country with an effective military at a realistic dollar value. That just isn't happening. And it's frustrating.

When you look at the testimony that's been given so far, you find that this committee has been given an enormous amount of very sound advice from a lot of people such as myself, not only with military experience, but also a number of years' experience teaching defence policy and examining and studying defence policy. Yet there seems to be more credence given to the people who are, frankly, amateurs in the field and are making recommendations based on ideology rather than common sense and the national interest. This is totally frustrating.

There's a basic lack of understanding of how a military force functions. If you put troops into a situation in Bosnia, using one example, you can't control the events in Bosnia. They're determined by outside forces. Putting those troops into Bosnia, ill equipped to protect themselves, is the kind of situation that many proponents of the new defence policy want to continue. The good advice that they've been getting from retired army people and professional analysts is to make sure the military is able to protect itself in all conditions. If not, don't commit it.

They're basically saying that the future world is safe. We guarantee the future world is safe. And a lot of the defence groups and public advocacy groups that have been coming forward to this committee have been showing the same sort of shallow understanding of international affairs with the same misplaced belief that we have peace in our times, which was prevalent all the way through the 1920s and the 1930s as the Second World War approached. Many of us have been trying to convince this committee to use a little caution. Please. It's too early to embark on a disarmament program.

As I mentioned earlier, there is one group that's advocating that we give up our capability to operate fighter aircraft, to conduct anti-submarine warfare operations, to operate tanks and other armoured vehicles, that we no longer need heavy artillery in the belief that those capabilities are not called for in UN operations. In their place they advocate a low-tech, low-skill-level military force, committed to the world, that only will do traditional peacekeeping operations after the signing of a truce. And by the same token, they expect that Canada will still be respected on the international scene. This is the hypocrisy that I find galling.

It's naive to believe that you can put a military unit on the ground and still control the environment around it. A warship is different. You can put a warship into a situation that is uncertain and the warship inevitably will extricate itself because it only has itself to move. Put an army battalion into a place and all of a sudden it becomes surrounded by the people it is supposed to be observing and is held captive.

There was the one situation, I think it was Gorazde, where there were Canadian soldiers who were surrounded and their release had to be negotiated with the Bosnian Serbs before they could come out. Canada had absolutely no control over that situation whatsoever, and those people were in there without adequate self-protection. That's criminal.

The heart of the political problem today lies in the use of force. There are those politicians who believe that there is no longer a need for any country to use force to stabilize a situation in say Somalia, Yugoslavia, Haiti, whatever. Events, as they unfold, are proving them wrong. The related fallacy is that it is not appropriate for Canada to be in coalitions of nations using force, that Canada has attained a moral high ground through its long tradition of Pearsonian traditional peacekeeping.

There's an important point to look at here, and it's very simple. How many nations are there who have the professional military forces who can do difficult things in the name of international stability, and how many are there that have got militaries that are unstable, unreliable and cannot do the difficult things? If you count the stable, professional militaries, you've got probably about a dozen, and nearly all of those are the NATO military forces because we've trained together, worked together, practised together for 25 and more years as combined forces. There have been Canadians under multinational control for in excess of 25 years. We've learned a lot. We are good at it.

If a new defence policy suddenly says, "Take Canada out of that international security process," the ability to maintain order in the world is not as strong as it was before. It's been reduced by Canada. Who's to say the Dutch, the Norwegians and the remainder wouldn't start leaking and very quickly, as medium powers, start walking back from their commitment to international security? You're going to be left with the big powers running the world, and that is a direct contravention of what Mackenzie King and the other world leaders set out to do in April of 1945 at the San Francisco Conference when the UN was formed. They were absolutely clear that they did not want a situation prevailing that would be run by the big powers alone. The role of the middle powers was important. So in some respects what we are going through at the moment is an attempt to remove Canada from the role it saw itself assuming all that time back in 1945. That's wrong.

The committee of 21 (Canada 21 Council) very simply says the Canadian Forces should not use force. Period. Except in self-protection by individuals through the use of light weapons. They do not see the Canadian military having the capability to extricate itself from a problem or to use force as part of a collective security undertaking. It, very simply, is demilitarization.

If you look at that whole process again, you're back to the very simple argument that I think has been made by Colin Gray and many others, and that is you cannot predict what will happen in the world. You have got to retain some flexibility in your thinking and some flexibility in your policy so that you can react, as and when you determine appropriate, to situations that threaten your security, your sovereignty or your national interests. And that's the key point. The committee of 21 would remove that ability and would not allow Canada to be sovereign in making decisions in the international system of the future.

The United Nations has no military command structure at the moment. It has to borrow the military command structure of somebody else or it has to attempt to cobble something together as it has done in the former Yugoslavia. That doesn't work very well. The chain of command in the former Yugoslavia is not good. Although through NATO you've got a chain of command, it is subordinate to the UN political officer on the ground. And this is where, when the strikes are being ordered, you are having difficulties.

If you don't have a credible military structure, you can't expect to be at the discussion table when the operation orders and the operation plans are negotiated. You are therefore saying to whatever formation is ordered and under whoever's command it comes, "Just take my troops and do with them as you think fit." You're losing your sovereignty. By maintaining an effective military structure, you then turn around to say to somebody, "Yes, I'll take some of the risks and, by the way, the cost of my taking some of the risks is that I want to be part of the team that writes the Op order, determines the objectives and establishes the rules of engagement, thank you very much." And that is that.

So, to sum up, what is the problem with Canada's military? OK. First thing, lack of funding for capital programs to provide individuals and units with the protection necessary for them to do their job. Two, lack of public respect through a steady erosion of views that the military is not a force of warriors but an international peace corps and boy scout troop that just does odd jobs around the world. Third, there has been a systematic erosion of the military ethos in this country to the point that senior officers have become, effectively, bureaucrats. Decisions are made not on the basis of the military need, but on the basis of the political objective. And that is a slippery slope downward on which professionalism will be lost, on which, essentially, you will have lost the good name that Canada has gained on the world stage through its military in the earlier part of the 20th century.

Because of this politicization of the military, the military leadership have become, not the guardians of the Constitution, but a part of the political process. They are not, first and foremost, upholding the requirement of Canadian independence and Canadian sovereignty.

DAVID HARRIES

Colonel (Retired)
1994

*C*olonel Harries was interviewed in 1994 while he was on the
staff of the National Defence College in Kingston. Trained as
a combat engineer, Colonel Harries served in Cyprus and with
UNPROFOR. He later obtained his doctorate and spent some
time working in Indonesia.

My background is a mix of regimental duty, combat engineers in the
Airborne and professional development. I began my peacekeeping
activity in 1974 as a member of the Airborne Regiment's tour in Cyprus,
in the middle of which the Turkish forces invaded the island. It was that
experience that made me determined that I was going to learn more
about the United Nations and international affairs, especially international organizations.

Virtually every country in the world is eligible to be a troop-contributing
nation, whether that's uniform-troop contributor or non-uni-
form-troop contributor. The variety of competence and the variety of knowledge which they bring to the theatre means that the

United Nations is very, very different from what it was even five years ago.

We've always had something special to bring to the arena because we've always been professional soldiers, volunteer soldiers, sailors and airmen. With our relatively high level of competence in soldiering and near soldiering, we can do much to help new nations, new contributors, people that have not been in the field before, learn a lot of the skills that are needed.

We have laws that no other nation in the world has. We are a haven and a magnet for people from all over the world. The more peaceful the world is out there, the more peaceful we are. And therefore if we can play some part in doing it out in the field, if we go and fight the war over there, perhaps it won't come to our shores. But I believe strongly that we should continue to be part of hopefully well-thought-out United Nations missions.

Peacekeeping

One of the really interesting debates, but it is also very frustrating, is that of definitions of the different forms of multinational operations in the interests of peace and security — peace support operations. Peacekeeping, peacemaking, peace building, peace enforcement, personally I am taking less and less time worrying about definitions. Canada's contribution in the former Yugoslavia was certainly right for its time. We were lucky and fortunate, well placed and well timed, coming out of Germany with a full-blown operational capability. We went there as well prepared and as well equipped as anybody else. It's my professional opinion that equipment is often held up as the weak link when it isn't. The weak links are more on the human side.

The peacekeeping that is taking place in the former Yugoslavia is very different from what anybody did in Cyprus, for instance, but I don't know whether definitions or terms are the way to study how to react to the differences. In the old days, in Cyprus, I can remember again and again being told force, minimum force, only in self-defence. Then, post–cold war we passed to self-defence and defence of mission, defence of mandate. Now it appears to be on the brink of moving up to the right to do harm to someone or something that is interfering with the mandate or the mission or your self-defence. We seem to have gone up three steps.

We're not going there to fight a war. We have not declared war on any of these parties, whether there's one of them, three of them or 12 of them. It's a moot point whether you adhere to the principles of war, secrecy, offensive action, victory or maximum force to make sure that you completely wipe out the opposition. By the same token, you want to be in the best possible position to do what it is you've been told to do.

Forces large and small, new and old, good and bad are put in the position where they might be shot at. The confidence of those forces is a function of their equipment and also their circumstances. If they are well-trained troops and well-trained peacekeepers, overlapping conditions but not the same, and you can provide them with their own safe havens from which they go out to do their work, and the equipment which makes them safe at an acceptable level, it's arguable that you've met the requirement for equipment.

The old, quiet, stable positioning of troops between two parties that have agreed in full to your being there and to your watching them on a day-by-day basis is unlike a war. You're always out in the open. You must not be secret. And even if you had the best weapon in the world for your mission, you would almost be obligated in the UN situation to make it known to everybody. Whereas in war fighting your best secrets are some of your best offensive weapons. And we haven't come to grips with this.

Rules, Rights and Risks
Hundreds of years ago there were rules of about peace or war between two individuals. We had boxing rules, wrestling rules, rules for sports, rules for debate, golden rules on the wall, and when states became a major issue in the international system, over the years we built up rules by which states operate, one to the other. In peace. In war. And in those grey areas in between. We have conventions for how you treat prisoners of war, and we have rules about diplomacy, about how you treat one another's diplomats.

But over the last few years we seem to have spread the spectrum of our concern. At the one end we have human rights; the individual is paramount. At the other end we have dealings between international organizations. But we do not have a framework. We do not have Queensbury rules and we do not have Oxford debating rules about how NATO and the UN will deal with each other.

In situations like the former Yugoslavia, people in positions like mine had a treasure chest of opportunities to do things, any of which, had we the resources, we could have done. Often we thought up ways to do small things better, but all the progress was going to be on the margins, almost certainly. The policies that we saw that were reflected in direction to the United Nations Protection Force in Yugoslavia were either an iteration of, or a sudden input from, advisors — the academics, businessmen, consultants and policy makers — from back there. From over there. And the policies come to the field and they're given to the people, military, civilian, new, old, very good, not so good, to carry out, together.

The feedback in quieter days could make it back to the places where the advisors and the policy makers were building up the next iteration of policy and so on. But things are changing so fast today that the imperative of having that feedback in the type of conditions we're finding in peacekeeping missions is made more difficult because we aren't in the discussion at the start.

Canada's Role
Whether it's something in Canadian genes or whether it's just because we have been doing it for so long, we seem to be good at helping or participating or contributing. So there's almost a personal thing about being over there. You can see it even in soldiers who have been on three rather rapid missions. The level of the skill that we bring to the field is proven by the very, very, very low number of casualties and deaths. If you're confident, you know how to do your job well. If you are confident in your skills and in your equipment and in your colleagues and in your leadership, you can do marvellous things. Marvellous things.

Because my field was engineering and it spanned mine-awareness training, mine lifting, fixing roads and bridges, doing reconstruction, trying to get infrastructure in Sarajevo, people that I worked with, for and around did incredible things every day of their tour, whether it was six months, four months or a year. And as long as there are people who come back from tours who feel they've contributed, I argue that the people here in Canada will be willing to see them and their brothers and sisters continue to go over and contribute.

But nobody can stop the fighting or the troubles except the people that are doing the fighting and the troubles. And it's a choice of Canada's government whether we go or not. So whether Yugoslavia continues or not, it's entirely up to us here in Canada to decide how long we stay. As long as Canadians stay there, I have confidence we can do a lot to help, both in the theatre and for our colleagues.

We're one of the luckiest countries in the world and if there's an impediment to Canada realizing what's going on out there in the world, it's that we're one of the luckiest countries in the world. We haven't been invaded. We've got lots of space. We don't have to worry about a war over water. The immigration, far more often than not, enriches the country. We live next to a superpower. The other superpower that was our enemy is gone. We're able to travel freely within our own country. And we have little signs all over the country of how lucky people are to come and live with us and become Canadians. The impediment is that we are very comfortable. Maybe too comfortable. I honestly believe that the case could be made that by not having a test, we are not quick to realize or even to be interested in what's going on out there.

Being Prepared

During cold war times the major discussion in most NATO meetings was the capability-commitment gap or the other way around, depending on whether you were seen to be ahead of the game or behind the game, which was a neat method of starting any discussion. The capability that we require to do peacekeeping is still under development.

We've always known in Canada that a well-trained soldier or sailor or airman was definitely the starting point, was a foundation. But now that these missions have become so complicated, conditions in all these missions change on an almost daily basis. To keep up with that, even being confident that you know enough about what's going on, you need a base of knowledge of the theatre. We used to say, "In war, one of the most important things is to know your enemy." Well, now you not only have to know your — you can't use the word "enemy" of course — know the people you're there to help, you also have to know all of these friends that are there helping you as well. Because they might be on one side or the other of you.

Back in the old NATO days, because you'd trained again and again and again, you knew that a certain party was going to do something a certain way if a certain situation arose. Now you don't. If you don't know anything about that person, and you don't know anything about the conflict-ridden groups you're there to help or their history, you're at a tremendous disadvantage when things change quickly.

How do you prepare for missions like Somalia, Rwanda, Yugoslavia or even Cambodia? I don't have the answer to that. But each country that provides the resources, the armed forces, the police forces, the humanitarian groups and the money has to decide what it is they're going to put in the kitty.

I don't think there's a country left on earth that can do everything. So everybody will have to choose. Some can do a helluva lot more than others. And it comes to a choice by each state of what it is they are going to be willing to commit to doing well. Acceptably well.

The business about riding for free or not is different now than it was in the cold war. There was that tremendous focus, the almost perverse stability of black spy, white spy, good guy, bad guy, the team thing and knowing what you were supposed to do. If you didn't or if you chose not to do something, it was almost allowed or accepted because there was someone there on your team, invariably the boss member of the team, that would pick up the slack or would cover. As long as you didn't seem to do that too often and played enough of a role, you were still in.

But there were only 10 or 15 main players then, main state players. Obviously the United States and the Soviet Union and their allies were part of the environment. And peacekeeping's a good example of that. Each peacekeeping member had to be chosen by one or the other side.

But now everybody's eligible for everything. Democracy is the way to go. Everybody agrees with that, but we haven't defined it very well. Nobody's decided exactly what the final picture is. So everybody has a choice. If you want, you can withdraw, you can pull out when you want and you can argue the right to do that on first principles. But you've got to assess what that will cost you. First of all, it will cost you competitiveness because if you pull out of the game, there's going to be somebody else training or interested to get in. And if there's anything I've learned personally and viscerally in the last two years in my experience with the country of Slovakia and the armed forces of Slovakia and the government of Slovakia, it's that there are a number of new countries or renewed countries or reappeared states who are keen to the point of almost quivering to get in to be part of this big show.

At one point the combat engineer battalion was taken out of our commitment in Bosnia and I was left with no force engineers. I had no force-level resource with which to do all the mine-awareness training and to do the planning for the mine clearance and the reconstruction. What happens in cases like that is UN headquarters is asked to canvass the members and find us more engineer units. Only one country replied. Slovakia. Virtually days after it became a state. I spent as much as three days a week for nearly eight months with them, helping them build a force. They started from scratch, a new country that is not well off, and they were willing to go to all the trouble and cost, to come to a place which is not a nice place and become the single unit doing one of the most continuously dangerous jobs. They wanted to be in.

And there are lots like that. The Malaysians came to Yugoslavia and the Jordanians doubled their contingent. These are countries that have never been very effective in winter because they've never had to worry about snow. The Nigerians. Some of their tribes don't have a word for snow. They're all eligible. They are all equal. They have a vote at the table. We don't have a system for that yet.

I don't know whether we have a world that is the old, established international community in a new world, or whether we've got a new international community — because of all these new countries, all the new globalization, all the new economic circumstances — in an old world. Perhaps the last 50 years or so have been an aberration because we had two great big people keeping the lid on some overwhelming Armageddon that artificialized everything. We marginalized all the important things and now we've got debt and drugs and refugees and so on that everybody's got to handle. Right now I'm leaning to the view that it's a new international community with old problems that have been dormant for 40 or 50 years, in which case, whether we're doing peacekeeping or managing military affairs here at home, they present great challenges.

I'm happy we haven't been tested. I'm happy we've escaped horrible things happening to our country. But the number of Canadians that fought and died overseas — in two world wars, Korea and in the peacekeeping situation — is no small potatoes. We're respected for that. When the whistle blows really loud, certainly in the last century, we've done a lot. But we have been quiet and happy — peace, order and good government — here at home.

I don't think we're anti-military. I just think we're "amilitary" because we've never had to see if there's a difference between "amilitary" and pro-military.

PATRICK STOGRAN

Lieutenant-Colonel
1994

Patrick Stogran was the commanding officer of the 3rd Battalion PPCLI deployed to Afghanistan in late 2001. Attached to the United Nations UNPROFOR mission in Bosnia in 1994, then Major Stogran was a firsthand witness to some of the most bitter fighting and ethnic cleansing in the former Yugoslavia.

I joined the army in 1976, went through the military college program and graduated in 1980 with a degree in electrical engineering. I've served as a platoon and support-weapons commander with the 3rd Battalion of the Princess Patricia's Canadian Light Infantry, I've served with the Canadian Airborne Regiment, and prior to going to Yugoslavia I was with our 1st Battalion in Calgary, as a company commander.

In June of 1993 I joined the United Nations Protection Force in Yugoslavia as a military observer in Croatia on the Serb side. I spent the remainder of my tour in Bosnia in Gorazde and in Tuzla.

Medak

While I was in Sector North in one of the Serb-held areas of Croatia, I saw my share of action during the period of the Croatian offensive into the area that we called the Medak Pocket in Sector South, where the Croatian army attacked and massacred all the Serbs living there.

In January of 1993 the Croatians made an attack into the Sector South area where there were UN forces positioned and, disappointingly, the UN forces did not live up to the mandate that they had at the time. That undermined the credibility of the entire UN Protection Force. In meetings that I had with Serbs following the attack, the Serbs would say that the UN didn't live up to their commitment and they were going to defend themselves now. In September there was the attack that went into the Medak Pocket and our troops went in after the fact to clean up the situation. Now, when I say attack, I mean it's basically a full-blown offensive. There were large amounts of artillery that were fired, tanks were in the area and there was small-arms fire, anti-aircraft artillery, the full range of offensive weapons.

In early September the Croatians were being very aggressive in my area of responsibility, and we expected that there was going to be a major Croatian attack into Sector North. We called the local commanders on both sides to talk over the event. Things quieted down very quickly after we brought this to their attention. I feel that we probably compromised the plans on one side or the other of the warring parties, and shortly after that the Croatian army attack into the Medak Pocket took place. Our Canadian soldiers were tasked to go into the area and they basically drew a line, or had a line drawn for them, between the two warring parties. This is where peacekeeping becomes really what I would call war making.

We were going in there to make peace but the way we do that as soldiers is to make war, and our young Canadian soldiers had the line drawn for them. Our commanders made it very clear to both sides the line that they were going to seize, and they seized it aggressively, from my understanding. I wasn't with them, but they seized the line that they were to take and they held the area. I was in a meeting subsequent to this with two Serb corps commanders and one deputy corps commander. At this meeting it was pointed out by the Serbs that the Canadians should be setting the standard for the rest of the United Nations Protection Force because they were completely professional. They were totally objective in what they did. They were committed. They didn't take any excuses from either side and the Serbs respected that. I think that the incident in September of 1993 went a long way to restoring the credibility of the United Nations Protection Force in the Croatian area of the mission.

From my understanding the Canadians were fired upon and they did not hesitate to return fire. I think in my own mind that this went a long way to settling the hostilities in the area very, very quickly. The Serbs understood that the Canadians were not going to be overrun by the Croatians. The Canadians took every possible means to move the Croatians out. The Croatians were being belligerent and were not prepared to move out in accordance with the agreement. The force commander, a French general at the time, was brought in for the negotiations, and the Canadians stood fast and the Croatians evacuated the positions. The Serbs had a great deal of respect for our soldiers.

Gorazde

When I went down to Bosnia I was the team leader for military observers in Gorazde during the Serb offensive in March and April 1994. We were the only United Nations military presence in the pocket.

The Serbs on or about March 28 attacked the pocket. At the time I was in Vienna having some leave with my family, following it very closely on CNN whenever I could. I was inserted into the pocket on about April 7 with a team of SAS of the British Army, and I lived in Gorazde through the main part of the offensive.

I should make a differentiation between the United Nations Protection Force that was in place and the military observers. Our role as military observers was basically that, to observe and report. We didn't take part in any of the interposing of forces between the Serbs and the Muslims. We were restricted to being on the Muslim side, that is, within the pocket itself, and while I was team leader, I made a conscious effort to get out and meet as often as I could with the Serb commanders. It was that type of relationship. Our battalions, on the other hand, the United Nations Protection Force, interposed themselves between the warring parties, in particular in Croatia, the area that I'm familiar with, and their role was to try and keep the two warring factions separated.

I would like to make it very clear that we are in a war there. We are peacekeeping and I think that satisfies our collective conscience that we're doing something good for the world, but we are in the middle of a war. The Croatians, the Serbs and the Muslims, in my opinion, want to kill each other. And it's our presence there that has a stabilizing effect. There's a very fine line between being combatants and peacekeepers. And as long as we maintain our professionalism and are very disciplined — and our soldiers are extremely disciplined — we manage to stay on the peacekeeping side.

The Airborne Regiment

I don't know exactly what happened in Somalia but I would like to point out that the Canadian Airborne Regiment are amongst the highest trained airborne troops in the world. They're the kind of soldiers that if we had a punch-up in Yugoslavia where one of our battalions was taking a beating, and if the Canadian government was committed to its policy in Yugoslavia, I can say to a man, every soldier in the Canadian Airborne Regiment would jump to his death on behalf of this country in order to reinforce that battalion, in the unlikely event that we decided to take that approach. The Canadian Airborne Regiment has had a lot of bad press and they are extremely disciplined soldiers. They were living under terrible conditions there, from my understanding, and what the public should understand is that they were living in a war zone. They were dealing with death every day. And perhaps some soldiers lost it. Our soldiers in these war zones are under a tremendous amount of pressure.

I can understand the criticisms that have been raised toward the Airborne Regiment in Somalia, but I can say that, having served in a war zone, having been fired upon by every type of offensive weapon that I ever read about, until you have been through the paces, until you've been in the trenches, you should not be passing judgment.

Since the breakdown of the cold war we have committed more troops into war zones than we've had since, to my knowledge, Korea. If we are prepared to put lives on the line, then we need a force such as the Airborne Regiment, the cream of the crop. They are our strategic reserve. If a problem erupted in Haiti, say an embassy problem, of all of the units that I've served with in the Canadian Forces, the one unit that is ready to do an operation on behalf of Canada would be the Canadian Airborne Regiment. And I would challenge anybody, any member of the press that would be prepared to sit down and debate the issue of the Airborne. We need soldiers of that calibre in Canada.

By sending soldiers to the Canadian Airborne Regiment where they receive very good training, we increase the standard of training and readiness throughout the Canadian infantry.

I don't want to pass blame to our politicians. I don't want to pass blame to the senior military leaders. I think the blame lies with the Canadian media. When the Americans mobilized in Haiti, there was all sorts of news on the television and in the newspapers. However, since I've been back from Bosnia I have been clinging to the television set to find out what's happening to our soldiers over there. I've been scouring the newspapers to find out what's happening in Croatia with our young soldiers. And there is no information. There is very little information coming back out of the war zone that can inform the Canadian public. Our media in Canada has an obligation. We have soldiers deployed in a war zone and I know that Canadians want to hear about it. They want to know about the conditions and the only way that can be conveyed is by our own media.

Tanks

Our lives are on the line every day. And I can honestly say that I would go tomorrow, commanding Canadian troops in any area that I was called upon to go into. Granted our equipment is getting old. Much of the equipment is as old or older than I am. However, I am prepared to go into a theatre with the equipment that we have. I would love to have Bradley fighting vehicles, but the reality is that we have a problem with our debt. I think that there are actions under way to try and enhance our capabilities, but it has to be done realistically. We are not a superpower. We have to be realistic in the types of equipment that we think we can deploy with. And from my perspective I think that we have the equipment that's capable of doing the job. Just barely.

You take our tank, for instance. While I was in Tuzla the Serbs had attacked one of the NORBAT's positions and were shelling it. This is the Nordic countries' battalion, a composite battalion, and the NORBAT headquarters warned the Serbs to cease their attack. They refused and the Danish tank company deployed four tanks out into the area and fired, if I remember correctly, 72 rounds at the Serbs. They took out bunkers. They took out trench positions. There was quite a significant firefight. That incident gained the respect of the Serbs. I think it was a begrudging respect, but there were no more problems with NORBAT and the Serbs from there. That's the same tank that we have in the Canadian Forces. It's not a Leopard 2, but it definitely gets the job done in the areas that we might conceivably deploy to these days.

The most predominant tanks that I saw in Yugoslavia were T-34 or T-55s; that's stone-age technology, even compared to our Leopard 1. I would love to have state-of-the-art equipment, but I think that the roles that we're being committed to are realistic for our capability. If we were to deploy the Leopard tank into Bosnia, it would be a significant force to deal with, but I don't think it's completely necessary. Are we going to go in there and try to fight our way out? I suggest we're not. But the Leopard 1, although it's an older tank, is still effective on the battlefield.

Take a look at the Israelis. I don't know if they're still running Centurions but that's real stone-age technology that they've been upgrading and keeping in the field. It's very expensive to run a tank. Extremely expensive. We could use better armoured personnel carriers, and I understand that we're working toward that. I don't want to come across like I'm defending the politicians. I know my life depends on the type of equipment that we bring in. But it's not as easy as saying, "We need this equipment, let's go buy it."

For instance, I was on a project team that was investigating purchasing a new light armour vehicle for the infantry and we were looking at, if I remember correctly, upwards of $4 billion to put a fleet in place. Can we afford that given the current financial climate? I don't think we can, and I think that we can make do with what we have and what our senior leaders are planning on bringing onto line. Quite honestly I think I've got a realistic approach in the equipment world.

There's a lot of people that disagree with me, and perhaps by coming across hard core and demanding that we need new equipment that might sway opinions. I'm speaking based on my experience, and I am quite prepared to go into the type of missions that we have today with the equipment that we have. And I do that in full knowledge that at National Defence Headquarters we are looking to the future. We're looking to see how long we can push the current generation of tanks.

We're looking at the different options in purchasing an affordable armoured personnel carrier for the types of commitments that we see ourselves getting into.

I don't want to come across as the eternal optimist. There are improvements that we have to make, but I'm confident that things are in place and if the budgets are not cut too drastically, I think we can make do.

SCOTT TAYLOR
Corporal
1994

Scott Taylor spent three years in the infantry before he became the publisher of Esprit de Corps, *an independent magazine voicing the views and opinions of Canada's military community — serving and retired. Published since 1993,* Esprit de Corps *has a wide readership, especially within the Armed Forces, and has earned the enmity of many inside NDHQ for its unflinching examinations of defence issues. Taylor is the author of several books about the Canadian army, including* Tarnished Brass *and* Tested Mettle.

In a sense I've never really left the service. I've stayed with it through this publication. As a journalist I've visited virtually every single UN peacekeeping operation where Canadians have been deployed. That's part of our ongoing mandate. We try to bring back a little more background, explain why they're being deployed and how they're being equipped.

Information About the Military
Given media budget restraints, and given the number of deployments and the duration of these deployments, coverage hasn't been all that it

could be. But I think the information that comes through from the Defence Department's resources is sadly lacking. If the information coming back wasn't managed to the degree that it is, the civilian media would have more to work with. As it is, peacekeepers' deaths have been deliberately misrepresented, in terms of how these guys have been dying. Peacekeeping casualties include instances where our troops have been deliberately targeted or attacked by the belligerents.

I don't think it's a conspiracy, it's attitude that's the problem and it's been so since the unification of the Armed Forces and since the Trudeau plan to bureaucratize the military. Officers are now often simply managers and managers don't like surprises, either good or bad. And day-to-day occurrences are surprising. I mean, stuff happens.

Look, war is a four-letter word with any HQ brass. There are other words that they don't like to hear as well, like casualties or hostilities or battle. Anything to do with putting our soldiers' lives on the line in open warfare.

I think that the lack of coverage is definitely having an effect now. Canadian troops are leaving their families and going back in for their third and in some cases fourth mission to the same country, and what they're accomplishing or the dangers they're facing isn't making it back to their families or their friends. Your average person doesn't understand or really recognize the dangers that these guys are facing.

That's where the public relations policy at DND is sadly lacking. I don't think Canadians would lose the will to support UN missions if they knew the real dangers. I think if you herald the heroism of our young men and women out there, people would still take a sense of reflective pride in that, as Canada has inevitably done in wartime.

They want everything to follow the "no-surprises" blueprint that they've set up, and peacekeeping is a guy in a blue helmet with a child and a teddy bear. That's Canadian peacekeeping. It's not returning fire or giving covering fire while your wounded are withdrawn under the cover of smoke. This isn't what they want to project. I think there is a fear that perhaps Canadians will lose the will to support real armed forces. UN and peacekeeping are their ticket to the future, the ticket to retain their budget, with the absence of a cold war threat.

The families of the soldiers that are serving suffer when the truth is not being told. It's tough to give a medal to someone who's saved a life if you can't admit that the life was ever in danger. One of our guys was killed by an anti-tank rocket. The story line that was given to the media was "accidental mortar fire," mortar fire that just happened to be landing near his carrier. That wasn't the case.

Their defence was that they were saying this to protect the family from the gruesome details. I don't think that was the case. One year after the fact they finally admitted it was an anti-tank rocket. By that time it didn't really matter.

There are buzzwords that everyone keeps using and overusing now. We've gone from "peacekeeping" to "peacemaking." Well, they're certainly taking their sweet time making peace in Bosnia. I don't think that anybody's got a clear blueprint for success there. I don't think the problems in a region wracked with warfare for 600 years are solvable by the presence of blue-helmeted troops.

There is warfare going on, despite the presence of the UN. They're able to deliver aid, but when you go in and you sustain these people with humanitarian aid, you allow these things to go on ad nauseam. These things are not being solved.

Those soldiers that have gone back three and four times question why they're there. The first time the guys go in they can see progress. They can see that a village that has been ethnically cleansed is being rehabilitated and people are starting to grow things. But once you've seen your 100th cease-fire being violated, it starts to mean nothing. I don't think even the Canadian public believe the next cease-fire agreement. It's a blunt nerve now.

Manpower and Leadership

There's rumbling amongst the ranks. I wouldn't say it's at a crisis point yet, but it's getting there with recent incidents, such the Kyle Brown trial, in Somalia, where the lowest-ranking guy ends up going to jail for five years and the colonels and majors that gave the order don't even get a reprimand. They were let off the hook. At the same time these troops are being asked to give more and more. And there's no relief in sight. The key? The army's got to get 2,000 more regular troops.

They took the cream of the crop of the militia as an augment to these regular force units. They were given the first crack at becoming a regular soldier and most of them jumped at it. So most of those 2,000 soldiers that increased the numbers came from our own militia. But the militia was not then authorized to go and recruit an additional 2,000 troops. You've taken away the 2,000 best-trained and best-experienced militiamen from the units that are providing the reinforcements now.

It's a case of beginning to eat your young, if you will, by simply moving the cockleshell over one and then claiming it's an increase. The army can't complain because they've got more men. You've got the same men but you've just simply named reservists as regulars and moved them over on the ledger sheet. A leader would say, "I see through this cockleshell game." That didn't happen. The head of the army, Gordon Reay, is not stupid. He knows what they've done to him. But he didn't get up and say, "Unless you give me the tools to work with, I'm now Mr. Reay."

He didn't do that. He accepted it. They touted this as a real commitment to Canada's army and to our peacekeeping manpower shortage. It didn't change anything. The troops aren't stupid either. They know. They know they're packing up now, in the case of the engineers, for their third, fourth or even fifth tour. These guys are really stretched.

Management is leading by attacking the traditions and the inner fibre of the military. The only thing that's going to see them through is if they've got a strong cadre and a strong sense of tradition and a strong sense of morale. You can survive that. But when you've got the Kyle Brown situation added to the overtasking, you've got yourself a serious highway to trouble. It's coming apart because you're losing the senior NCOs. They're not accepting it. They've been around long enough to know that this isn't how it should be happening. They see the future and the future is no change.

I mean, being a soldier is a young man's game. A lot of troops are getting out because of what they're seeing. The writing on the wall says more of the same. They don't like what they're seeing. Officers don't take responsibility for their actions, or stand up to the bureaucrats. They don't demand that they get the proper support until the families come forward and scream.

But I think you're always going to find soldiers who will volunteer to go. You could probably equip these guys with even less, pay them less, feed them hard rations and you're gonna find young Canadian men that would go and do it. And if you put an ad in *The Globe and Mail* and cite the dangers and say there's a 50/50 chance of coming back alive, you'd probably still get a surprising number of young men that would turn up to do that. But would they still go and serve if they knew they might end up in jail for five years for accidentally shooting a non-belligerent?

Responsibility

Having the restrictions, worrying about who's to blame or who's going to be responsible for orders given in a situation where you have to open fire has limited the efficiency of the troops. It affects not just morale but also the hierarchy of the military. The orders have to come top-down but the loyalty has to be bottom-up. When something goes wrong the officer comes forward on behalf of his men and takes the fall. But that's not happening. And it's not a healthy thing. What came out of the Somalia trial was that those who came forward with information were the most heavily punished. So instead of appealing to a soldier's honesty and integrity, you've punished him for that.

The message now is, "If something happens today, nobody saw anything."

I've been speaking to some of the officers who planned those operations. The number-one option was for the Airborne to parachute in, in their normal role, to secure the area they were landing in. There weren't any parachutes. No parachutes. I believe that. The problem with logistics comes back to this idea that they're managing and not preparing for war. You've got people in the logistics branch who do a nine-to-five job. They don't often go into field and don't have to see or be responsible for any mistakes they made. I mean, it's OK to make a mistake if you work for Canada Post. Something gets sent to the wrong address, no problem. In the army that doesn't work because the guy in Kuwait ends up with wool socks and guy up in the Arctic ends up with a package of condoms.

This is not the army of yesterday where your supply technicians were with the army. From the time they joined they knew what was happening. They followed it through. Now everything's computerized. Everyone is virtually unaccountable. What you've got is a supply system that's almost untraceable.

It's going to take a strong leader to emerge. We've had strong leaders come through the ranks. General MacKenzie has gotten out and has continued to trumpet the military's shortcomings. There are other leaders in there; the problem is the system works against them. It keeps them at a lower level where they're ineffective. They need to clean house, pick the right man from two or three rungs down the ladder, make him the CDS, clean out the whole top end, bring in a new deputy minister, someone who perhaps has military experience, and get back to basics.

This is not a social-welfare department. This is the Defence Department. If it doesn't pertain to defence, it shouldn't come out of the defence budget. You don't need more money. You don't need $12 billion to get the military results that you're getting now. You could probably do it with less than $9 billion, if you were to cut out all the attention and detail that's spent on research projects going nowhere, huge salaries and an overburdened civilian equivalent to the generals. We have more civilian general equivalents than we do generals, and we have three times as many generals as we need.

The thing is, it cannot clean itself up. It's virtually impossible to ask somebody to eliminate their own position or those of their colleagues around them. It has to be done with a deliberate purpose. The U.S. picked Colin Powell and made him head of the armed forces. People jumped ship because they were passed over for promotions. The same thing could work in Canada. I think it's overdue.

BOB KENNEDY

Captain (Retired)
2000

Bob Kennedy spent five years at Ontario Command HQ as editor of The Garrison, *a newspaper for the army in Ontario. He was fired after criticizing DND's public affairs branch and publishing in* The Garrison *detailed statistics on casualties in Yugoslavia. He is currently working as a freelance editor specializing in Canadian military affairs. He wrote the essays in the recently published* To The Trace Imagery of Soldiering, *a photographic portrait of the citizen soldier in Canada.*

My background included a number of years in a small radio station in the town where I grew up, and then five years in the Parliamentary Press Gallery in Ottawa. After that I went back to school and after finishing school I joined the army. They're not necessarily compatible, being a reporter and being a soldier at the same time. But the unit I joined has nothing to do with public affairs. It's a reconnaissance unit, a unit of scouts for the armoured corps, and a very good unit of scouts in the armoured corps, the best in the militia.

The beginning, of course, is basic officer training, which is a challenging undertaking, especially when you're 30 years old and your classmates are, you know, 19, 20. But I think I survived that episode on two strengths. First, the lack of perhaps youthful vigour was compensated for by just ordinary maturity, I would say. And on the other hand, I've always believed that anything one can define as temporary can be tolerated. And temporary is an elastic concept, you know.

In those days the cold war was still under way. The Pershing II missiles were being deployed in Europe. The Canadian Forces had a regular force at that time of about 75,000 and an army reserve of fewer than 20,000. I joined partly because it struck me as a place where one could make a difference. You know, the eyeglasses model, which argues that although contributing an old pair of eyeglasses to Colombia or somewhere makes no difference at all to the global gap of north-south wealth, it makes all the difference in the world to the person who gets the eyeglasses.

The Garrison
The return to journalism happened when I was essentially recruited by the public affairs people here in Toronto during the Gulf War. The task I was recruited to do was to create and then edit a newspaper, *The Garrison*, for the army in Ontario. As it developed it gained quite a national character by way of its distribution and by way of its story selection. There was no equivalent newspaper in the Forces at the time.

At the outset the constraints were far less than what I expected. Indeed, the constraints were not really greater than one encounters in an ordinary newsroom. There are a lot of constraints on journalists in Canada to start with, in terms of libel and slander, in terms of obscenity, in terms of accuracy and in terms of the clock. I remain convinced that the biggest constraint on reporters is the clock.

My supervision at the outset was by actual soldiers, colonels and generals who were from the combat arms who had no particular political axe but were most interested in the rest of the world knowing what their soldiers were doing, how good their soldiers were, what their tasks were, and from a sort of argumentative point of view, why we even have an army.

One of the advantages I had at the outset was that the general in command of the formation I was working for was a militia soldier whose civilian experience was as the manager of public affairs in a large automobile manufacturer in southern Ontario. He understood fully what should be done and what I was supposed to be dealing with. When controversial items came up, he had no problem with my reporting what had happened.

A good example is the pay system. The pay system of the reserve force in Canada has always been abysmal and has caused a great deal of grief to thousands upon thousands of soldiers. By this point it has cost the Department of National Defence a few hundred million dollars, I'm sure, trying to get the software operating up to the point where part-time soldiers can be paid with something like the frequency that a company like McDonald's can achieve.

The army's problem is no more complicated than your average large company with a large number of part-time employees working strange hours irregularly and so on. But they took decades to solve the problem and I'm speaking in the past tense, believing that it's much better now than it used to be. But at one point early in the career of *The Garrison* newspaper, it was discovered that about 1,200 soldiers had never been paid for the summer, and this was about November.

As a reporter it was easy to recognize that as a story. And so I wrote the story as well as I could, and many of my more senior colleagues were quite skittish about reporting so plainly the incompetence of the pay system. But the commander said, "Well Bob, is it true?" And I said, "Yes sir, and not only is it true, but it would be hard to find a soldier in the army in Ontario who did not already know that the system had collapsed, and therefore surely my role in the paper is to first acknowledge that the thing has collapsed, explain how it collapsed if I can, and most importantly, from the army's point of view, explain what's being done to fix it."

What developed was that the supervision of the public affairs activity here in Toronto, that is, with the army in Ontario, was no longer by combat arms soldiers but rather by the — I hesitate to say it — the professional public affairs people from Ottawa. One was dispatched to our cell here in Toronto to essentially get a grip on these wild-eyed militia soldiers who were operating the shop entirely to the satisfaction of the soldiers, but definitely off script when it came to the view of public affairs at National Defence Headquarters.

The Casualty Story

I came across the casualty story, like many good stories, by accident. I did not set out to write a story about how inadequate was the tracking of our casualties in the UN operation in Yugoslavia. The initial idea was to publish a kind of educational piece for the recruiters and the platoon commanders and the troop leaders, the junior leaders back in Canada, who were more or less constantly in the business of training and exercising their troops, teaching them how to dig trenches, how to drive under dangerous conditions, teaching them, essentially, tactical behaviour in a dangerous situation — that is, in a war zone. I thought that if I could demonstrate to the people in Canada that most of our casualties in Yugoslavia were being caused by, for example, mortar fire, then your average platoon leader should be able to point this out to his soldiers as they are digging yet another trench. Or perhaps most of our casualties were being caused by mines, and then you can say, "And that's why we're doing yet another mine lecture today."

So initially it was intended to provide fuel for the trainers to emphasize ordinary tactical imperatives, and I set out to find a list of what our casualties had been and what the causes were. This turned out to be not an easy list to find because the medical people were not tracking it at that time. In fact, I could find no one, really, who was properly tracking it, until I discovered that a former classmate of mine was working in the operations cell at National Defence Headquarters on the public affairs side, and he had a list which they used to answer questions that might have come into the operations centre.

The list itself was being compiled by a couple of clerks deep within the bowels of the building. These clerks were thoroughly overwhelmed by the task and getting help from virtually no one, including the chain of command. So I published that list as a sidebar to the story of two soldiers from Ontario who had been shot up on New Year's Eve one year in Yugoslavia, and one of whom had been quite badly injured, half a dozen bullets ending up in various parts of him. Both of those soldiers survived, but their jeep had 54 holes in it. That was a good story. The list was published simply as a sidebar on the page.

There are two categories which have to be accounted for in each case. The first is the cause and the other is the severity of the injury. For causes traditionally there were only four items. War (being hostile action of any kind on the part of the enemy), disease, accident (having nothing to do with the enemy) or "other." "Other" in Yugoslavia would mean suicide, essentially.

No one went missing; no one was being captured that we didn't get back. But in the category of war we had things like someone running over a mine, two guys in Srebrenica that were attacked, a bombed building collapsing on someone, since it's a result of hostile action.

When that issue hit the streets I was flooded by e-mails and voice mails and letters and phone calls. I was buttonholed in hallways by soldiers who essentially said, "Nice list, Lieutenant, but I should be on it. Let me tell you why." Some of these guys were quite upset that a list which purported to be a complete list of our casualties had left them out, when they knew very well that they had been shot, and indeed had come through the medical chain and come back to Canada.

That was clearly a story worth pursuing. I had a couple of pretty good reporters working for me on the paper, and they went to work. In part they simply scanned every wire service story from any part of Yugoslavia in the previous two or three years in the search engines, just correlating "Canadian casualty," "United Nations," "Yugoslavia." That process generated another dozen or so names. We also interviewed several battalion commanders, particularly the commander who had been there with the first unit, who had gone into Croatia straight from Germany that spring, and he provided us with a list of another 20 or so soldiers who had been injured, none of whom had appeared on the list, which, incidentally, began around the first week of July 1992. The troops had been there for two months before that, and in a most dangerous environment, so surely there were casualties.

After combining all of these I subsequently published a much longer list, along with a story which I thought explained how it came to be that the list was so poor. Now, there were a number of reasons why the list was so poor. Some of the reasons were transparent and can be explained simply through bureaucratic inefficiency. For example, UN Canadian military observers who had been injured and shipped home from Yugoslavia were under a different chain of command. That means that they were not, strictly speaking, part of the Canadian battle group and so had gone through a different set of paperwork. Nevertheless, they ended up in the National Defence Medical Centre and others had to be sent to replace the people who had come back to Canada. So there was no doubt at National Defence Headquarters that people had been hurt. Those were the easy ones to explain.

Others had no apparent explanation at all, particularly names which appeared on the list as having been injured accidentally, who in fact were combat casualties. How someone is listed as being accidentally injured when they are in fact casualties of combat truly remains to be answered.

An outstanding example would be a couple of soldiers, Jordie Yeo and Jeff Melchers, who were part of the reinforced company group that went to Srebrenica. Srebrenica was declared a UN protected zone by the French commander at the time, and he did that without really having the means to protect it.

Shortly after that a Canadian reinforced company was sent there, and by reinforced I mean, as well as 100 or 120 infantrymen, they were reinforced with extra anti-tank assets, extra medical assets, extra engineering assets, I believe, up to a strength of maybe 175, 180 men. They established a camp in Srebrenica, a defended camp, and proceeded to patrol the perimeter.

One day while two of them were out, just two soldiers and a radio, they came under fire from a machine-gun point, I believe it was a Serbian nest, around Srebrenica, and both of them went down. One of them was quite badly injured in his lower legs. The company commander dispatched a platoon to collect these guys and bring them home. Eventually they went into the medical chain and their injuries were treated. These two guys had apparently "accidentally" walked into a stream of machine-gun bullets The inaccuracy of the accidental description was pointed out to me by the company commander himself, who was thoroughly upset to discover that a couple of his soldiers, who really had been attacked, were listed as merely having accidents in Yugoslavia.

The result of publishing the revised list was to get yet more letters and e-mails from guys all across the country pointing out that it wasn't perfect yet. Several iterations of the list were published, longer each time, along with summaries of the notes that I had been sent, pointing out the mistakes so that each episode could be described and the reader could draw his own conclusion about what might have gone wrong.

But the authorities certainly were not happy to see our diligence at the newspaper. No, I was not congratulated for filling in the gaps on that list. The outcome, in short, was that Captain Kennedy returned to training recruits rather than editing a newspaper. That is to say, I was fired.

The Garrison eventually died. After I left there was not much enthusiasm for pursuing it because the professional public affairs person who was then in charge of the shop in Toronto had an entirely different concept of what these things should do. In other words, her view was not that it was truly a newspaper, come what may, but rather just an inhouse sheet to pat people on the back. It was certainly not to reveal, as they like to say, the dirty laundry of the army in public.

Now, the Yugoslavian casualty story was the outstanding effort of the paper, which annoyed the public affairs branch, but of course that was not the only story that I had published. It certainly would not appear now in the Force's newspaper called *The Maple Leaf*, which is vetted to death before it ever leaves NDHQ.

The System and the Image of Peacekeepers

The system was not prepared with a casualty procedure even though one existed, very clearly, in what were then Canadian Forces Administrative Orders. That is, one of the CFAOs, as they were called, described step by step what must be done at the originating unit when one of their soldiers becomes a casualty. That procedure simply was not pursued, was not observed. And back at National Defence Headquarters it clearly had been so long since we were coping with anything like this that the burden of effort was not directed toward tracking the causes or looking after the soldiers when they got home, but rather being absolutely sure, from a bureaucratic point of view, that all of the documents were in place to prove, before we put someone on this list, that he had indeed been shot.

It's like some of these overseas trusts, whereby you get a pension if you had your leg amputated in Malaya in 1958. Well, every year the guy has to come and confirm that yes, he remains eligible for the pension. It was that kind of mentality which really got in the way of even the possibility of doing it well.

The authorities in NDHQ clearly were not pleased with the amount of noise that the whole story caused, particularly by the stories which resulted from my being fired. Indeed, quite a large inquiry was undertaken inside NDHQ, although, typically, the person who was assigned to explain all of this to the minister was the person in charge of the unit which was tasked with collecting the data in the first place. He of course said we need an entirely new system, failing to notice that the system he had was very good, if it had been worked properly.

It is irresistible to imagine that the masking of combat casualties in Yugoslavia does not coincide with what the policy is. That being of course to obscure, really, the dangers of these overseas deployments. The impression, clearly, that we are supposed to get is that when we send the army on a peacekeeping mission, it is to help people, which indeed it is.

The picture of Canadian soldiers handing out teddy bears and sharing their rations with starving refugees and fixing the roof of a schoolhouse is all true, but it's what they're doing in their spare time. What the soldiers are really going to do is to intervene in a war zone where for the most part the belligerents have stopped fighting reluctantly. And it becomes a test of wills.

Peacekeeping, of course, is sold as something less dangerous than warfare, something nicer, something which a non-threatening, helpful, non-imperialist country like Canada is well suited to do. At the political level, the distinction between peacekeeping and warfare seems to be considered absolute. From the army's point of view, peacekeeping is simply another form of warfare, and indeed it happens in war zones and is in many ways more dangerous and certainly more frustrating for soldiers than a clear-cut friendly-and-enemy scenario might be.

The army trains for peacekeeping as if it were going to war and if it arrives in the theatre and discovers that the place is actually much more calm than they expected it to be, so much the better. But the assumption from the military side is that they must be prepared to fight, and indeed their credibility on the ground in a peacekeeping scenario depends on their being seen to be capable and ready and prepared to fight. That's how you prevent people from shooting at you. You shoot back with a bigger weapon.

So the distinction between peacekeeping and warfare is not nearly so sharp as it has been sold. Peacekeeping can cause many more casualties than simply the accumulated stress of being forced to watch bad things and be able to do nothing about it. In a conventional warfare scenario, the soldiers would be intervening.

The fact that my conclusions varied so radically from the picture which we have been trying to paint for so many years was certainly upsetting to them. Although, even in Cyprus, when our armoured vehicles patrolled the Green Line between the Turks and the Greeks, they went, as they say, fully bombed up. They did not go out on patrol without a full load of ammo. They understood that their credibility depended on being able to fight, not on having a blue flag. The blue flag helped, but credibility depends on looking serious.

PART TWO

SEAN HENRY

Colonel (Retired)
2000

During his career in the Canadian military Sean Henry was assigned to a wide range of command and staff appointments in Canada and overseas, including deputy commander of the Special Service Force at Petawawa. As an exchange instructor at the U.S. Army Command and General Staff College, Fort Leavenworth, he was cited with a commendation from the president of the United States and in 1988, was appointed an Officer of the Order of Military Merit by the governor general for his work as a senior policy analyst at National Defence Headquarters. He is currently a consultant in the fields of strategic analysis and government relations and the senior defence analyst with the Conference of Defence Associations.

Canadians for many years looked to the colonial power, first the French and then the British, to provide the defence capability for them, and that persisted right up until the beginning of the last century. There have always been difficulties in Canada with providing Canadian armed forces. It goes a long way back.

At the beginning of the 20th century, of course, the British Empire was a mighty and proud entity. Canada was an integral part of it, and when the British Empire was under threat, or it was thought legitimate to go to war, Canada felt that it should do its part and we responded in first-class fashion. There are many who say that the nation emerged as a nation after Vimy Ridge in the First World War and went even further toward full independence after the Second World War.

The Cold War

The problem has been that, once the immediate threat of major war had been removed, there was quite a bit of backsliding into the old colonial mentality, in other words, a reluctance to provide resources for our Armed Forces. Now, this started to change in the 1950s when it became evident that the cold war was going to present a new kind of threat and Canada was going to be on its own, so to speak. We had Mr. Pearson who was, on the one hand, a person who was very peace-oriented, but on the other hand, was very much a pragmatist and knew the art of the possible as far as peace was concerned. He was a great supporter of the UN, but by the same token, he knew that something had to be done with respect to the Soviet threat. We went to Korea and we got involved with NATO and went on that way for the next 30 years.

Our early contributions to NATO were absolutely outstanding. We had 12 squadrons of fighter airplanes in Europe and we had a very good brigade over there for many years. That was the case until the late 1960s when a number of events occurred which have been very debilitating. And we are living in the legacy of those events today.

The role of "Honest Broker, Helpful Fixer" goes back to the inter-war period, between the First and the Second World War, when people like Mr. Pearson were just getting started. There were other people out there, the "Ottawa men," like O. D. Skelton and Robert Rice, who were very determined to define and firmly set down a Canadian persona, or a Canadian position that was going to be separate from Britain, and show us emerging from the colonial past and establishing a Canadian entity out there. For a variety of reasons, particularly because of the horror that came out of the First World War, there was a great interest in seeking peace and there were many people in Canada that were focused on that sort of initiative.

So there was a very great dedication to peace in the world, but also a determination to set up a distinct Canadian identity within diplomatic circles and the international arena. Then the Second World War came along, and Canada felt it necessary to participate very, very strongly — which we did — and when it was over the United Nations was formed to try and take the place of the League of Nations, which had collapsed before the Second World War.

Within the context of the United Nations after World War II, this Canadian entity, so to speak, was more fully developed by people like Lester Pearson. They were still trying to base it on an independent foreign policy and a benevolent foreign policy, based on the principles of human rights and peace. But Pearson, being a pragmatist, knew that in the face of threats you have to hold your nose and do some things you might not like to do. Now, in the mid-1950s there was the Suez crisis, to which Lester Pearson made quite a large contribution, but his contribution was somewhat different than the myth that has come out of it.

He did not invent peacekeeping. The idea was put forward by the British, but since they were one of the aggressors in the war, they couldn't put it forward themselves. So he decided to put it forward at the UN, and did a magnificent job. I'm not taking that away from him. But it got lodged there in time as the defining point in Canadian history.

For the remainder of the cold war Canada did contribute a reasonable amount to peacekeeping operations. But the peacekeeping operations we were involved in were always a peripheral part of our military contributions to NATO and elsewhere. It was not until 1988 when there was a great outpouring of emotion over the world's peacekeepers being given the Nobel Prize that all of this sort of came together, and then it was followed immediately by the end of the cold war. Before we knew it our history had disappeared, and many people were saying that all we had ever done was peacekeeping, and of course that's totally wrong. Peacekeeping was a peripheral part of our heritage, a proud one, but peripheral nonetheless.

Unfortunately, after 1988, in conjunction with the financial deficit problems and debt problems of the government, peacekeeping was looked on as a convenient way of cutting defence spending. And of course that was a big mistake because since the end of the cold war we've had more very serious peace enforcement and peace support operations. The old blue beret peacekeeping died with the end of the cold war. That style of peacekeeping is long gone, and what they call peacekeeping today is really low-level operations of war.

Pacifist Movements and Human Security

In the 1920s there was a very strong pacifist reaction to the horrors of the First World War. Many of the people who were strong supporters of that approach were upset with Lester Pearson when he advised the government in the 1950s to enter NATO and to provide a strong Armed Forces. There was even a political movement in the late 1950s and on into the 1960s to try and make Canada declare itself a neutral, non-aligned nation. This was a developing thrust within Canadian domestic politics, and there are many groups out there that believe in this.

What brought it to a head, of course, was the coming to power of Mr. Trudeau, when he really took off with his program in the 1970s. There are those who will tell you that Trudeau was probably both a crypto-Marxist and a pacifist, and he certainly didn't believe that the Soviet Union was a threat. He was very uncomfortable with Canada being a member of NATO and providing forces in Europe. At the beginning of the 1970s he tried to take Canada out of NATO, and when he failed to do that he reduced the Armed Forces down to a real shadow and cut the military budget. Of course, that is the background to the problems of today. The Armed Forces never recovered from that period.

As far as human security is concerned, we have to look into the early 1980s when the peace movement in Canada, building upon the earlier thrust that I mentioned and building upon Mr. Trudeau's personal agenda, became much more widespread and much stronger. At that time the Soviets took an interest in it, as the English did under Wilson, and they saw Canada as a weak link in the Western alliance, so they determined to support the Canadian peace movement.

The peace movement became stronger and stronger throughout the 1980s, and by the time the 1990s arrived, even though the cold war had ended, they were still going full blast, and they produced a study based on hearings that they undertook across Canada. They produced a document, the *Citizen's Inquiry into Peace and Security* (also called *Transformation Moment: A Canadian Vision of Common*

Security), and it emerged with a central theme related to something called "common security."

While this was going on Mr. Axworthy was a very committed member of the peace movement and, being a former Cabinet minister, he was very important in this context. When the Liberals were in Opposition in the early 1990s, he took this study that the peace movement, the Canadian Peace Alliance, had done and developed some of the themes into items that were incorporated into the Liberal Party *Red Book*, and he changed the wording of "common security" to "human security." When he eventually became foreign minister, he took it on as his personal crusade.

Mr. Axworthy has not really acted alone. Human security now, within Western nations, has supporters other than Mr. Axworthy, particularly in places like the Scandinavian countries. And of course what they are trying to do is use the United Nations as a springboard.

I think what you're seeing out there today is a divergence of opinion and a diverging set of agendas. There is no doubt that Mr. Axworthy states that from time to time you do need armed forces to implement the human-security agenda. But it is very difficult to believe that he really means it because he is very much immersed in human-security issues. What is being missed by him and other people who support him is that unless you have a framework of stability in any of these places where civilians are being slaughtered and mistreated, then there's nothing that can be done. Sierra Leone is a perfect example. Until you send some strong, competent armed forces in there to impose peace, then there is no way you're going to start implementing a program of human security.

When you cast aside all of the rhetoric, particularly in a place like the Balkans, very few nations are going to go to war or go into a strong peacekeeping mode unless there are national interests at stake. Now, it can be shown that the motivating factor behind the NATO contributions to Bosnia, to Kosovo, was really not concern over humanitarian values. They were the shop window, the smokescreen, so to speak. What's really at stake, of course, is the stability, or the instability, of the Balkans, and the impact instability would have on Middle East oil. A big factor in the Balkans is not being seen to be moving against the Muslim population because there is a delicate balance going on in the Middle East, and what would be an absolute disaster for the West would be for

Muslim fundamentalists to topple the royal houses in Saudi Arabia and other countries.

This is the sort of thing that's behind what you've seen so far. That sort of national interest almost doesn't exist anywhere in Africa. So it is realpolitik, and yet many people out there today, including Mr. Axworthy, say that realpolitik is out of fashion and is no longer a factor, and that we must deal with all these other aspects in human security. But unfortunately that's not the way life works.

Military force is a fact of life, and, going into the philosophical side, war and conflict and aggression are hard-wired into the human psyche. That's unfortunate, but it's true. Differences between groups can only be resolved to a certain extent by negotiation and diplomacy. Once you get into vital national interests, generally speaking, force or war is the only way you're going to sort these matters out.

I will say something that makes an awful lot of people very upset, but by the same token, it can be shown and proved that, generally speaking, war leads to progress. Now, there's an awful lot of horror in the short term. But beyond that things get better, generally, after the war. Why is that? Well, one of the things that war does is that it imposes change. And the one thing that human beings resist more than anything else in the world is change.

So the main reason to impose military force is to impose change. And what is very interesting is that in the long run it is good change that wins out. And all you have to do is look at, say, the Second World War with Hitler and Mussolini and the Japanese, and then look ahead to the cold war where the Soviet Union represented another type of very, very unhealthy dictatorship.

Defence Contributions
To put it quite simplistically, Canada would like to have its cake and eat it too. With respect to our G7 membership, it has a lot to do with the fact that the Americans wanted another North American partner in it and therefore supported Canada. There are other nations out there, such as the Netherlands and Spain, who had their noses out of joint because they see themselves as being more economically advanced than we are, but nonetheless, we are in the club, and it is certainly incumbent

on us to pay the dues of the club. And one of the dues that a lot of people believe is important, with respect to international trade relations, for example, is that you pick up your share of the cost of defence. But of course Canada, for the last 20 or 30 years, has been a notorious deadbeat freeloader. It may not be quite that bad, but our contributions to defence since the Trudeau era have gone downhill very sharply, to the extent that today we only contribute 1.1 percent of our GDP to defence. The NATO average is 2.1 and that's probably the same within the G7.

There's a mistaken perception amongst the public, which is cultivated by other interests, that because there is no direct threat to Canada then we don't have to spend money on defence. And what these interests overlook is that Canada lives or dies by trade. Our trade is immensely important to us to maintain our prosperity and our quality of life. Although 85 percent of our trade is done with the United States, the other 15 percent is done with other parts of the world, and if things go wrong with international trade, then that will have an impact on the economy of the United States and that will ricochet onto Canada. So it is hugely important for Canada to assist in maintaining international peace and stability.

We have not had capable Armed Forces for a long, long time. And all you have to do is go back to the early 1950s, when we had come out of the Second World War and were a major contributor to NATO, to see when our stock as an international player was way up. We'd built up a bank account that you wouldn't believe. But from about 1970 onwards that bank account has been drawn down, and some would say it's in a deficit condition today and we do not get much respect. That has a bearing on things like human security because, if you come up with projects and initiatives under that, people are not likely to listen to you. You're not a serious player.

It became very evident in the 1970s, behind closed doors in NATO, that many of the allies were very unhappy with Canada. When Mr. Trudeau was going to withdraw us from NATO and when he cut back on our troop contributions and, in particular, when he was going to get rid of main battle tanks in Germany, he was taken aside by his German counterpart and was told, quite bluntly, that if Canada did not reconsider and improve its contributions, and in particular stay with main battle tanks, then the German government was going to retaliate with trade restrictions. Those who were there will tell you that keeping those tanks was a tradeoff for six shiploads of plywood from the West Coast of Canada which the German premier was going to cut off. That is a small but telling point.

When I was at the NATO Defence College in Rome, I shared an office with a Dutch diplomat. And the Dutch are immensely grateful to Canada for liberating them at the end of the Second World War. To this day, there are all sorts of celebrations in Holland to celebrate Canada and the Canadian army. One day my Dutch colleague looked up from his desk and looked straight at me and he said, "Sean, what has happened to Canada?" What he meant was, what has happened to our Armed Forces, our commitments to NATO, our defence responsibilities? When you have criticisms coming from people like the Dutch, who are our greatest supporters, I think you know you're in trouble.

I think that there is an agreement, I would not go so far as to say an outright conspiracy, amongst like-minded people, and this goes back to the Trudeau era when an awful lot of very bright and enthusiastic people joined the civil service and have now worked their way up to the deputy minister, assistant deputy minister level. They in particular were very committed to Mr. Trudeau's vision of peace and committed to downplaying military contributions to peace. When the Conservatives took over in 1984, there is some evidence that these people took it upon themselves to preserve what you might call the Trudeau agenda.

And of course, when the present government, the Chrétien government, emerged in 1993, there is evidence that they simply picked up where they had left off. The way this transpires is through constant pressure on the defence budget. In other words, advice to the government not to increase it. Constant pressure on the government not to make any exceptions for defence as being a special part of the government. In other words, the Department of National Defence is treated like just any other government department, and this is extremely debilitating.

Understanding Defence and the 1987 White Paper
There's a generation of people out there that don't understand defence and how it contributes to national well-being. And they are dead set against defence because they feel it is morally wrong to spend money on armed forces. There are still people like that within the civil service and within the government.

This is the challenge of people like myself who work hard to try and inform the public. The public, not just in Canada but in most countries, is not really hands-on with defence issues, and certainly in a case like Canada there is no threat that is evident, no barbarians at the gates. But if you go back to international trade relations and how they are very much hinged on peace and security, and how Canada lives or dies by trade, then this is the sort of thing that you have to put across to the public.

It's very difficult because the people that I call the anti-defence forces are very skilled in developing and maintaining public ignorance by using slogans and manipulating the media. So it's not just a question of people like me trying to develop the reality. I, first of all, have to beat down all the disinformation and the misinformation that the other side is putting out there.

The 1987 white paper was a very valid document because the government attempted, virtually at one stroke, to undo much of the damage that had been done during the Trudeau years. Of course today, with the benefit of hindsight, many people will say that it was preposterous, because the cold war was ending and did end. But I would point out that the cold war ended very suddenly in 1989 and the white paper was put together from about 1985 forward, and there were few hints that the cold war was going to end that quickly. In terms of its content it was very realistic and useful. Of course, there was quite a large price tag associated with it, but it was approved by the government in the face of an awful lot of opposition from the top civil servants because a number of them were starting to realize just how fragile Canada's fiscal situation was getting because of the huge debt that was built up. There were others who were horrified by spending that much money on defence.

So although the 1987 white paper was approved at government level, it would probably have been very much diminished in terms of being implemented, regardless of whether the cold war had ended or not, because the civil servants I'm talking about were successful in imposing on it a very severe funding formula. The formula was built around not increasing the defence budget more than two percent per year, which had been the amount that had been enforced since about 1976. And they convinced Treasury Board and others that all this extra money that was going to be needed should be dealt with in so-called bumps, that each time a big project came up, it would be dealt with as an isolated entity on its own merits. I don't have to tell you what that was doing. That was "divide and conquer," and their aim was to block each one of these projects as they came forward. It emasculated the white paper.

There was one good thing that still is a legacy of that white paper, in spite of everything that's happened. It allowed a foundation to be put in place for planning in DND. As a result of all the things that happened in the Trudeau years, which by and large brought in an era of "ad hocery" in the department, it was impossible to plan force development because you were planning on a bed of quicksand. The 1987 white paper installed a firm foundation for force development.

At the time the 1987 white paper started to be developed, I was serving in the ADM (Policy) branch of National Defence Headquarters in a rather unique job, something called a senior policy analyst. There were four of us that occupied that type of job and we were almost an independent group of advisors, on the one hand, to ADM (Pol) himself, and on the other, to the service chiefs, navy, army, air force. There was a civilian member as well. We had a lot of independence and we were often called on to render advice. I was there from 1983 to 1987, and so I was hands-on with the process leading to the white paper and with the guts of the white paper itself.

There was a basic difficulty. A lot of the staffing that was being done by the military people to produce the framework of the Armed Forces within the white paper was being undercut by other people, possibly acting on behalf of others in the central agencies outside of DND who did not want to spend money on defence. It was not all Trudeau being anti-defence. The whole massive structure of social programs that were put in place under the Trudeau regime in the 1970s certainly didn't leave any place for spending very much money on defence. From the point of view of the civil servants in the central agencies, whether or not they were pro- or anti-defence, they were faced with this very great problem of financing all the social programs. And if defence was eating up a number of the resources, obviously they were not going to be friends of defence.

It was quite evident to me that there were people that did not agree with the policy aspects that were emerging. They were quite determined to pull the Armed Forces out of Europe. It was a throwback to the early Trudeau years. That thrust had never really disappeared. It had gone underground.

I was involved with a number of people who were able to keep rational policy on the table and to encourage the development of organizations to implement that policy. But there is no doubt there were people, generally within the ranks of the officials in government, and certainly the Liberal Opposition at that time, probably including Mr. Axworthy, who were very much against this as well because they were still embedded in the Trudeau years.

From my point of view, the minister, Perrin Beatty, was well briefed on the contents of the white paper. He was caught up in this ongoing debate and this ongoing battle between the people in the Department of National Defence, particularly the military people on the one hand and the civil servants and the central agencies on the other. It is debatable whether he was well briefed on the possibilities of running into great difficulty with respect to funding the white paper. That was a factor that had to do with, not just the end of the cold war, but the looming crisis over Canada's fiscal situation.

The CAST Brigade

It was in the summer of 1986 and by that time the idea of consolidating the Canadian commitments in central Europe, which was going to eventually be reflected in the white paper, was well under way. At that time we had the brigade permanently stationed in Germany and the so-called CAST Brigade, stationed in Canada, was supposed to be loaded on ships and airplanes and moved over to north Norway. However, it was beginning to be decided that it would be much better to have a divisional commitment in central Europe. There were difficulties with respect to carrying that out because the Norwegians were going to be most unhappy if Canada pulled out, and there were a number of other political and just plain practical problems associated with doing that.

It was decided that a live exercise, which would involve actually moving the brigade over there, would be done, and by so doing would show that it was not going to work. Well, I actually visited Exercise Brave Lion. I was still in the policy branch, but I spent a week or so over there, and, generally speaking, the exercise was a success. They moved the brigade over there, it manoeuvred in war games and so on, and they loaded it back on the ships and it came home.

The spin was that the exercise had been a failure so that they could justify moving the commitment to central Europe. However, it was not all spin and we have to be very clear on a couple of items that emerged out of Exercise Brave Lion in 1986.

I had been involved in a study some years before that had to do with the viability of NATO's plans to stop Soviet invasion of north Norway. That very extensive and well-put-together command-post exercise done by the SHAPE Technical Centre in the Hague as a computer-generated war game showed quite conclusively that, even if all of the reinforcements to north Norway — and the Canadian brigade was only one of many reinforcements that would be sent to north Norway — were deployed in time, in an ideal situation it would be impossible for them to hold out more than about 13 days, 19 max, 13 average.

This study had shown that, for the Canadian brigade, north Norway would have been another Hong Kong. That was another factor that was influencing the Canadians to change that commitment, and a very valid one. But as far as Exercise Brave Lion was concerned, it was successful. The brigade went over and it was deployed and it came home.

The Gulf

I became aware of what Canada's approach was going to be to the Persian Gulf crisis, and then eventually the Persian Gulf War, when I arrived back in Ottawa from Rome roughly the first week of August. So this was very early in the game. In spite of that there had been some assessments made within DND, and the first one I had seen was quite disturbing because it virtually said, in advance, that Canada should not under any circumstances deploy land forces and that it should simply go with the relatively small commitments of airplanes and ships. The reasoning behind this was that there were going to be huge casualties and that it was going to turn into another Vietnam. There were all sorts of great flaws in logic and misplaced facts within this appreciation.

By that time, mid-1990, the cold war had ended and the Trudeau agenda was re-emerging out of the woodwork. There were many people that were committed to Canada getting out of Germany and devoting itself, forever after, to blue beret peacekeeping and sending a brigade of fighting troops into Kuwait. This just flew in the face of what these people were trying to achieve. So they were pulling out all the stops to try and derail such a development. The brigade was still sitting in Germany and, despite what anybody tells you, could have been deployed and could have acquitted itself well in Desert Storm and could have re-established Canada's stock away back up here. It was a huge opportunity that was missed. But it was done largely as a result of people who were dead set against Canada maintaining combat-oriented commitments.

It was my impression that the main thrust was to avoid ground forces, under any circumstances, by saying that the allies did not want us to join the campaign. I disagree with that very strongly. They would have welcomed our land forces because they wanted to get a wide set of representational commitments from various nations, and they knew that our brigade was damn good.

The naval and air assets that we sent over there in the first place were operating strictly under the United Nations and in a very restricted mode of operation: to simply enforce sanctions at sea and to enforce some sort of no-fly zone. Even afterwards, when we committed those resources to the war phase, there were still severe restrictions on them. The ships were still virtually outside the war zone, and until the very last day of the war the aircraft were not allowed to engage in combat operations.

Now, to be fair, the weapons those airplanes had were suited to combat air patrol and we did not have precision-guided munitions at that time. But it was beyond that. There was a political determination not to have Canada involved in the combat operations. At the very end the government gave in because it became apparent to them that it was going to be important for us to do a little bit of combat.

It was my experience, having been at NATO Defence College for three years, that many of the allies were getting extremely fed up with Canada's lack of commitments, and let's not play games because this is going on out there today. "Our allies have not asked us for any assistance." The way the world really works is that they come to you behind the scenes to find out whether or not you are willing to contribute, and if you say no, then they don't ask. Then you can go away and say, "Our allies have not asked us to contribute." That's what's going on in the UN right now. And it certainly went on at the official level at NATO, but behind closed doors. I am sure that the allies were again making nasty remarks about Canada.

The Balkans

On the other hand, the same people who supported our lack of commitment of land forces to the Gulf War saw what was going on in the Balkans as a golden opportunity for Canada to re-launch itself in a blue beret peacekeeping configuration. This was going to be the big turning point, the big turnover era. So they quickly set about sending two battalions down there from the brigade in Germany at the same time that the brigade was being taken apart and sent home.

Well, of course, once they got into the Balkans it became quickly evident that it was not a normal blue beret peacekeeping operation, and over the next three years it flirted with disaster. One of the aspects of that situation was that many of the peacekeepers started to take casualties, including the Canadians. Well, this was going to place in jeopardy the commitment and enthusiasm which was trying to be drummed up for Canada taking on the peacekeeping role forever. If it became apparent that peacekeeping was now going to generate casualties the same as combat operations, even the public would start saying, "What is going on here?" That's point one.

Point two is that within the military itself, particularly the army, there was a very big mistaken impression that, after pulling out of Germany and with the cold war ended, the Armed Forces, particularly the army, was going to have to justify its existence, and they jumped aboard the peacekeeping bandwagon as being their saviour.

I had just finished a one-year study of peacekeeping and sounded all sorts of alarm bells that old-fashioned peacekeeping was long gone and that new peacekeeping was going to be much different and much more combat oriented. Nobody was willing to listen. We also sounded the alarm bells that Canada should not commit itself fully to peacekeeping because if you did that, you would find it very difficult to build your forces back up. Your combat-capable forces can always do peacekeeping, no problem. But if you draw down, you can never go back up.

But nobody was listening. The military were very reluctant to admit to having casualties because they had jumped on the bandwagon. So if the casualties were being admitted and the government was forced by public opinion to pull troops out, then the army felt they would be left with nothing.

I don't want to say there was a conspiracy, but these factors were all floating around out there. In a couple of cases I saw the reports concerned, both from Somalia and from Bosnia, where Canadian troops were under fire, but the incidents were never reported. To my mind this was a big mistake. They should have been much more transparent as far as the public was concerned because that would have helped to justify increasing the defence budget and maintaining combat capabilities.

Analyzing the Problems

There are two seminal factors to the overall problems of the Armed Forces today and how they developed back in the early Trudeau years. Everybody knows about underfunding, the lack of money. The other one that is equally important and debilitating is the demilitarization of the Canadian Armed Forces. Back in 1973 there was a conscious decision taken to meld the civilian and military parts of the Armed Forces, and everybody knows about that. But what many people don't know is that out there, amongst the central agencies, particularly at Treasury Board, there was a policy invoked whereby DND was not going to be treated any differently than any other government department. So we have now arrived at a stage where the Armed Forces are not much beyond civil servants in uniforms. That's overstating the case but it's true enough, and it's caused very great problems.

From the mid-1970s onward, the personnel, material and finance branches of the Department of National Defence were less and less capable of supporting military operations because their attention was taken away from operational military matters and focused precisely on all the other things that go on within the federal bureaucracy. Process is more important than results, and they forgot all about looking after the troops.

That is a great problem and it has not been totally resolved. It's just an act of God that we didn't have more casualties in the Balkans and elsewhere, and it's a tragedy that those we did have had to be the ones that were mistreated before a number of these problems were dealt with. They have been by no means overcome, and they never will be until some very, very strong action is taken to reinvent the Armed Forces and to make the central agencies accept the fact that DND is different.

The whole question of unification is another element in the situation, and a number of the problems that the Armed Forces have today predate the Trudeau era. They come in at the end of the Pearson era, and the focus, of course, is unification, not integration. The 1964 white paper, with the benefit of hindsight, was not bad. The integration it proposed was OK, bringing together the top level of the navy, army and air force into joint operations, which everybody's doing today. Where it ran off the rails was when it went a step further into unification. The unification of the three armed services was a mistake of the first order. It created chaos; it was unnecessary and probably was one of the greatest tragedies that has occurred in the Canadian military scene since the Second World War.

In spite of all the other things we've talked about as being problems, the chaos emerging out of unification is a central problem. If there had been benefits that arose out of it, you could offset the bad effects, but as far as I'm concerned, and as far as most people are concerned, there were no benefits, and everything that came out of unification was bad.

There is no doubt that forcing the entire Armed Forces into a base configuration had all sorts of very bad effects, particularly in the army. The air force's bases of operation are their bases. The army is the exact opposite. For the army the base is a temporary structure where they live for a while and then they go out in the field. The field is where the army is supposed to carry out its operations. The navy is somewhere in the middle. The navy has bases but they also go to sea. This virtually undermined the entire army system and it's been a long road back. To this day there are still difficulties out there, particularly with the support because the support facilities for the army are needed in the field.

On a day-to-day basis the commanding officer was no longer the god, so to speak. You had a slow erosion of the unit commanding officer's ability and responsibilities to look after his men, in that a lot of the functions such as pay, logistics and medical were taken away and administered from a base organization, even though when he went back into the field he had to take these people with him. He had to adjust to the fact that somebody else was dealing with his troops in some very important functions.

Looking at the other end, you had people on the base side carrying out these functions who did not really have the same commitment and feeling of responsibility that they would have if they were in the unit. That was one step in the direction of becoming civil servants. They were interested in process, not in the results.

And, of course, dealing with DND as just another government department was beginning to emerge in Ottawa, so it was starting to occur at the top of the organization. People here began to see themselves as civil servants and that began to percolate down through the organization at the same time as this other factor was coming up from the bottom.

The interface between underfunding and demilitarization was also a factor. In the face of dwindling resources in units, there were not enough people, the equipment they were using was rusted out and the taskings were such that everybody was being double-hatted. That was occurring within the support resources as well. It was just a great big eggbeater of people that were running around trying to do two or three jobs at once, and doing none of them very well.

Under those conditions many commanding officers, and others, were virtually willing to give up. In the army combat arms, and presumably in navy ships and in air force squadrons, commanding officers tried to the best of their ability to insulate their troops from this terrible instability that was going on around them. But over a period of time their efforts were less successful. Over a period of time non-commissioned officers and officers were beginning to say, "We do not have the support from the government or anyone else to do our jobs properly, so let's start looking after ourselves."

In the old days, when you came in as an officer, you understood there was a certain noblesse oblige, that you had to look after the troops, and nobody had to tell you about that. But under the emerging conditions of the 1980s and 1990s, you were telling these new people what was expected of them. We have been developing a group of people in the Armed Forces who are more and more self-centred and who are not as willing to put service before self.

The Charter of Rights and Freedoms
The Charter of Rights, in its pure form, has had a very destabilizing impact on the Canadian Forces. There are people who say that there should have been some exclusions but, of course, the Trudeau government refused to do it, and it was refused again during the Mulroney

years. But untempered application of the Charter of Rights is not good for the Armed Forces. You now have a chain of command out there that is very gun-shy of doing things that need to be done in a disciplined way because they're afraid that people will jump up and say, "My rights!" You have a lot of people coming into the Armed Forces who think this way, that they've got rights all over the place. You also have a whole generation of predatory lawyers who are going to be encouraging them.

The Future

We have to set about reinventing the Armed Forces in Canada and do something along the lines of what was done in the United States after the Vietnam War in the late 1970s. Although it comes from a different source, the condition of the Canadian Forces today is not unlike the condition of the American armed forces after the Vietnam war. And although there are all sorts of individual remedies being applied out there, these remedies don't really get to the heart of the matter. They are dealing with the symptoms rather than going after the disease.

When I say reinvent the Armed Forces, it would take first of all a prime minister who understood the situation. It would take a minister, a deputy minister and a chief of the defence staff who all really understood what was going on, who committed themselves to doing something about it and then applied dynamic leadership, including knocking heads, to reinvent the Armed Forces. High on the list is to take measures and to make it known that the Department of National Defence is not just another government department. The minute you do that, you're going to have all the senior civil servants lined up against you, so you have to have dynamic leadership and knock heads. There will have to be exclusions within the Charter, or some sort of understanding that the Charter cannot be applied in blanket fashion in the Armed Forces. Some more money, always. There will be a number of expansion programs to make people in the Armed Forces, particularly the leadership, understand that they are not civil servants in uniform. You've got to galvanize them again.

There was a survey done by social scientists of what has happened to the militaries in most of the Western nations since the end of the cold war. We're talking now about the Americans, the British, the French, the Dutch, the Norwegians, the Germans, the Italians, the Australians, the New Zealanders and Canada. In all cases they were dealing with things like women in the forces, homosexuals, peacekeeping and so on. What jumps out at you when you read the Canadian one is how the Canadian defence establishment of the Armed Forces have really lost sight of what it is they're supposed to be doing. In all the other countries there was no doubt that their armed forces were still there to conduct conventional combat operations. In the Canadian case it's completely dominated by all of these other social-engineering, Charter issues. That is why you have to reinvent the Armed Forces.

When you join the military you take on a contract of unlimited liability. You are putting your life on the line, firmly. In no other human organization is this the case. Policemen and firemen — not quite the same thing. In the military you must be willing to lay down your life to execute your contract and you must be willing to do it in terms of your country's national interest. So when you bring people into the Armed Forces these days, you have to be very careful to ensure that they understand this. It is my observation that some of this is being overlooked, partly through ordinary shortfalls, but in other cases through a reluctance to deal with it because of philosophical and psychological reasons. Also because it might scare off recruits. You pay the price because you get people out there who object to doing some of the things that they are obligated to do.

The military is unique. It is a commitment of unlimited liability. Therefore, within reason, you have to operate the military in a different way than you operate any other organization in human society. Now, having said that, I am not a dinosaur. I am the first to admit that things are changing at the speed of light out there, and there are all sorts of changes you have to make. But when people start saying that you have to change the military culture simply because it is not in step with the culture out there (and by the way, this is becoming a mantra within the Department of National Defence), I disagree.

What you have to do is reinvent and preserve the military culture in the face of all these other things that are breaking it down. If you break it down, then I'm the first, as a citizen, to object to spending $11.5 billion on a military organization when all you need to do is go out and hire a bunch of armed security guards. Because that's what you end up with. If you do not accept the military as a very special organization, you might as well go out and hire security guards.

The military culture does not need to change. It needs to be modified in certain ways and reinvented in many other ways in line with modern society, but still as a separate culture. A lot of mistakes are made by people who get enthusiastic about this sort of thing and think you pull a lever and go from here to there immediately. You can't do that in a human situation. You cannot impose change arbitrarily because if you try, you get a counterrevolution and before you know it you've gone back again. So change is going forward and then stepping back, going forward and stepping back. Keeping the hierarchical approach to the military well into the future is going to be essential. Where it ends up 50 or 100 years from now, when you're talking about space stations, it may be different. But as long as you have grunts down in the mud, you're going to need a hierarchical organization to deploy them in battle.

I have had some limited experience working with the Department of Foreign Affairs, and generally speaking I have found the people over there to be extremely bright people and highly motivated. Certainly many of them have understood and still understand the value of armed forces. But having said all that, there always have been a number of them who are much more supportive of what they see, mistakenly, as the "pure" Pearsonian approach: the Canadian reputation for being a helpful fixer, honest broker, human rights specialist and so on.

There are fewer and fewer people out there who have had the experience that Pearson himself had, who understand the art of the possible, and understand that you have to hold your nose and get on with the practicalities. I'm not alone on this. I have attended seminars where some of the older generation of the foreign affairs people, who are now retired, have stood up and decried what they see developing over on the diplomatic side of the Department of Foreign Affairs with a newer generation of people. I think you would find a different situation on the trade side. They understand the realities and are more able to support armed forces because they know that there's a place for armed forces to create that stability you need for trade.

Somalia and the Airborne
One thing that must be made clear that is very much confused in the public mind: Somalia was three separate operations. The ones on each side were UN operations, UNOSOM I and UNOSOM II. UNITAF had nothing to do with the UN. UNITAF was the Unified Task Force that

was put together by the United States and was a replica of what had been done in the Gulf War. It was a coalition and it had a mandate which was approved by the UN, but it was not an integral UN mandate to go in and defeat the warlords. It was a military, conventional-warfare operation. Canada initially got involved in the first UN operation, UNOSOM I. That was going to be our commitment as a blue beret operation. When that shifted, in December 1992, into the Unified Task Force, UNITAF, a replica of the Gulf War coalition, Canada had to cast about for what it was going to do.

You have to keep in mind that this was like jumping on a train going at 150 miles an hour, and the people that were involved were sorting it out as they went along each hour of each day. You then extrapolate that into trying to explain to the public and to Parliament what was going on and to get it all wrapped up within 24 hours, so to speak. There was a practical difficulty involved in doing this.

The approval had already been given to the Airborne Regiment to go in as a blue beret force, but the way in which the government was briefed, and whether or not there was still a reluctance to admit that Canada was taking off the blue beret and putting on the red beret and going to war, I cannot give you hands-on knowledge of that. I would say that, based on what I do know, hands-on, from what happened in the Gulf War, it is highly likely that this was the case. They didn't want to rock the boat or stir up the pot too much and simply wanted to get on with it. They paid the price because they should have done a better job of preparing the public for what that force was going to do. And don't get me wrong, I am not justifying what happened to Shidane Arone. That was totally unacceptable under any conditions. But in terms of the broader context of trying to look at some of the other things that became a problem as far as Somalia was concerned, it is quite likely that, had they made more efforts to explain it to the public in the beginning, it would have been easier for them down the line.

The End of the Blue Berets
At the end of that year-long study of peacekeeping we declared blue beret peacekeeping over. It was a cold war device. It performed reasonably well, but what was happening in the early 1990s was not going to be suitable for blue beret peacekeeping. And as Canada got involved in the Balkans, in Bosnia, and later Croatia and Kosovo, that prediction

was held to be true, it was proven. Blue beret peacekeeping for Canada ended at the Medak Pocket and at Srebrenica. If you needed proof, there it was in spades.

There are two aspects that we have to look at when we talk about the end of blue beret peacekeeping. One has to do with the necessity of imposing deadly lethal military force upon the sides that you are dealing with in the controversy. In the old days in peacekeeping, you only did that very much in self-defence. What started to emerge in Bosnia and the Balkans was that you had to start applying deadly force in order not only to defend yourself but to guard the mandate that you'd been given: to maintain the peace and to protect the innocent people caught up in these various wars. It took awhile for that to sink in. Mind you, there was a precedent. All you had to do was go back to the Congo in 1960 and you found the same problem. People's memories are short. And even in the early days of Cyprus there were some examples of this occurring, but it came on like gangbusters in Bosnia and Croatia.

The other aspect has to do with the dreadful things that occurred as a result of ethnic cleansing and the genocide, and the fact that a lot of our people were exposed to quite horrendous scenes of burned bodies and hacked-up bodies and bashed-up babies and so on. The Airborne and the infantry battle schools used to, within that training, get guts from slaughterhouses and use them as part of the hardening process. I doubt you can get away with that today. When we try to do it we get criticized for the inhuman things we are subjecting our troops to. But we have to do a better job of preparing our troops because if we don't, we're being unfair to the people that we're going to send into places like Bosnia and Sierra Leone.

JOHN A. ENGLISH
Lieutenant-Colonel (Retired)
2000

A fter completing a 37-year career in the Canadian Forces, John English taught at Queen's University and at the Royal Canadian Military College in Kingston. In 1999 he accepted a position as professor of strategy at the U.S. Naval War College in Newport, Rhode Island. He is the author of the widely respected tactical manual On Infantry. *His most recent book,* Lament for an Army, *was published by the Canadian Institute of International Affairs in 1998. In September 2002 John English joined the Minister's Monitoring Committee in Ottawa.*

I just knew I always wanted to be a soldier. I was born in Delburne, Alberta, a little Prairie town, and I saw a bunch of dam busters on parade one day, and I had visions of joining the air force. Then I decided for some reason that I would join the army, and I joined the cadets when I was 13.

I went to the Royal Military College and gained my commission in 1962. I really wanted to go to the Queen's Own because it's an ancient and honourable Canadian regiment and I stayed with the Queen's Own until I went to Duke University in 1964 to study the American Civil War. Somebody once told me that Canadians had to understand two nations, one was Britain and the other was America, and to understand Americans you have to understand their civil war.

I got a good sampling of Britain after I got a good sampling of America. When I returned to the Queen's Own Rifles in Calgary I was offered a position on exchange with the British Army. So off I went to England for two years to serve with the Queen's Own Buffs and the Queen's Royal Surrey regiment. I served with the British Army of the Rhine in Germany, fought against the Canadians (in exercises) with some success, I might say. I went with the Queen's Own Rifles to Cyprus after that and when we came back from overseas we listened to the chief of defence staff tell us that the Queen's Own Rifles would never be disbanded. The chief of defence staff drank our wine and told us we weren't going to be disbanded, and lo and behold, our second battalion was immediately disbanded. That's when I began to doubt what senior officers said.

I was prompted to get involved intellectually with the study of things military when I was teaching at the combat arms school between 1974 and 1977. I was in the infantry school, and I realized when we were trying to teach people about infantry that there wasn't really anything written on infantry. It was always assumed that everybody knew everything there was to know about being a foot soldier.

The armoured Corps could go to books by Heinz Guderian, the great German Panzer commander; they could go to the Russians and read about tank warfare. But what did an infantryman read about? So I set myself a task there of writing a booklet for our students at the infantry school on the subject of infantry, and it turned into a book. I sent it off to Praeger Publishers who decided to publish it, and the U.S. Marine Corps were the first people to pick it up. Major-General Al Gray made it compulsory reading for his 2nd Marine Division, and he went on to become the commandant of the Marine Corps and made it compulsory reading for all the warrant officers and junior officers in the Marine Corps. Meanwhile the army in Fort Benning had also started issuing it to their advanced infantry course.

I never really had any intention of taking a Ph.D. degree while I was in the army, but I applied for part-time Ph.D. work as something to increase my knowledge of the military profession. But when I went to the army staff college at Kingston as a directing staff member, there was a progressive general in the chain of command who called me and asked if I would like to go to Queen's for two years to get my Ph.D., with the proviso that I would come back to Kingston army staff college as a directing staff member. So there I was, graduating in uniform with a Ph.D. degree. But I did not get the degree to become an academic; I got the Ph.D. degree to become a better soldier. By the time I got it I was getting rather long in the tooth and there is a retirement age in the Canadian Forces at 55, which ultimately came up. So after 37 years, counting my militia time, I retired.

Queen's University came along and offered me a full-time position, so I went there for two years and then taught for a while at the Royal Military College. One day I happened to see an advertisement for the United States Naval War College. I applied and they asked me to come down and be a professor of strategy, which is a much higher level than tactics or operations, which I had been teaching up until that time.

Here at the War College I am in the strategy and policy department and we are one-third of the course. The other blocs are joint military operations, for three months, and national security decision making, for another three months. Then we teach three months of strategy and policy. This study was set up after the Vietnam War and it's war at the highest level. What we are concerned about here is making sure that our strategy matches our policy.

A lot of people in the American forces thought that we had lost the war because of a failure of policy and therefore we didn't have a strategy to match. We wanted to correct that. Not having the people on side to fight a major war was probably error number one. So here at the college we remind people that there are sociological dimensions to strategy. Keeping the people and the armed forces as one is very important. We also look at things like war termination. Before you start a war, think about how you're possibly going to end it, which we rarely do.

There is great debate today on what is the true nature and purpose of armies. There is a school of thought which says that war has changed, and what we will face in the future are merely intrastate conflicts, for either ethnic or ideological reasons, and that we are going to be consumed with this internecine warfare, waged along guerrilla sorts of patterns. I would say that is obviously a distinct possibility, but I do not think we can make great sweeping assumptions that there are going to be no more interstate wars of a large nature.

If we look at the nuclear dimension today, we can see that perhaps nuclear deterrence worked in northwest Europe during the cold war. Perhaps it didn't. There was no way to know absolutely that it was nuclear deterrence that stopped us from fighting one another. There are a lot of people today saying we've got to be prepared to fight a nuclear war. Then there are others who would argue, like myself, that we will be lucky to keep wars from being nuclear, but it doesn't necessarily mean that they won't involve massive armies or that they won't involve huge logistic infrastructures. I would say the true purpose of armies is still fundamentally to protect states, like a rainy-day insurance policy, and to be prepared to engage a first-class enemy.

Armies and the People

I think there is absolutely no way that an army of any state can sustain a war-fighting role without the full support of the people behind it. I think this connection between the army and the people is more important than the connection between the army and the government. The army will always do what the government says, but it could be one wing of the government that sends the army off to battle, and if it doesn't have the support of the people from which that army springs, then it will probably fail.

Sir John Hackett's suggestion that if a nation looks at its army it will see its own face is one of those things that we accept as a given. But there is argument in some quarters that says, no, armies will not necessarily reflect the face of the societies from which they spring. If you take a democratic society like Canada and then you take an armed forces society which is more along fascist lines, those people are subject to another code of service discipline and are not entirely reflective of the general population. If you look at that army and you don't see a cross-country representation in the faces, it probably isn't an army of the people.

There is something about Western armies, the American army, the Canadian army, the British Army, which seems to reflect a humanitarianism, as compared to some armies in the world that have been brutal in their approach. I think those values reflect the values of the society more than the society assumes those values from the army.

Some people suggest that the threats today have changed from being threats from states to terrorist groups, guerrilla groups and ideological groups within our society itself. I think that we have to look at some of these threats. A terrorist with a nuclear bomb in a suitcase is the extreme statement of that. We should be concerned about that, obviously, but let's look at some statistics. Something like 1,000 people a year die from terrorism. What we're worried about is somebody pulling off a Trade Center attack and killing 250,000. But right now, despite all the poisonings on the Japanese subway, about 1,000 people a year die in terrorist attacks. Compare that with 45,000 people a year dying on American roads. Which is the greater threat to society?

On the other hand, if an interstate war comes along, perhaps it will cost our citizens something like 37,000, the number of Americans we now think died in Korea. These are bigger threats. Are we sure that we aren't going to have a second Korean war on the Korean peninsula? And will desperately trying to contain it to that peninsula keep it from spreading? Are we sure that this kind of situation is never going to come up and that they're all going to be peace enforcement operations?

If the threats today are more environmental in nature, is the military the right means for addressing those threats? Obviously, no. The military are not in the business of sorting out the environmental threats to us. Loss of the ozone layer is not a military problem, that's a civilian problem, and civilian agencies would be better off dealing with that.

One of the big problems we have, though, is the perception that we're going to use armed force to do things like this. We're going to use armed force for drug wars. I would say this is a misapplication of the military arm of government because it's ill suited to do that. Its primary purpose must be to defend the nation against external threats and internal threats if it can. But when you get into armies fighting their own people, they will probably always go to pieces.

Peacekeeping

The essential question is whether peacekeeping is good for an army. My tendency is to say it is not.

To a certain extent militaries, before we had sophisticated states, have always done law enforcement duties. The metropolitan police department was a more recent development than armies. Armies used to collect taxes. Armies used to police places. They still do in certain countries like India. There'll be a soldier that will conduct police duties in certain Indian towns, with a .303 rifle, but this is not what we would prefer in our societies today. We would like a civil arm to do our policing. We would not like the military to go around collecting taxes. We would like that military really to focus on military threats to our internal security from outside and possibly revolution from within.

We have definite historical grounds for believing that military forces that engage in peacekeeping operations will not, by the time they finish them, usually be in a good position to deal with a threat from a first-class enemy. The British Army between the wars took on garrison duties, within the British Empire primarily, and peacekeeping duties in India, and when British battalions came back from India after two years' internal security duty, they were perfectly useless for going into action against the German army or any other army of a first-rate power on the continent of Europe. Perfectly useless for that.

Clausewitz talked about his "big battle." He was always saying the big decisive battle was key. We've always misinterpreted this. We've always said it's always us looking for the big decisive battle, but it rarely comes about and we fail in seeking it out. Western armies are notorious for going after this big decisive battle and not ending up with one.

But Clausewitz reverses that and says to watch out for the big decisive battle because it might be visited upon you by the enemy. That to me is one of the big concerns about why you have an army. We've seen Saddam Hussein create a huge army that no other nation but America could have handled because of its sheer size. What do we do when we meet an army like that? We're going to have to deal with it conventionally, probably along more traditional lines than the new world order might lead us to believe at this particular point.

As I mentioned, the whole idea of peacekeeping is not to bring maximum force to bear, so right off the bat you've got a different approach and officers tend in those circumstances to do mediation duties. It can be very exciting, going to an exotic country, but you're going to act as a mediator. You're not going to be involved in the management of violence, which essentially is what armies are all about. If I had any certainty that peacekeeping wouldn't detract from conventional fighting expertise, there wouldn't be a problem with that. Perhaps in theory, an army can do both, and I think a big army can probably do both because it would not neglect the conventional war-fighting aspects of it while another portion of that army is doing peacekeeping. But in the case of the Canadian army, it is so ridiculously small right now, it's preposterous to think that it can carry out peacekeeping duties and then turn around and be able to conduct conventional warfare with any great amount of effectiveness.

There is obviously an argument about whether peacekeeping detracts from conventional fighting expertise.

I'm going to start by asking the question, "Can war be learned from books?" I would argue that since the development of general staffs, yes indeed, war can be learned from books. The reason we try to study war and peace is because there's not enough time in war itself to learn the lessons of war. The German general staff taught us that.

Go back in history a little bit to the time of the Franco-Prussian War in 1870. The French army had officers who fought all over the world and the empire. They were tremendous individuals. They were a full-time professional army, they were great swordsmen, they were great horsemen. They performed incredible individual feats of honour and of fighting. But they were beaten by what I would describe as a nerd army, the Prussian army, who, with their spectacles on, studied in the classroom. Part of the problem with the French army was they thought they were masters of the profession of arms and they took up arms against the Prussians, who they thought were just a bunch of reservists, little bookworms. And lo and behold, the little bookworms beat them.

So if you have an army today that's engaged in perpetual action, flying to Cyprus, flying back and forth to Bosnia, they're not studying war from the books. They're not even exercising in Wainwright or Camp Gagetown on major conventional warfare. So how can they possibly be as good? We know that they can't be as good because they're not doing those things in Cyprus or in Bosnia. In Bosnia they're not going around as groups in war-fighting mode; they're in observation mode and they're not in the training mode for major conventional war. So I think it's preposterous to think that peacekeeping doesn't detract from conventional war fighting.

I've seen a number of battalions come back from peacekeeping operations when we used to have our concentrations in Wainwright and Gagetown, and those battalions were not as good as battalions that had been working as a group on the ground in those training areas. They had to relearn a lot of that stuff because they hadn't been doing it. Peacekeeping was a great corporal's war where the corporal looked after the sections on the hill and played a tremendous role, and that was good training for corporals. But for the higher level, in the higher practice of war, at the tactical level and the operational level, it was not good because the officers weren't involved in that sort of stuff.

The entire challenge of armies is to translate theory into practice. That's the thing that's always done the poorest. The Germans did this quite well prior to World War II, where they took a blitzkrieg concept, using little mock tanks with bicycles, and built a real system for war fighting, taking that concept from theory and putting it into practice. An army that can't take concepts and put them into practice is probably useless. Now, we've been so busy with peacekeeping that we've lost the time that could have been spent on the development of artillery fire plans, for example, and it has bumped some important aspects of conventional war fighting out.

So you have a problem of emphasis. Then there are the people who come back from peacekeeping who say that this is the role of armies of the future. Why bother training for a mini World War III because it's not going to happen? However, are we sure it's not going to happen? Who would have thought that the British would fight a war in the Falkland Islands? Who would have thought in 1988 that we were actually going to fight a war in the Gulf against Saddam Hussein with NATO forces? Nobody could even envisage these situations coming up.

Erosion and Change
Our staff college system is not as good as it could be. On the other hand, what is left of the Canadian army, the expertise that the Canadian army

acquired over the years, is reflected in the training of the army staff college at Kingston. It is the rump of the old Canadian army and the old Canadian army staff system.

But instead of being built upon as a firm foundation, we've tended to let the staff college system erode over the years. I gather we're starting to try to rebuild it by providing a research basis for finding out how operations really run, which, I think, is commendable. But for the longest time we just lived on borrowed experience, and then we let it disappear. We didn't build on it. We had a very good exam system, which created an intellectual basis for the officers that went there and eliminated people who didn't have the intellectual ability to go to staff college.

I think the Paul Hellyer reforms were based to some extent on the fact that our Armed Forces were more responsive to coalition requirements than they were to national requirements. In other words, our navy felt it should be at sea when the Americans put the embargo on Cuba. They felt that they would respond to American strategic direction before they would necessarily respond to the Canadian governmental direction. Now, I think his idea was to create a global strike force for Canada which would be joint army, navy and air force.

But one of the problems with having a joint army/navy/air force strike force for Canada is that it is clearly beyond our means. As I said before, we are not big enough to have a global reach. We don't have a strategic lift capability; we have to go to the Americans for that. So we really are too small a power to be able to deploy an army and a navy and an air force together. If we were going to make the best use of those resources, we would have to plug them into a coalition, which means the air force would have to plug into the coalition air forces, otherwise it would be a waste of the air force to be providing support to a small brigade or division formation when they should be collectively husbanded at a centralized level.

The same with the navy. I think this was a lesson we learned in World War II. We actually had a unified Department of National Defence from 1922, but when the war came along we had to break it into an air ministry, a naval service ministry, and the Department of National Defence, the army ministry. We needed three ministers to run each one of these because they were so complex and so large.

I think Paul Hellyer, with a bunch of fanfare and fuss, was talking nonsense because we weren't as big as we thought we were in his perspective.

Operations in Europe

In regard to the deployment of our brigade to Europe, I think there is a timeline we can look at. When we had our brigade group and it was with the 2nd British Division and British Army of the Rhine, it was a very good brigade. It was indeed a heavy brigade. The 2nd British Division knew that it was a great fighting force with lots of punch. But once we unified the forces we moved out of the British zone, and there was a joke going around at that time that Prime Minister Trudeau wanted to bring the army out of Europe. And they got as far as the airfields in Lahr and Baden and the Germans said, "If you do that it's going to cost you trade relations." So we kept the army there, and not in a very good position. To put an army on an airfield was probably not a bright idea. It might have been a good target as well. It was ridiculously small and it had ridiculous tasks, like supporting 2nd German Corps or supporting 7th U.S. Corps. It was a mere shadow of its former self as far as a fighting brigade went.

But we had lots of options and there was lots of swagger about how important we were as the Canadian brigade. But in a pinch it was very, very limited compared to what it was in northwest Europe under the British, when we had a real army in the field. I think that period is the crossover point when the Canadian Forces, and the Canadian army particularly, became less reliable as a war-fighting instrument.

In the mid-1980s we ran exercises on the CAST Brigade, one of our NATO commitments, which was supposed to deploy to Norway. We were going to use CN ferries or something to help transport them. It was logistics nonsense. It was a political commitment made to a country, Norway, which wouldn't let foreign troops be stationed on its soil. I think it was a dodge to get out of putting more troops on the central front. People used to argue that strategically it was silly to put the CAST Brigade into Norway because by the time it got there, they may have just gone into the bag in time to surrender to Soviet airborne forces landing in Oslo. Strategically it was probably a very poor decision to have gone that way, but as a political gambit, I suppose you could say it was successful. But we knew for the longest time that it was probably militarily untenable.

The Gulf

There were many reasons given for not putting a land-fighting formation in the Gulf. One was that we wanted to send an entire brigade, and unless we could send an entire brigade we were going to send nothing. We had lots of questions, like were our tanks good enough, were our M113s good enough to transport infantry, when the Americans had Bradleys and the British had their new MCV-80 fighting vehicle? I always thought that was a nonsensical question because there was a lot of capacity to support M113s logistically in the Gulf, and in many cases they probably would have done all right at that particular point.

Of course the government was concerned about body bags, so that may have prevented people from putting land forces in there, but we could have made a case for sending a battalion to the British division, which really needed infantry. We would have probably been supported by them enough to have been able to have a battalion in there and gained an awful lot of credit for it. But we chose not to do that, we chose to wait to have an entire brigade and then it fizzled out, so we sent nothing. Of course from one perspective that's very good because we didn't incur any casualties, but it wasn't necessarily a very good show. It showed that our army couldn't deploy a formation because either it didn't have the will, or the means, to deploy.

Discipline

One of the things that the Canadian army always had going for itself since the development of the Canadian Corps was very harsh, strong discipline. We were noted to be a highly disciplined army. That presupposed a great trust and confidence between officers and men. There was an argument in the Great War about Canadians being more and better disciplined than Australians because Australians had a great desertion problem. The Australians refused to let Australian soldiers be executed because of the Breaker Morant problem in South Africa.

They said that if a man went 6,000 miles to fight and he showed cowardice in the face of the enemy, let's just send him home, let's not execute him. Canada executed. Out of the 295 members of the British Expeditionary Force who were put before a firing squad and shot, 25 were Canadians. So people argued that Canadians were a much better disciplined fighting force than the Australians, and some people argue that because of that, we were indeed the better corps. Of course, that's an argument an Australian will obviously disagree with.

The Canadian army in the old days, when it was at its finest, was marked by a really good, strong discipline. Discipline is the backbone of armies and that was something General Simonds continually emphasized during World War II. Of course, in the American army General Patton's attitude toward discipline was very similar to General Simonds's. I think Patton was the one who said there's no such thing as discipline except perfect discipline, and that was what Canadians had in bags. We were noted to be a really well-disciplined force. I would suggest a better disciplined force than the American army, by a long shot.

Over time we allowed that to erode in funny little ways, for example, in the role of our NCOs. On the one hand, we started giving our NCOs more responsibility. That was sort of the outward manifestations that we were treating NCOs better. But if you actually looked at what was happening, officers were starting to do NCO jobs, which happens in many armies that don't have strong NCO corps. The young officer was down at 8:00 in the morning doing the sergeant's job and getting people on parade, whereas in the old army it was more like the German system: few officers, rarely seen.

The Canadian regimental sergeant major's position was eroded. In the British Army, the old regimental sergeant major saying was, "The CO commands this battalion, gentlemen, but I run it." They were much stronger, and the stronger NCOs in all armies, British, Canadian and American, are the ones that work for officers, any officers. They do not pick or choose their officer; they work for the officer and the greater good of the unit as opposed to the individual.

We started eroding when we made everybody a corporal in the army. It was sort of a technical promotion. When I joined the Queen's Own Rifles, when a soldier talked to a corporal he stood to attention, and when the corporal dismissed him he made a proper about turn and marched off. Corporals had great respect. It might have been begrudging in some places, but it was respect nonetheless. Along comes unification, everybody's a corporal.

The NCO has always been described as being the backbone of the army. Without a strong NCO corps you might not have as good an army. Now, certain armies have stronger NCO corps than others. We, following the British practice, had a very strong NCO corps, and some people described them on the regimental level or the battalion level as being regimental property. The officers come and go; the NCOs were always there. They were the bridge between the officers and the men. They were, in fact, the men, but they were the ones that were responsible for effecting discipline, a very, very critical role and great care should have been taken.

When I joined the army the regimental sergeant major was a god in the army, to junior officers and to senior officers. How many junior officers in the Queen's Own Rifles saluted the regimental sergeant major by accident? He would pick them up for it because he was Sam Brown. He was the epitome of the NCO. We adopted the American practice of having brigade sergeant majors and command sergeant majors so that regimental sergeant majors from battalions could follow a career pattern to the top. But you didn't need to make him the brigade sergeant major or the command sergeant major. He'd reached the peak as a regimental sergeant major and was a wonderful person. He knew everything about that battalion.

This highly disciplined nature of the Canadian army persisted through the time the brigade was stationed with the British Army of the Rhine. The outward manifestations of this discipline were very pronounced. Of course, it continued in certain units in the south as well, but I think there was an erosion of discipline over time to the point where, when we got to Somalia, here's a whole bunch of chaps drinking beer and cleaning weapons with live ammunition around.

Certainly you can trust troops to a certain point, but I would say any officer worth his salt is inviting disaster when he allows troops who are cleaning weapons to have live ammunition in their possession, and to be drinking beer with no supervision at all. You merely have to wonder whether that would that have happened in the brigade when it was up north with the British and you'd say no, it wouldn't have happened. Nor would it have happened under some very fine officers who did, in fact, command the Canadian Airborne Regiment. There was no nonsense in that Airborne Regiment when they commanded it because they were disciplinarians and they were also great leaders.

Somalia

I think the situation that developed in Somalia was probably a symptom of what was happening. It was only a matter of time before something like that happened. I was surprised by the Somalia affair, even though, looking back on it with the benefit of hindsight, you can see that there were problems in our Armed Forces, a lot related to discipline, a lot related to employment, and I guess I was outraged by how we handled it. As heinous as the acts were, the problem was in how we handled it. That showed us to be completely amateurish.

First of all, and rule number one, we should have fired the commander. In the old army he would have been fired, he would have been gone. Now, people will say, "Well, he's never been promoted." Well, most certainly he shouldn't be promoted. He should have been fired. Before we went after the private and put him in jail, before we went after the major, the higher commander should pay the price. It's his command. You see the Americans do it all the time. They fired the commander of the Marine fighter pilot who took off the Italian ski lift. It's a harsh rule but it was an old army rule in the Canadian army and it was a good one. There but for the grace of God go a number of us.

The issues of Somalia actually strike at the root of the problems that we face today, partly because we haven't ever thoroughly investigated it. The royal commission was terminated, which was an unfortunate mistake. We're quite content to let the truth be buried.

But the biggest black mark that we suffer from Somalia is the fact that the high command, to protect the image of the Canadian Forces, decided to cover things up. I think it is quite clear that they did, and they haven't ever come out and said it really was more than just a bunch of bad apples. They haven't ever admitted that.

Except for one major who was found guilty, there weren't many officers who carried the can for anything in Somalia, and part of the reason for that was because there were a number of senior officers involved, and the senior officers are always most able to protect themselves. It's junior officers and ranking soldiers that are less able to have the clout to protect themselves, so naturally they can be picked on. And this is what happened, to our shame, in Somalia.

It wasn't just a problem of the private soldiers. There were some fundamental problems here. Some people don't look at the death of a prisoner as being as heinous a crime as I do because the exigencies, the circumstances of the time, sort of make it all right. "After all, they were trying to protect vehicles and headquarters and people and he could have carried a bomb."

But what we used to learn at our old exams was that we didn't kill women and children, and we didn't kill our prisoners because they're not our prisoners, they're prisoners of Canada under international law. The chap was a ward of the Canadian state, and the Canadian state guaranteed his well-being. Somehow we didn't know that, which I think is inexcusable, from the commanding officer's point of view, or from the NCOs who walked by the compound. It's entirely inexcusable. I made a very severe judgment by saying that it compared to the 11th SS Panzer Division killing Canadian prisoners in Normandy. Essentially it's the same thing, except that they killed 139, we only killed one, but that doesn't absolve us from responsibility in the commission of that crime.

I have written that I thought it was the greatest crisis in Canadian military history and I think I'm on reasonably firm ground to say that. If you look at past crises, they've been national crises over conscription. In World War I we had elections over it, the khaki election of 1917. Then we had two conscription crises in World War II, but they were more national crises. This was a crisis that hit the military establishment itself and tore it apart. If you went into an officers' mess at that particular time you could divide the room. It split friendships, for example, over which side people were on about whether the Canadian Airborne Regiment could be or should be disbanded by the minister. Of course, regiments have been disbanded in the past. We had mutinies in World War II out in Terrace, B.C., in a regiment called the Prince Albert Volunteers, and where did they go?

The Somalia affair is significant insofar as it's never been properly investigated. I would wager, however, that it will be investigated. Students of Canadian military history will now revisit this situation and I guarantee that at some point in the future a historian will probably thoroughly investigate this from beginning to end because we did a terrible thing. We terminated the royal commission. The minister of defence, Doug

Young, terminated the royal commission, and my belief is he did so because it was getting too hot.

Admiral John Anderson, who was the CDS when this started, went off to become our NATO ambassador in Brussels, and Robert Fowler, the deputy minister of the department, who had a rather unique position in the department compared to the chief of the defence staff, went off to become our United Nations ambassador. Both those individuals should have been called before the Somalia inquiry, and they were not. That is a shame, but it might have reflected adversely on the government itself. The whole process by which Canada got involved in Somalia might have come under public scrutiny at that particular point. I would challenge any young prospective historian to dig deeply into this, get the documents under Access to Information, and try to ascertain the truth, which our government should have done, but which it didn't.

People used to say in the British Army, from time immemorial, "There's no such thing as a bad soldier, there's only bad officers," and that probably says it well. If something goes wrong with the soldiers, officers have to pay the price. We used to have a rule on the grenade range. If there was a grenade accident, the range officer was fired and it hurt his career. It was not his fault, normally. It could have been an NCO's fault putting the grenades together, or how things were fired from the grenade point, but the rule of thumb was, "grenade accident, the officer fell." When you had a blind on the grenade range, only the officer blew it. He had to walk out in front of that blind and he had to blow it. An NCO could not do that in our army, which is rather neat. Some armies call in the ordnance disposal teams, but our army insisted the officer go out and personally blow the grenade that could have gone off and killed him. It was a great thing to earn the respect of men. But you carried the can if anything went wrong with that grenade range. Officers have to take responsibility.

I think the reason things have changed is obviously because of leadership. If I recall, on the royal commission, the chief of the defence staff, John de Chastelain, was chastised for inadequate leadership. But a lot of people have said that he shouldn't have been. The army's now in the process of proving it by having him made the colonel of the regiment of the Princess Patricia's Canadian Light Infantry. The army really doesn't recognize some of the things that happened. In fact, you could criticize the leadership at the highest levels, and possibly above the CDS. Why was Canada involved in Somalia in the first place? Why did we agree to go in as part of an American force at that particular time?

The final judgment is still to come on Somalia. Whether it'll have any impact is questionable, but students of Canadian military affairs will continually revisit this. I would say the army hasn't learned its lesson over Somalia. It's like the Holocaust deniers. Nobody has said, collectively, "mea culpa." This is probably what's really wrong here. If we can't see something wrong with Somalia, then there might be something wrong with us.

Military discipline was always based on justice. Certainly we wanted order, and obviously, in the Great War, where we executed 25 soldiers, we wanted order, and some people have said what we did to those soldiers was unjust. At the time I suspect it probably wasn't. There is such a thing as good order and discipline, but essentially there was a basis of trust between the officer and the men. There was a feeling of a social contract between officer and man that was very important. Sometimes, when we get too legalistic over these things, that sort of common understanding disappears. Canadian law was always set up based on what a reasonable man would do. Today perhaps we're having more laws based on what an unreasonable man would do, and that might cloud the issue.

Defence Policy, Parliament and the Public
From a national perspective, in theory, and hopefully in practice, policy should be established first and we should effect a strategy to carry out that policy. What does this mean for the average soldier who joins the Canadian army? I would think he wants to be fully supported, not only by the government, but also by the people. If he's not supported by the people, the army will probably fail. If he's not supported by the government, he will probably become antagonistic to that government, perhaps like our army was in World War II when they booed the prime minister. This soldier has a right to expect certain things from his government, that he will be given attainable objectives within the resources that he has been given. I believe that's where the soldier can fault policy.

Policy should never put Canadian soldiers in an untenable position. High command should not tactically or operationally put their soldiers in an untenable position. Of course, we know that military history is replete with people putting soldiers in untenable positions, but we normally say that's bad generalship, and you could also add that it's often bad policy. In the past we have been accused of doing it, in the case of Hong Kong, for example. We sent troops there with no hope of surviving against the Japanese and they went into the bag.

This idea of the social contract between an army and its people is very, very real. Contrary to all sorts of interpretations, I believe we had this in the Great War. We had a prime minister, Sir Robert Borden, who was dedicated to making sure the Canadian Corps was supported in the field in France. We had a Canadian public that was totally behind that army. I gather in the streets of Toronto, if you were an able-bodied man of a certain age, a little lady might come up and give you a white feather and say, "Why aren't you over there with the rest of the boys volunteering?" There was tremendous public pressure that was put on, but there was always tremendous public support. The Canadian Corps never lacked for reinforcements. It never really lacked for anything. It probably cost the prime minister his political prospects eventually, but you had an almost ideal wedding of the army, the government and the people in the Great War.

In World War II, in contrast, an argument can be made that the government of Mackenzie King did not support that army to the extent that it should have. The people supported that army, but the government sort of just wanted them to die quietly on the Scheldt and not cause political problems back home. In fact, they did cause great political problems back home because the people exposed them.

One of the problems is that we've fallen into this approach where the government has committed Canadian troops all over the world in the guise of peacekeeping, but they've never been responsible to the Canadian people. They've never been responsible to the Canadian Parliament. This is where you can say a good thing for Mackenzie King because Mackenzie King insisted that the Canadian army should not be deployed overseas until Parliament had debated it and had approved it. I think that's something the Liberal government should probably go back to. That was a good policy. But over the years we got into this business of deploying peacekeeping forces by order-in-council or by Cabinet decision. They will go over and there will be no parliamentary debate called, and there will be no debate within the Canadian public at large. The Canadian public has largely been kept out of knowledge of these operations and therefore they won't support the army. I shouldn't say that, they do support the army, but they don't know the implications, necessarily, of those foreign engagements.

The problem with parliamentary oversight of Canadian operations abroad is that an MP doesn't have the resources at his disposal that the defence minister has in the Department of National Defence. One of the problems may be with the parliamentary system itself. You hold up your fist in the House of Commons, à la C. D. Howe, and the majority votes, and it doesn't matter what the debate is. But perhaps these debates should be taken to the people themselves, and maybe we shouldn't be so secretive in our Armed Forces. One could argue as well that our Armed Forces have tended to develop into fiefdoms where generals think the Armed Forces belong to them. Armed forces have never belonged to the generals; they've always belonged to the people.

The gulf that can develop between an army and the people is a serious matter. It's a traditional concern of armies, and going back to Sir John Hackett, you should look in that mirror and see something that reasonably resembles you. If you're a Brit and you look into the mirror, you shouldn't see the army of the Third Reich, you should see the army of Britain. The same goes for Canada. But we've been very secretive. We've always overclassified documents, even the most mundane documents. We won't let the public see them because, "Oh, they shouldn't know anything about it." On the other hand we complain about lack of public support, but if a public doesn't know what an army's doing, it will probably be less prone to support it.

Some people say, "We just have to hire a better public relations firm," but it's not a matter of public relations. I would argue that public relations got us into trouble in Somalia because we were always trying to present the most favourable image, when in fact John Q. Citizen doesn't necessarily want the most favourable image. He wants to see our warts, and it's arguable that some of our best soldiers are the ones who have warts, not the ones who are absolutely politically correct. I think society at large will tolerate them, and we've got to work beyond a public relations machine to get back into the hearts and minds of the Canadian people.

Politicians want to keep cards close to their chest. They don't want to play them until the last minute or until they have to, whereas strategies have to be founded on a certain amount of long-range planning.

In the Great War the war aims of the British were never discussed in Parliament because they would have been far too contentious. So you had some war aims — for example, restoring the territorial integrity of Belgium, which seemed to be the reason Britain went into the war — that seemed to be accepted, generally speaking. But then the foreign office got into the de-Prussification of Germany. Now, how do you translate that policy into military terms so the military can carry it out? Soldiers need a hill. That's not a problem that's resolvable by armed force. It has to be done by different methodologies.

An example from World War II in the Canadian case is that the army general staff knew that the Canadian people would call for an expeditionary force. Government policy at that time was that we would not train or prepare for an expeditionary force. But the army general staff beavered away quietly and prepared an excellent mobilization plan, and when we went to war they put that mobilization plan into effect, which is what the people wanted. I would say in that case the general staff, with a dearth of government direction, were able to sense the feeling of the Canadian people and react accordingly, and I think that was very, very good.

Today what we have is a military establishment which is too prone to jump when the government says, "Another peacekeeping operation here, please." Everybody says, "Yes sir, yes sir, three bags full, sir." They don't question the policy itself, which is correctly the purview of statesmen. They just blindly say, "Yes sir," and try to carry out that tasking. They never say, "No sir."

Lament for an Army
When I wrote *Lament for an Army* I took as my example George Grant's *Lament for a Nation* and I wrote it because I liked how he described lament, that something positive can come out of a lament, where conditions would be better because of what we had learned in the past. He said that if you ever have any doubts, go with tradition, and we had a very fine army in the past, so I wrote the book with that in mind, to see if we can turn our army around.

My problem in *Lament for an Army* is that I thought in Somalia we'd hit the bottom of the barrel. The question is, how do we get back to that fine army? I ended by saying there is a way, and I think that we will ultimately be able to return to that, and if we can't return to that, then God help us.

When I walked around in Cyprus as a young officer, the Queen's Own Rifles officers refused to carry sidearms. We carried swagger sticks. A little bit of panache or silliness perhaps, but we were respected at that time by the Greeks, not because of what we were, but because of the reputation that the Canadian army had earned in the past, the exploits of "the best little army in the world" in World War II. That's why we got a leg up over other nations' armies who were then on peacekeeping. We got respect. We didn't deserve it, but because our fathers and grandfathers had earned it, we got it, and we benefited by it.

I would say that the development of professionalism in the Canadian army came with the Great War, where we realized that you couldn't be an amateur, that there is something to the professional ethic, this sense of expertise, this sense of corporateness, corporate responsibility for running the force. Study was very, very prominent in this. You had to know what to do in war.

I think we must return to our professional basis in the future and I've emphasized the general staff idea. In the Commonwealth armies and in the American army we have rejected the concept of a dedicated staff corps, like the German general staff, for reasons that don't necessarily have to do with the military. Maybe suspicion of the military is why we don't want these corps. The German general staff prized function and knowledge over rank, whereas our armies have tended to become hierarchical. The opinion of the senior officer present is the tactical solution. That's not acceptable in the German system. A captain can have a better solution than a general, and this is a great strength. This is the sort of thing that I see us evolving toward, getting a very professional group of officers.

At the Royal Canadian School of Infantry a lot of our instructors were back from Korea, very confident, very proud, wearing their military crosses on their chests and their DSOs. They'd been in a war where they thought they'd done quite well, and they tried to pass on some of that expertise to us. We were taught by people like General Dextraze, who was the chief of Canadian defence forces from 1972–1977. Dextraze's great thing was that you had to have sacred fire, *feu sacré*, burning within you to be a proper officer. I always thought that that was a tremendous approach to officership, and without that you couldn't be an officer. You were part of a sort of monastic order. It was a calling, like being a priest.

This was sort of the epitome of professionalism at that time, and I thought it was quite good. I think the appeal of that is still good, that there is a higher calling than just your own career advancement. It's a search for professional military knowledge and performance. To be the best battalion commander is far more important than being a high-ranking general sitting on a chair in National Defence Headquarters.

Professionalism and Lessons Learned
The advocates of a return to a warrior ethic have missed the significance of the idea of professional militaries. Before the rise of the German general staff we had a concept of officership, certainly, that concept being to control the troops under your command in good order and discipline. But when you get to the professional ethic, we go beyond the warrior cult.

In ancient Greece up through the North American Indians, you fought for macho reasons, to prove yourself as a man. With the Indians you wore an extra feather in your hat. In the case of Greece you got a leg up with the gods. It was sort of a savage warfare ethic and it was individually based. By the time we get to professionalism, it's state interests, *raison d'état*, that is governing the conduct of armies. We put armies in the political context of attaining a political aim for the greater good of the state as opposed to the individual.

This is why armies that were so imbued could easily defeat warrior-ethic armies, who were nothing but a bunch of individuals trying to attain an individualistic aim. A professional force would in fact attain a collective aim, and the first duty of an officer was to train the man who would succeed him. It still is. The first duty of an officer is to train his second-in-command so that if he were cut down by a bullet, his place would be taken immediately. The whole idea of the German general staff was that a staff officer was faceless, and that cuts out careerism.

Brigadier Freddie de Guingand was the chief of staff to General Montgomery and he said in his book *Operation Victory* that if you're going to train a future army, make sure you test commanders. Before the war it was all too prevalent for the British battalion commander or the divisional commander to say, "I'm running an exercise to test my division," but he would not test himself. He would go around and jump on people for making mistakes within his division, but he didn't test himself.

You could see this happening in our Canadian army, especially after unification. All of a sudden there was no general officer to test the brigade commander, so some brigade commanders tested battalion commanders, but didn't test themselves. I think there was only one general who perpetually tested himself and that was General Kip Kirby, who always put himself under a tremendous amount of strain. He would pretend that he received his orders, give orders to himself and then react within that time frame. He would actually try to test himself because he too had read de Guingand's book.

In the year I was company commander the only people tested were company commanders. So, as they were tested two or three times, you ended up with possibly very competent company commanders, but the battalion commanders were never tested. Once you get high rank, you feel that you know everything, when in fact you know very little. Once you've jumped through the hoop, there's a tendency not to go back.

To learn from experience you have to study it, and it's amazing to me that we don't study anything. For example, we don't study one of our great battles, the Battle of Amiens. In fact, we don't study any battles in which Canadians were involved at any of our military institutions in any depth. We don't look at them to see what lessons could be used. We certainly don't do it on the scale of the Americans. They examine their battles operationally, tactically and strategically. They use case-study methodology. The British probably don't do as well in that regard, but the German army still studies the Battle of Amiens, which was a great Canadian victory of World War I, at their staff college. Here you have the old enemy talking about what the Canadians and the British did and still learning from it.

The Canadian army became very, very proficient by 1918. Canada's greatest moment was during the 100 Days, which started on August 8 — which General Ludendorf called the black day of the German army. The Canadian army, with the Australians, spearheaded the advance of the British Expeditionary Force for 100 miles, crashing through one strong German defence line after another, breaking them all, and ending with the armistice on November 11, which we still wear poppies for and quite rightly so. That was a tremendous string of victories sustained by the Canadian Corps and it was done under tremendously arduous circumstances. Every day they got up, they went to war in a gas environment and they did extremely well.

They were masters of the set-piece attack. They could attack a line in great depth and sustain those operations; they were that good. Everything was modern. We had close air support from planes flying at that time, we had tanks and we had tremendous artillery capability. This whole orchestra of arms was put into effect by General Arthur Currie, and it was a tremendous achievement.

He did it by building in electronic deception, where he put wireless nets in other sectors of the line so the Germans would think the Canadians were there. He even put his medical section, and this was quite a risky thing to do, in another part of the line where they would think the Canadians were. Of course, that was a problem when you went in and incurred casualties, but overall it was a very successfully conducted series of operations. I would say it was the zenith of Canadian military prowess. This is where Canadian arms earned the adulation of the world, not just the British Empire. We were that good. We may not make that all the time, but perhaps that's the star we should aim for.

A lot of people thought that we were good because we were Canadian, but we weren't good because we were Canadian. We were good because we learned. We actually studied the problems. Sir Arthur Currie went to Verdun, studied the problem in great depth, learned from the French and of course learned from the British. We couldn't have done it without the British because we were taught by the British. We learned a lot from the British. I wouldn't say there was a Canadian way of war, but in the conduct of war at that particular time, we did things extremely well. I would also say that in World War II we did some extraordinary things, particularly in the Battle of the Scheldt, where we were easily the match of other armies.

The Canadian Corps was an exceedingly good corps but we shouldn't ever kid ourselves to think that there wasn't a good British corps as well. There were incredible British divisions. Remember, we won one of our biggest victories in the battle of Vimy Ridge under General Byng, who was a British commander. We had Byng boys' clubs throughout the country because they remembered Sir Julian Byng and loved him, possibly more than Arthur Currie, who was more of a stodgy Canadian and very insistent on standards.

The Australians also learned well and if you go to Australia they'll maintain they were the best. But it's a harmless little competition, really. They were both very good.

I would argue that the American army that fought in the Gulf War so successfully really represented a return to the traditional army methods after the disaster of the Vietnam War. The whiz kids had come in and said, "Oh yes, this is a new way of waging war," adopting new methods, which ended in utter, abject failure for the American army in Vietnam. They turned around and went back to their professional principles. They rejected the business-school approach that was so pronounced in the McNamara era and went back to traditional methods of how armies fight, the relation of troops to officers, using your brain, fighting smart and studying past lessons of war.

They did it with very much a traditional army, a traditional approach. With high-tech equipment, yes, but it was the men and women behind that army and their training that really sustained them throughout. I would say, in contrast, that the Canadian army in Somalia was indeed a new army. It was not based on traditional army principles or else it wouldn't have had the conclusion that it had. We would have done traditional army things like fire the senior commanders involved. But we didn't do things like that. We took a new approach. So it was really not the old Canadian army that went to pieces, it was the new Canadian army, with all the foibles of integration, unification. All of those things foisted upon it saw it explode, or implode, in Somalia.

The corrections that the Americans took following the failure of the army in Vietnam were a very commendable effort. They managed to turn themselves around and they did it through a series of debates, reforms, local initiatives by officers, and they began studying history.

The American army was a bit of a disaster around 1979, but they went back to fundamentals and managed to turn themselves around over a 10-to-15-year period to become a very professional fighting force. One way they did it was that they admitted that they had failed. They said, "mea culpa." They admitted it up front and took corrective action. Now, in contrast, I don't believe the Canadian army after Somalia said, "mea culpa." It still denies a lot of what happened there. If it denies it, it can't reform itself. It probably has to be reformed from without.

The Nature of Casualties

Battle shell shock is obviously a factor in war, and possibly this is how you're getting casualties in peacekeeping. The question that has to be asked, though, is, "Are the casualties any greater than they would be in a shooting war?" And I would say they couldn't possibly be greater.

It could be that we really don't want to know about traumatic stress coming out of peacekeeping operations. Perhaps it's increased, and maybe the increase comes from commanders being confused as to what their precise role is. What are they supposed to be doing? Are they supposed to be peacekeeping or are they supposed to be actually going to war? It must be a terrible situation to be in, trying to determine that. One of the great examples was Rwanda, where there's mass genocide being conducted right before your eyes. And what are you supposed to do, stand by helplessly and just watch it like a football game? Maybe somebody should be responsible for making sure these mandates are more clearly defined so that our commanders going in will know what they have to do, which in turn will make it easier for soldiers to know what they have to do.

RMA and the Future

When you look at the roots of the Revolution in Military Affairs, you can say that the term was first coined by the Russians, who saw several Revolutions in Military Affairs occurring throughout history. But are we in an era of a Revolution in Military Affairs? If so, what does it mean? It doesn't just mean technological advance; it means the organizational developments that go with it, plus how you implement these technological changes and adapt them to your benefit within the service. But is it evolutionary or is it revolutionary? Are these things going to transform warfare entirely, or is it like a second industrial revolution where all these things will go to all armies whether we need them or not? In the beginning there was the Ford truck but it was only in the United States. Eventually the Ford truck and the internal combustion motor went into all armies. Was that a Revolution in Military Affairs? They all changed at the same time. Some may have had a better transmission, but for the most part they were all pretty even on that score. Are we going to enter a new era with computers? Should we emulate the United States in that regard?

We should probably try to emulate the United States because they seem to be the front-runner in this thing with few challengers on the horizon. At the same time, do you think we're going to be able to compete with the Americans when their budget is $270 billion and ours is $7.8 billion? How on earth can we pretend that we're going to keep up with them? Maybe that's not necessarily what we want. Maybe we want to look at the RMA and the antidotes to it. We would probably perform a good function for the Americans by finding out how to defeat some of these things that we're using right now. Sometimes they can be defeated through better tactics. There are tactical responses to technological developments, as we've seen from the Great War all the way through. Maybe that's something we can focus on.

But the role of policy comes into this. What is Canadian government policy in the use of armed force? If we're just going to chase after the Americans for equipment, where's that going to lead us? Just to flood down to the States to try to get a better tank will not necessarily be the answer to the Canadian security or defence problem.

If you go back to what armed forces are all about and decide that they're in the service of the state, you'll realize right off the bat that the Canadian state is different than the American, and therefore the response of our Armed Forces will be different than the American response. When we were part of the British Empire, we decided to form our own Canadian army as opposed to just joining the British army. It was important for Canadians to fight as a group, which we managed to do, sometimes by refusing to do things that a reasonable man would have done.

For example, when the great 1918 offensive was launched, the 5th British Army went to the Canadians and asked them to commit divisions. We said, "No, we fight as a corps. We won't commit divisions." The Australians allowed the British to commit individual divisions, which was probably very responsible at the time. We wouldn't commit the divisions, so the corps never saw action there. Fortunately, by the time of the 100 Days, the corps was in very good shape to start the offence, so we benefited in that regard from British and Australian blood that was spilt first. I think this business of Canadians fighting as a collective in principle is good, but I don't think we're going to be able to do that if we get involved in a major war because our air force will probably fight with coalition air forces. Our navy will probably fight with coalition navies and our army will have to plug in with a ground coalition of sorts. So we're going to have to be very good tactically.

We are now such a very small professional force that personnel-related costs are something in the order of 60 percent of the money that goes to the military. That's on pensions for soldiers and keeping them gainfully employed over a 20-year period. It's something similar to universities with tenured professors. They can't afford to hire tenured professors anymore because they're just so expensive. They have to pay them $90,000 a year and give them huge, lucrative pension plans at the end. They're better off getting the extra piece of knowledge from short-term contracts of five years. I think the army is entering that same sort of situation. We can't afford to have a Cadillac regular force anymore; it's bound to get smaller. So one of the challenges is to see whether we can get more mileage out of the citizen soldier, or maybe some more innovative approaches toward keeping the art of war fighting alive in peacetime.

We are paying one of the lowest defence budgets, certainly in comparison to the Americans. Of course, some people would criticize me for saying we shouldn't compare ourselves to the Americans with their $270-billion budget, which would mean Canadians should have a $27-billion budget, being one-tenth of the U.S., and that's unfair because America's a world power with world-ranging responsibilities and we don't have that. We're not even really a regional power, and we have a different geographical strategic situation because we can always depend on the Americans to defend us.

Leadership and Reform
I think we could do a lot of things to reform the Canadian army. I'm very concerned about regular army regiments being out of control, doing wrong things. As long as we had a general staff, regiments were kept in line.

We have my regiment, the Princess Patricia's Canadian Light Infantry, forming a guard to protect the interests of the regiment. They're doing this in imitation of the Vingt-Deux, the French-Canadian regiment, which has a group that makes sure that the Vingt-Deux gets certain jobs at certain times. Once we removed the general staff we had no control over these regiments and they became little entities unto themselves. That's got to be stopped.

There's no need for a regiment to have a guard. It should be banned. There's no reason it should have a former general officer being the colonel of the regiment. We should force them to have civilians as colonels of the regiment to create a connection between the military and the community. If the regular generals want to be colonels in regiments, let them be colonels of reserve regiments if the reserves want them, but we should stop them from being colonels of the regular regiments.

There's a lot to be said for the creation of an army general staff corps that's a collectivity which would look at how to introduce innovative methods of involving the citizen soldier more in our organization. Perhaps we could set up a training organization at Camp Gagetown which would induct people who want to serve their country directly off the street, and train them to go to Bosnia and not poison their officers. I think that could be done with a good training system. I know costs have to be taken into consideration here, but that could be done.

I've always steered away from gender issues because I'm not so sure that they were ever an important consideration, outside of us trying to keep things the way they were. I think there was a lot to be said for the old pioneers circling the wagons, women and children into the centre, because that's how you reproduce the group. But when it comes to flying a high-performance aircraft, there are a lot of human skills involved, and I'm sure that there are many women who have more dexterity and facility in that regard than many men. It's very difficult to deny them the right to fly that high-performance aircraft. As far as I understand, the Canadian Forces have gone to the total integration of women, down to the combat arms. The German army recently has been told it will integrate women into the combat arms, down to the infantry, because they have to respond to a European court judgment which directed them to do that.

The British were forced by the same European court judgment to allow homosexuals into the army, which the Canadian army already does. The American army, of course, is doing a policy of "don't ask, don't tell, don't pursue," but they've been accused of forgetting number three. They've been pursuing and throwing out homosexuals.

I'm not sure that this, in a wartime scenario, should necessarily make that much difference or erode discipline to the extent that we perhaps think it does. We know, for example, when the Soviets were fighting with their backs to the wall against the Germans in Russia, women snipers were used, and some of them were very good. You see the old girls coming out every now and again wearing tons of medals. They were snipers; they were in the frontline. Soviet women were members of tank crews, we know that for a fact, and they performed, presumably, well.

So I don't think this necessarily is an insurmountable problem that can't be solved through good leadership. To put a man and a woman guarding a rifle company at night when you double up the sentries, I don't think is necessarily a good idea. That might put temptation in the way of being professional. But if you put two homosexuals in that sort of situation, could you not have the same problem? And it may not occur at all. So I think that some of this business and some of these reactions can be dealt with through good leadership.

Clausewitz used to say there was one thing more important than creativity in an officer. He called it inquisitiveness. What we want to encourage is a thinking officer corps with inquisitiveness. I think in that regard we should also train ourselves to conduct critical self-analyses. When we make an error, let's openly admit it.

We should have wrestled the Somalia affair to the ground, debated it thoroughly and cleared the air of it entirely. That would have meant not cutting off the royal commission. We should have gotten to the roots of the problem. We should have done a thorough investigation of it because now we're going along somewhat in the nature of a Holocaust denier. It'll only be a leap to say it probably never happened if we continue to carry on this way. As long as we deny it, we won't be able to solve the problems that we encountered at that particular time and find out whether they were symptoms or results of a greater malaise.

The Americans have a great propensity to say, "We made a big mistake there; we're a real bunch of dummies. Now we're going to see how we can cure it." But we seem to be reluctant to do that. We want to put on this beautiful face, this image of the Canadian Forces which is more important than getting at the truth, and I think we've got to drop that entirely. Once we do that, once we say "mea culpa," we're on the way to reform.

DON MACNAMARA

Brigadier-General (Retired)
2000

*D*on Macnamara is a founding member and past president of
the Canadian Institute of Strategic Studies and an authority
on national and international security affairs and strategic analysis. He had a long career in the RCAF/Canadian Forces, including
appointments as director of strategic planning and director of
arms control policy. After he retired he joined the Queen's School
of Business in 1988, teaching international business and international strategy. He is now associate director of the Public Executive
Program and a senior fellow at the Queen's Centre for
International Relations.

It never occurred to me not to join the military as there was an
extensive family background in the Armed Forces over a number of
generations. I joined the air force reserve and went to university,
serving and getting trained during the summer. I initially trained as
an air traffic controller but, because I had a degree in science, there
were some opportunities to work in military research and development, particularly in the human-factor side. I eventually ended up

first as the deputy director of strategic policy planning, then as director of strategic policy planning, and finally as the director of arms control policy.

In my post-military career I've been teaching at Queen's, and I know that I'm a dinosaur in terms of age and attitude. But I've found the lack of knowledge of the young people coming into this university about Canada's history, about Canada's politics and political history and about Canada's military history, frankly appalling.

I have personally taken a couple of thousand young people, in groups, to battlefields in Europe, and without exception they feel that they know nothing about this. Many of them feel offended that nobody has taught them about this. We have a fantastic heritage in terms of our contribution to what we might call the Western way of life, the democratic way of life in our defence of Western Europe.

Many people in Europe, the French, the Dutch, can't figure out how a bunch of Canadians actually volunteered to come and put their lives at risk for their sake. And the gratitude that they have, even today, is overwhelming by any standards.

But our young people don't even know about that, except for the occasional television program when the anniversaries occur. Jack Granatstein's book asks, "Who killed Canadian history?" The fact that it wasn't taught killed it.

Canadian Concerns

From a global perspective we have to recognize that Canada certainly is the largest landmass in the Western Hemisphere and the second largest landmass in the world. We are second only, in terms of our landmass, to Russia. And we do have the largest coastline of any country in the world, bounding on three oceans.

But in terms of population we are 34th or 35th in the world, so that doesn't make us particularly large. But by other measures, we are among the G7 in terms of economic power and we have political clout which is consistent with the economic power. Some people would say that we don't use the political clout consistent with our economic power.

In terms of military capability, because we are so close to the United States on the one hand and so far away from other punitive threats on the other, we are very well down the list. We're something on the order of 122nd in the world in terms of the proportion of our population that serves in the military. We are well down the list in terms of the proportion of the GDP that we allocate to the military. We don't see ourselves as threatened, otherwise we would have a much larger force. People in Canada don't have to spend a lot of their income on defending themselves against whomever, and people in Canada have no obligation to serve in the military. So if you put all of those things together, it's a very, very good place to live and, not surprisingly, the preferred destination of millions of people in the world.

So what is our strategic position? I think that we have a potential that is not being realized. We try in our foreign policy goals to advance our values. I think we have a good set of goals there. But how many of our resources we really want to allocate to those goals is somewhat problematic. So there's a certain imbalance and inconsistency with our potential and the reality.

Whatever the government is prepared to ask the military to do, they're asking our sons and daughters to do. If we have any fundamental sense of political morality whatsoever, everybody should care about what the government is asking its military to do. We need to know how well we equip the military, what risks it is assuming on behalf of the citizens and what the odds of survival of your son or daughter might be in going off to some expedition on behalf of Canada.

One of the areas that I feel is very poorly served in Canada is how the national interests are in fact assessed and discussed at the broadest level in the country, in terms of why we should do anything in the world. The second thing is the degree to which any expedition is in our own individual national interest, and this is in direct contradiction with the United States, which takes this national interest approach very seriously. If something is not perceived to be in their vital interests, it's a tough road for the administration to put American lives at risk. Politicians will not accept that.

The world is really our marketplace and we are the most export-dependent country in the developed world. So if we are going to assume that our national wealth and well-being is dependent upon our being able to trade equitably and freely in the world, we had better participate in that system. With that participation comes some responsibilities to contribute to the stability of the world. That doesn't mean that we have to try to stabilize every country in the world that has some kind of an upset. But we have to look at what it is that we can contribute. To a substantial degree, some of the efforts in peacekeeping have been directed in this way. But we also have to remember that in our history peacekeeping, before the end of the cold war, was really the best thing we could do to ensure that a superpower nuclear war did not occur as the result of some kind of escalation of a far-off conflict that had divided the two sides, East and West.

Therefore we could exercise power in our own national interests, out of all proportion to our size, by intervening and preventing or stopping conflicts that could cause a nuclear war. After the cold war we've had this breakout of continuous tribal warfare around the world, much less international and much more intranational conflict. The question is, are we there protecting our interests or are we there protecting our values?

This is something that many Canadians simply don't understand, that is, that the role of Canada, and for that matter the Canadian Forces and many non-government organizations, is much less in protecting the direct interests or the perceived direct interests of Canada. Rather it's standing up for and promoting and indeed protecting, in the global sense, the values that we stand for — democracy, and with democracy the rule of law. The two go together. If you have a country in chaos, if it's not going to have a democratic system and if it's not going to have a recognized rule of law, it will continue in chaos.

We recognize and promote individual freedom. Under that individual freedom come all kinds of human rights, and associated with human rights we have this sense of social justice and the value of the individual human life. And we practise that both domestically and internationally. If we really stand up for those values, if we think that these are the values by which countries and people can best live and enjoy their lives, then we should do whatever we can possibly do to promote the well-being of others recognizing those values.

In the longer haul, then, our own domestic interests, and what you might call our own economic well-being and long-term quality of life, would be not only preserved but also enhanced. But not by placing our young people at risk by getting out there, standing at the frontline and getting mowed down. We've already done that to the tune of 100,000-plus dead in the 20th century.

We have to recognize that national security operates in political, economic, sociocultural and military dimensions. There are some treatments for issues that affect our national security that would be amenable to military solution and some that aren't. Economic sanctions are essentially an act of war. An economic blockade is an act of war. If you wish to exercise the full spectrum of responses in defence of your national interests and your national security in the broadest context — protecting of the way of life of the average Canadian — then you must be prepared to invest in having the elements of the spectrum as part of your political policy choices.

If you say, "We are going to limit ourselves only to non-military responses, to non-military threats," then you leave yourself open to all kinds of exploitation and potential threats from people who will see you as a weak-willed nation. That's a nation not really prepared to put its force and money up to protect its interests.

The major alliance that we have, NATO, recognizes that an attack against one is an attack against all. Through alliances we can turn our relative weakness into relative strength. But we also have to make sure that we contribute to the overall strength of the alliance by making a contribution militarily and financially proportionate to our capability and proportionate to our perception of the threat. But how big is the threat? How much should we pay to defend against it? At the very least we should recognize there's a responsibility. We can't be on the take without giving.

Now, some of our allies may perceive that their immediate threats, particularly because of the geographic proximity to them, are greater than ours, and therefore they've got a whole lot more people in the military equation than we do. Certainly during the cold war this was the case with Germany and most European countries, which had conscription and all kinds of other elements which could mobilize the whole population in the event of a land war in Europe.

Canada's biggest concern, of course, was not a land war in Europe so much as the possibility of bombers and nuclear missiles raining down on us. So our best interest was in preventing a land war in Europe that could lead to such a nuclear holocaust.

Our elements of prevention included contribution of forces providing the land-based deterrence, air forces and naval forces that would provide deterrence, not to mention the recognition that there was solidarity in the alliance.

The second thing we did was peacekeeping by contributing to the prevention of a problem that could escalate into a European conflict or another East-West confrontation. There was a lot of argument as to whether what we were contributing was appropriate, and the biggest difficulty in the discussion was whether we were actually able to do what we said we were going to do in support of NATO.

I was certainly present at lots of meetings on both sides, at a modest junior level, in which this discussion was common. We frequently had discussions and conferences on burden sharing and what this really meant and who was getting what, whose responsibility it was to give what share. Frankly it was somewhat embarrassing because, notwithstanding the fact that it was recognized that the forces that we were contributing, in quality, were among the best in Europe, in quantity they didn't really make a significant difference. So on the one hand they were telling us what great guys we were. On the other hand they were telling us what cheapskates we were.

The Capability Gap

The commitment-capability gap happened when we said that we were going to be able to send forces to north Norway and reinforcement to Germany and still be able to sustain ourselves. In reality we did not have the capabilities, we did not have the number of people, we did not have the appropriate amount of weapons, we didn't have the long tail of logistics. It was clear that we were really living on the very edge, and this was something that could have been alleviated by what I consider to be modest increases in the defence budget at the time. But there was no political will.

Realistic people recognized that if deterrence failed, there'd be a real sacrifice necessary. The aim of the exercise, really, was to be as strong and as professional as possible, to contribute as effectively as possible to the deterrent. Our whole strategic policy was to maximize our capability to contribute to the deterrence with the hope and expectation that this would work. If deterrence failed, then we were in grave difficulty. And most of the people on the leading edge really understood that. But then it was going to be pretty messy, no matter how many people you had.

Even in some of the darkest days of the cold war we had maybe upwards of 10,000 Canadians and families based in Europe. And while there were plans to evacuate these people in the event things got hot, many people recognized that their families were essentially there as hostages as well. If things really got bad, things would be very bad indeed. Thank God it didn't happen. When there was an exercise held in the middle 1980s to determine just how realistic our north Norway exercise was, people realized how tenuous it was and began to understand that we had a combination of Hong Kong and Dieppe on our hands if it ever did happen.

Analyzing Problems
At the political level, because we have very, very small armed forces, and we have effectively the smallest reserve force compared to the regular force of any country in the world, we have virtually no contact with the civilian population. The civilian-military contact is extremely limited. The numbers of politicians that have any military background are minimal to nil.

Add to this the assumption that "peacekeeping" is Canada's role in the world and, because the word has "peace" in it, people think that it isn't very risky. But peacekeeping now runs the full gamut. It used to be that we were standing between countries whose forces and diplomats had agreed to stop fighting and there were certain protocols under the United Nations mandate that these people had agreed to accept. But now peacekeeping doesn't have that connotation at all. It can involve walking into the middle of a civil war. And how many factions are there shooting at the so-called peacekeepers?

This is not peacekeeping: this is humanitarian intervention. This is peacemaking, this is peace restoration. This is what we used to call war. But no, because we call it "peacekeeping," people in this country, not knowing any better, are quite happy to have Canada involved. There is a huge lack of understanding of what it is to be involved in the world and therefore no particular attention is paid.

Frequently commitments are made by governments, by diplomats, by other departments on behalf of the Department of Defence, before the Department of Defence is actually consulted. And then the answer is, "What we can do is the following ... " There's a certain momentum that gathers and it's a bureaucratic momentum which leads to things that are often other than those that were intended.

People should understand that there should be time taken to thoroughly analyze things and understand what the risks are and do some calculations. We are often too much in a rush to get people on the ground, to respond to the request from the UN or to make an offer to the UN and then have the UN come back and say, "Yes, please do this, but it's not quite what we asked you to do, it'll be something over here," which is the kind of thing that happened in Somalia. There is a tendency to rush these assessments, if they assess them at all, and one of my personal major criticisms has been that the capacity for doing these assessments has been minimal, both in terms of strategic intelligence and in terms of the overall force capability and long-term force commitments. Now, the next question is, why is that? Well, there are a variety of reasons.

The staffing in those particular areas has been inappropriately small. I was told that in strategic intelligence there was one officer responsible for the whole of Africa. There were several responsible for Europe but one officer for the whole of Africa. You can't get the assessments, in quality, in depth, in timeliness, when you don't allocate the resources to doing that.

The second thing is that there is often reluctance in a bureaucracy, I would say particularly in a political or economic bureaucracy, to really trust analysis. There's a trust much more in impression and personal opinion. Very often highly placed personal opinion will override the analysis. So in retrospect you might find that the analysis was there, but it wasn't accepted.

The third thing, and I regard this as a particularly serious issue, is that outside the military there is no appreciation for how these expeditions are launched. For example, if you were going off to someplace in which there is some kind of disease for which your troops have not been inoculated, and somebody makes the misplaced promise to have troops on the ground in 48 hours, you are automatically assuming some disease risk for those people. If you are going to inoculate the main force, you may be able to get that done in two or three days, but it takes a couple of weeks for the immunity to develop. So a responsible commander — and I would hope a responsible government — would recognize that we can't make promises to react that quickly.

Marshalling the equipment, the supplies, and calculating the distances and how many people you're going to get there and how fast is in itself a time-consuming exercise. Then you look around and say, "Do we have the capability to do this in terms of air or sea lift?" What do we depend on? Well, we depend upon the good offices of the United States or the possibility of hiring a big transport aircraft from Russia. But that means that we only go if the Americans want us to go, or if it's in their interests to give us their aircraft to go, or if the aircraft for hire are available.

Now, if one looks around the world to see how many military forces have the capability to project their forces through air and sea lift, there are very few indeed, and Canada is in the top five. But we still can't do very much. So there is a major logistical issue that many people simply don't understand. If you are going into Europe, there are all kinds of staging areas, the distances are relatively short, and we probably have a better understanding of the terrain and cultural environment than a lot of other areas. And maybe all of the other factors, diseases and things of that nature, are easier to manage.

But if you're going into East Timor, as far from Canada as you can get before you start coming back, it's not simply a matter of loading people into an airplane and flying them there. Your crews can only fly for so long before they have to have another crew. And so you've got to pre-position crews.

You've got to get all of the aircraft together in the first instance, and they may be off doing a number of other jobs. No thought seems to be given to this by the policy makers outside people in the department who simply say, "Sure, we'll do this!" In the case of East Timor, for example, it took 30 or 40 days to get people there, and many people laughed about individual Hercules having difficulty getting there. Airplanes break, that's the way it goes.

But the real thing is that we simply didn't have the troops inoculated, and we had huge distances to go to get them there. Once there, we didn't have the capability to stage them because we didn't have the heavy-lift helicopters. The Sea Kings were being used there, and these are decrepit aircraft that require an immense amount of maintenance. While any individual flight is not unsafe, the amount of time and effort to make them available is out of proportion to the availability.

So one has to ask the question, is it a problem that we took so long to get there? No, I would say it's a miracle that we got there at all, if you take everything into account. There's a huge knowledge gap because people simply don't understand the various military and logistical factors involved in an operation.

I know that there are some specific circumstances in which an operation has been turned off because the senior commander has said, "No, we can't do that." Often the politicians still apply significant pressure, particularly if some kind of promise has already been made. It then becomes almost a matter of professional pride within the military to do it. But then you can only do this so many times before professional fatigue overtakes professional pride.

At the political-military interface in this country, we have some very competent senior officers. I would say that without exception our senior officers, generals in the Canadian Forces, are exceptionally competent individuals. They are military competent. They have served in the various command and staff positions with distinction or they wouldn't be where they are. But have we prepared them for the non-military environment? Have we prepared them for the policy making or political environment in the cut and thrust of the bureaucracy in Ottawa? The quick answer to that is no, we haven't.

Military Ethos and Education
Here in Kingston until 1994, we had a year-long course at the National Defence College on national and international affairs. It was intended to bring the military officers out of the monastery and into contact with civilians from all walks of life, the federal and provincial bureaucracies, industry, academics and so on. There were 14 military officers out of a group of 40 people, and they studied for a year, together, Canada's role in the world and some of the strategic interests that we had. That pro-

gram was arbitrarily closed down in 1994. Now we're just finishing the second round of the program (in Toronto) which was designed to replace it.

It is much shorter, much more abbreviated. Intensive graduate-level, master's level and beyond, quality of education. But there are few civilians, so it's the military talking to the military. And what's happened since 1994? In the last five years all of the generals that have been promoted are people who haven't had the benefit of this kind of education. So we're going to be, for a number of years yet, behind the eight ball. It's very difficult for senior officers to explain to a minister or the prime minister some of the details of the logistical problems you face, when in fact they don't care. All they want to hear from you is, "Yes, I'll get on with it, sir."

I don't think that I would put the blame on the officers in place. I think that they have been absolutely inadequately prepared for the responsibilities they've been asked to assume, and I frankly think that considering everything, they do an amazing job, being able to adapt to what is essentially a very foreign environment for most of them.

The military ethos includes loyalty and duty to the country and courage, honesty, integrity, the fundamental military virtues. It doesn't matter where you are in the system, if you're going to be a member of the military profession, this ethos, if you wish, has got to be yours.

At the political-military interface that ethos isn't going to carry you far enough into the civilian environment. You've got to understand that your ethos is in fact quite different from the people you're dealing with, and they don't consider your ethos particularly worthwhile. Frankly, I've had all kinds of people speak to me in very derogatory terms about the military ethos. Again, this is an expression of the lack of understanding in the country of the role of the military.

As we get further and further away from the Second World War and the Korean War, which was the last time that we were actually losing significant numbers on the battlefield, the awareness of what the military's all about has been diminishing and the veterans are going to die off. It's interesting that there seems to be a renewed interest in this particular time, in no small part due to the efforts of one man, Jack Granatstein.

One hopes that it will not be necessary to have another conflict before Canadians begin to understand where the military fits in Canadian society, but the military have to understand that their position in Canadian society is not a privileged position, in the sense that they have any particular rights that nobody else has. Theirs is a position of privileged responsibility because they are the only people who are committed, by law and by profession, to give their lives for the country. And that puts them in a completely different position from anybody else. They're the only ones.

If one says that the military ethos must better reflect the civilian ethos, I think we've got to be very careful because you will not have the capacity for the military to do what they have to do in the country's interests when it really comes to that. And because you're in the military, working in a bureaucratic environment, doesn't mean that you become a civilian bureaucrat like the rest. The difference between an officer and an official is that an officer has a royal warrant, a commission that can literally and legitimately order a man or a woman to his or her death. An official has no right to do that. An official doesn't have the right to order anything, comparatively speaking.

So there is a dividing line and military people have got to understand the difference. This is why there has to be some kind of, I would say, a formalized education process within the military, particularly as people progress through the system to the higher levels, to make sure that there is an understanding that there are two sides to the street.

It's that extra advanced-military professional education, to get people to think in two ways. One, to think strategically so that they're not commanding a ship anymore, they're commanding a force, and that is a mindset that is not easy for a lot of people to change. The second thing is that they are now thinking in terms of dealing at the highest national levels and not at the level of an individual military formation. These are two major changes that are not easy for people to assume without getting some experience before they actually have to assume it.

I've been in a strategic-planning environment; I've been in the National Defence College environment where there were civilians around me a lot. And let me tell you that when I left the military and I came to Queen's University, a totally non-military environment, it was a real culture shock, and I suddenly realized something that I had said to other people for a long time, about the military essentially being a monastic order. When I came out of the monastery of military life, there were lots of differences that I wasn't prepared for. I don't think that it depends upon one's formal education.

On the other hand, I was among the most privileged, in terms of being able to live and teach in this military-civilian interface environment. There are other people who have never been exposed to that, who have been almost constantly onboard bases or ships at sea, and they simply don't come in contact with this kind of activity. They are plunged into a senior position in Ottawa and they can't really understand the behaviour of the people who don't wear funny-coloured suits.

Strategic Thinking and the System

Before 1759 the strategic thinking for Canada was done in France. After that, from 1759 until I would say the beginning or middle of the Second World War, the strategic thinking for Canada was done in Britain. And since the Second World War it's been done in the United States, and Canada has been running alongside in any given time trying to find its place in the strategies of the great.

When it comes to the sort of manoeuvre side of strategy, we don't have a force now of significant size to really make a difference in terms of our own national military strategy. That doesn't mean that we weren't important in the Second World War because we ended up with the third- or fourth-largest army in the world, the third-largest air force, the third-largest navy, which is another thing that a lot of Canadians don't understand.

Even in NATO we had a very important air force, particularly when we had nuclear weapons on the CF-104s. So in terms of our strategic contribution and the awareness of Canadian officers of the importance of our strategic contribution, we had excellent people thinking in these terms. You can think of the Curries of the First World War, the McNaughtons of the First and Second World War, the Crerars and the Simondses and the like that have carried us down through the ages.

In Canada we can think strategically and I think that there is a lot of good strategic thinking going on. And strategic thinking has to take place before strategic planning. You can think strategically, but if you don't have the resources to do anything about it, then that can be a very frustrating process, and you can talk about what you should be able to do, or what you could be able to do.

When you start trying to think through the strategy of what you can do, this is probably the real test of strategic thinking. I would say that the capacity of the Canadian Forces to do as much as they have with so little, comparatively speaking, certainly since the end of the Second World War, but particularly in the last 10 years, is nothing but a real recognition of the competence of the military's strategic thinking in this country. I don't think that there's a lack of strategic thinking. I think there is a lack of strategic will on the part of the country.

I don't think that there has been any serious change in the presence or absence of strategic thinking within the military since 1974, when we started the Canadian Institute of Strategic Studies. In 1974 the number of civilian strategists in this country could be counted on the first few fingers of one hand. Through an effective national program in more than a dozen universities and centres for strategic studies, we have both civilian and military students who have gone into strategic studies and trained at undergraduate and graduate levels. There are resources there.

You can do all the strategic thinking you want before you have the planning. But if there's no strategic will, it doesn't matter what you want to do, it's not going to be there. I would say that one of the biggest problems in this country is that the vast majority of the population really doesn't have the understanding of what's going on in the world and how important all of that is to Canada.

You can start thinking strategically and say, "What is it that we can do best?" Is it best for us to postage-stamp ourselves with penny-packet forces in 50 different places around the world, with a total of 4,000 troops? Is that the most effective contribution that we can make? Is this really providing us with some kind of national satisfaction that we're doing something, and as long as you see a guy with a blue helmet on his head and a Canadian flag on his shoulder, Canada's obviously doing the best thing in the world?

Well, I think that that's a very shallow expectation. I think that it's an unrealistic assessment and I think that it is frankly insufficient in terms

157

of Canada's wealth, responsibility and what we gain from the rest of the world. When somebody calls your bluff, it only happens once because in this game they call your bluff once and you're out of the game, probably permanently. That's a real risk.

We're talking about what we can contribute to the alliance. Yes, we can contribute some things to the alliance that the alliance really needs in terms of NATO training, for example. We have landmass for training, which the people in Europe simply envy. We have weather and expertise in things like flying training, so that we are able to offer some of the best flying training in the world, and the new NATO flying training program is an example of how successful Canada has been in generating this.

So there are some things that we can offer to the alliance, and have been successful in doing, which have served as contributions instead of the frontline forces. This has been strategic thinking. How can you make the best with what you've got when you don't have anything else to do it with? That, I don't think, is bluff. I think that that is substitution.

But what happens if the cards are called and you have to put your forces in the frontline? If you have not adequately prepared them through training and education, if you have not adequately equipped them, if you have not provided them with the medical support and the necessary supplies to sustain them in the field, then you've committed them to their deaths. That is political immorality of the highest order.

There's an old saying that war is an event to which old men send young men to die. It's not just young men anymore, it's young men and women, and it is assuredly old men who send them, but it's even different from what it was in the past. The old men today have never faced that same challenge themselves. And that's a significant difference in the history of our country. The old men before at least had had a taste of it themselves, or at least a lot of them had been nearby. Not anymore.

If the resources are being pinched, what is it that you have to put in the shop window? You have to put the guys with the guns. Maybe you hope that you won't need as many doctors and nurses. Maybe you hope that you won't need as many transport aircraft and ambulances and so forth. You hope.

As a result of this, because we have not been in these wartime situations and have only been on peacekeeping, the experience of the support staffs has not kept pace with the broad base of military medicine. You haven't got the money left in the budget for the kinds of medical resources across the country and overseas that you have to have on a day-by-day basis to mobilize and to deploy when necessary.

The end result is that as this gets pinched down into a smaller and smaller number, the specialists are fewer and fewer. The attractions of civilian practice are greater and greater. And so when something does happen and somebody says, "Gee whiz, we didn't realize that we had all these war casualties," one reason is that, day-to-day, there wasn't the staff to know what was really going on.

What we're really seeing when this happens is not any negligence on the part of the military or the Department of National Defence. It's the ability to respond to the continued pressure for downsizing and reduction of costs that's being tested. We're now in the pay-me-later business and the pay-me-later unfortunately is at the expense of some people's lives. Not necessarily that they have been killed, but their lives have been ruined in the process, and that's as politically immoral as sending them off to their deaths.

This whole business of the military is not simply having a battalion of troops with bayonets, or it's not simply having a ship with a couple of hundred sailors onboard, but it's an increasingly sophisticated interlocking system. It's a system which involves everybody, from the guys pulling the trigger right back to the highly specialized combat surgeon who is operating in a third-line hospital somewhere behind the lines or back in Canada.

It involves the people who are loading the aircraft to get these things over there. There is a very involved and long system in this process. I don't know where you begin to understand, or where you begin to teach and inform Canadians of all of this, and I've tried myself. I know two or three things that I can't do. I can't get a letter published in any of the newspapers if it's any more than about 35 or 40 words long. Unfortunately the kinds of things I'm trying to tell you don't lend themselves to 35- or 40-word explanations.

Similarly, in various television interviews I've done, this doesn't lend itself to 35- or 40-second explanations. It's like education. Education is not something that we do part time on Saturday nights for a couple of weeks a year. Education is a lifelong experience and is a cumulative process. So you can't do it through a succession of snapshots.

I would say that one of the major strategic issues in this country, if not the major strategic issue, is the education of the Canadian population on the national security interests and needs of Canada. If we don't do that, I'm not sure that we'll be able to hold our heads up, least of all survive in the coming world, economically or politically. I think we have to question the legitimacy of people who try to get a ride on the cheap. It's like hanging on behind the streetcar to get up the hill on your bicycle. You do that at some significant risk.

Canada has not been particularly good at clearly articulating its interests. I think that certainly the Second World War was fought on the basis of values. If you talk to the Second World War veterans, the vast majority of them when asked why they went say, "This man Hitler had to be stopped." Now, they probably couldn't articulate the ideology of National Socialism, which was so abhorrent that it caused them to risk their lives to stop it. But it's a very small step from having your values threatened and not defending them to having your homeland threatened, either physically or morally.

If you allow your values to be undermined by saying, "It's not in my interest to protect these particular values over there," then you really run a long-term risk because you're being dishonest with yourself. If you're going to defend values, then you have to articulate clearly for the whole population what those values are, how they relate to your national interests and how you're going to go about defending them. If you're serious about this, you have to then articulate, for the population, what risks you are prepared to accept.

We committed in the 20th century over 100,000 people to their deaths in defence of certain values in the first 50 years. In the second 50 years we have, I don't know the exact number, 100 or so peacekeepers that have been killed defending those values. I think that we've been very lucky, frankly, that there haven't been a lot more. On the other hand, there have been a lot of people who have been irreparably damaged because we really haven't understood the circumstances in which they've been thrust. Our values are something that we really have to spend some time thinking and talking about.

If the public really understood what the politicians are saying, in a democratic society the public would have the responsibility to hold the politicians' feet to the fire. But we've got the whole nation imbued with the idea that if we can do this on the cheap, it's more money in our pockets and less spent allowing these soldiers to play with their toys.

National Interests

I was the author of an annual paper related to our commitments, capabilities and how much we should be spending and what, if any, increase there should be given to the defence budget. I was hauled up to a very senior political advisor and asked if I was trying to get the minister fired with this kind of recommendation. I said I certainly wasn't, but why was he thinking this?

And he said, "Well, let me tell you the facts of life. We do not increase the defence budget simply because we have to increase or decrease the capability. We increase the defence budget when the allies are screaming, and we increase it by whatever amount it takes to stop them from making a noise and complaining. And then we stop spending. And that is in the national interest."

That's not my definition of national interest.

No government is under pressure to increase the defence budget for a variety of reasons: (a) the government doesn't feel threatened at a military level; (b) the Canadian population doesn't feel threatened at a military level and therefore they're not putting pressure on the government; (c) there isn't a significant proportion of the population serving in the military to represent a constituency that has to be recognized and served; (d) our neighbours to the south have been infinitely tolerant in picking up the bill because it doesn't matter what they do. They're doing it in their interests not ours, and it just happens that it's in our interests as well.

I'm not surprised.

If the "national interest" is only putting in as little money as is necessary to keep the allies happy, how little money is necessary to keep the Canadian population happy that their sons and daughters are not being put at unreasonable risk? Two different questions but the latter one I think is the one that the population should be asking, not the first one. Unfortunately it's the first one that they often ask.

The question of how much we should spend should fall out of a serious analysis of what it is that we want to do. I think that the British had a strategic defence review a few years ago where the military said to the politicians, "Tell us what it is that you want to do. Do you want to defend British interests outside our territory? Because we can assure you that, as far as we can determine now, there is no threat of invasion of Britain. Do you want to invest in protecting your interests abroad?"

To make a long story short they said "yes," and the military came back and said, "Well, here's what it costs to be able to mount this kind of force. This is the bill," and the British government accepted that. There was a very interesting dialogue between the military and the government and the bureaucracy as to how this was going to be effected. They finally ended up with two task forces that could be sustained for a significant period of time, each with an integral sea-lift support, airlift support, helicopters and close air support.

This demanded the integration of the fighters of the air force and the navy, the integration of the helicopters of the army, navy and air force. Huge changes came out of this. But, as you saw recently, the British were able to send 800 troops into Sierra Leone very quickly because they had the capability and they had the national will.

Soft Power
The "walk softly and carry a big stick" is one thing; "walk stickly and carry a big soft" is another, and we seem to have adopted the second. If we talk long enough and loud enough, somebody will think we've convinced them to behave differently. Unfortunately I don't think that human nature is that way. I don't think that international politics operates that way.

Sure there is soft power, but it is one end of the spectrum. The other end of the spectrum is hard power. If you are trying to make your way only with soft power, what is the interest that anybody should have in listening to you, unless you're prepared to back up your wishes with increasing coercive capability? And that's what the history of the world has been all about. If we think we're going to change human history, we've got another project on our hands.

When it comes to human security, this is very much a values-oriented look at the world. Perhaps this is going to be the most difficult kind of discussion in terms of the use of military force. At what point do you accept the loss of life of Canadian young men and women in defence of some far-off land that their parents have never heard of? And perhaps not even defence of the far-off land, but maybe the defence of a few civilians in that far-off land against a bunch of irrepressible and irresponsible rebels?

This question is going to have to be discussed at the national level. If we're going to take this human-security issue on, we're going to have to think clearly and thoroughly as to what it is that we are prepared to commit, in terms of our national assets, national resources and national lives. Because as Sierra Leone, Congo, Rwanda, Kosovo, Bosnia all tell us, the world is not a pretty place out there. If we think that we can send our young people off and they're not going to get shot at, we're whistling in the dark.

I think that many of the people who have been indulging in that thinking have found that the events of Kosovo, in particular, have changed their minds somewhat, that you can talk as much as you want but in the final analysis you end up with coercive force. As the Americans have concluded, much as they want to alleviate humanitarian disasters, and it is in their national interest to promote the humanitarian values of freedom and social justice and the like, these are not vital interests affecting the survival of the United States. Therefore no American lives will be consciously committed to that kind of activity. Hence you have the rather sterile high-altitude bombing done, as in Kosovo, that put none of our lives at risk, effectively. People don't understand why this happens, but it's a function of our lack of understanding of what's going on in the world.

We teach in our staff colleges and war colleges all kinds of principles and doctrines associated with land, sea and air warfare, and strategic bombing, as opposed to tactical bombing. You have this group of professional military people, at various levels, who are there to advise the politicians. "Right, according to our doctrine, if you want to terminate this war through strategic bombing, here are the things that you do," and with Kosovo, I think there were something like 168 primary targets that they showed to politicians and said, "This is what we're going after and it'll all be over in two days."

The politicians said, "No, no, no, no, those aren't the targets you're going after at all. We won't let you." I've been told that not one of the original strategic targets was allowed to be hit.

Often what happens is that politicians, who are taking the decisions on behalf of the country, call up the use of military power, get the advice of their military professionals, often choose not to take the advice of the military professionals, and tell the military to do something else that the military professionals don't particularly think is going to be effective. But being loyal, democratically oriented officers, they say, "It's not what we advise but that's what we'll do." Then the politicians and the population have the nerve to blame the military because this wasn't used effectively. I think that is absolutely disingenuous. And once again, people don't understand what went on.

I think that the military is quite prepared to be more transparent. The military in a democratic society is subservient to the elected civilian political power, and I would not want to change that at all. It may not be in the military's best interests to be kept quiet, but that's what happens. Is this in the better and broader interests of the nation? I don't think it is. I think that having a lid put on the military by either politicians or senior officers is not serving the country well. And indeed it contributes to the very level of ignorance that I've been complaining about, that the average Canadian doesn't understand a lot of what goes on.

So it goes round and round in circles. Who is responsible for this? I would hope more journalists would be looking at what the military does rather than trying to castigate the military in terms of its errors. It's hard to find a news story talking positively about the military. They dredge up the unfortunate behaviour of individuals, very small in number, and try to generalize that across the force. It's demoralizing. In a democratic society dependent upon an all-volunteer force, you can carry on doing this to your military for only so long before the soldier looks around and says, "Why am I doing this?'

Don't ask us to get our feet dirty unless you give us the mandate to be able to protect ourselves accordingly. The reluctance of the Canadian military leadership to contribute combat troops to certain areas historically has been when that mandate was going to be unrealistically putting people at risk. Remember that in the Golan Heights, where we have people, they serve there unarmed. They're truce observers that don't have any weapons at all, and they're out there in ones and twos. They're absolutely defenceless.

What if you then put a body of troops out, armed but lightly armed, and they're supposed to enforce, like heavy-duty policemen, and the other side chooses not to recognize their authority? What if they take you on and your mandate is not to kill or be killed, your mandate is to sit there and take it until somebody can call a halt at a higher level? There's got to be a more realistic understanding of the environments into which people are being sent by the United Nations bureaucracy.

One of the United Nations officials speaking on the situation in Sierra Leone said, "It never occurred to us that it might get like this." If we are putting people into these kinds of hostile environments, it has to occur to us that the worst can happen. And we have to equip our people for the worst and give them the authority to defend themselves when the worst happens.

You'll notice that the British have sent their people into Sierra Leone to defend the airport, and now they're defending the British civilians and they're helping the others defend the city, but you can be assured that they are not there in a passive, benign way. Those guys will fight their way out if necessary. They're not there under UN auspices: they're there because they're protecting British interests.

The Future
With the coming together of a new joint operations group here in Kingston, the intention is to bring together the army, navy and air forces to put together a task force that can be deployed, of various sizes. The white paper in 1994 says that the maximum overall task force deployed

should total 4,000 personnel. Right now we've got almost 4,000 in various parts of the world and it's not in a single task force.

The Joint Task Force, JTF 2, has a quick reaction capability and would be available for the evacuation of Canadians from certain areas. It would be up to the Canadian government to decide to commit them and get them there. There is a capability to do these kinds of things in a very limited way, like a few hundred.

We have to be careful about how we represent what size force can go, how fast and where. Our forces have participated in exercises with other forces in terms of evacuating civilians across beaches and from airports and things of that nature. I don't think that it's against the Official Secrets Act to say that there is a limited capability for this in Canada.

The interesting question is, what is the government's will to use this if the time comes? Because these people are trained to defend themselves and will be equipped to defend themselves. Another question: how large a group like this do you want? If it's just a matter of evacuating a few civilians that's one thing, but if you are going to defend the capital city of whatever country you wish to name, then that's another matter entirely.

You've got to be able to have air and sea lift to take in heavy equipment as well as the lead-time to do that. So to a substantial degree this is where we live now, six years after the white paper of 1994, which puts some numerical constraints on the size of the Canadian Forces on the one hand, and also some equipment-capability constraints on the other. The final constraint is, of course, a seriously limited budget, one really stretched and strained to meet its objectives.

It's time to ask what we really want to do in Canada's interests. We have to recognize that the kinds of wars that are being fought in the context of values that we want to protect, not only on our own behalf but on behalf of others unable to protect themselves, require a broader discussion. It will probably require more people and better equipment — and *more* equipment.

Our national security choices may be threefold. One is to do as little as possible to keep the Americans from screaming at us, knowing full well that in the worst case of any attack in North America they're going to look after us in their interests. That I regard as morally unacceptable. It is totally irresponsible to work on that assumption, except it seems to be the cheapest way to go, and because it's cheap, it's acceptable in the eyes of many. I don't buy that.

A second approach would be to look at the rest of the world and say, "We are prepared to benefit from all of the activities that go on in a trading context, and we will enrich ourselves to the maximum degree through commercial means, and we will contribute to the stability of the world by contributing our business acumen and our natural resources through export and import and so on. But please don't ask us to commit any of our lives to that, because we would rather just sit back and take the profits, thank you very much." That I regard as morally reprehensible as well, irresponsible and unacceptable.

The third route, one infinitely more responsible, is to sit down and take a look at the world. Identify where we get our benefits from, where our and others' benefits might be enhanced. If there is instability in those areas that may threaten those benefits, then what are we prepared to do to reduce those threats? What resources are we prepared to commit to that, and what are the risks that we're prepared to assume in terms of the lives of our young people on behalf of their parents? And that's the responsible position in my view. I'm not optimistic, but I think it would be a worthwhile discussion.

Defence 2020 is a document looking at a strategic framework within which to operate, and for that reason I think that it's very good because it can mean a lot of things to a lot of people. In it there is a comment about the Revolution in Strategic Affairs, the Revolution in Military Affairs and the Revolution in Business Affairs. And these are not the same kinds of revolutions.

The Revolution in Strategic Affairs means that you're not necessarily only going to be threatened by missiles. It means that you can be as easily threatened by a shopping bag in a shopping mall. And that shopping bag containing a bomb might've been put there by a terrorist from your own country or somebody else's.

The Revolution in Military Affairs means that the bomb could be a whole lot more powerful than it has been in the past, and that the capability to detect that bomb, either coming in or out of the country or being made, may be enhanced. So the revolution in strategic affairs really is saying that, unlike the time during the cold war when we had the real luxury, if you like, of only having to worry about nuclear war, our worries have intensified. They now run the whole spectrum up to and including nuclear war, from the lowest level of some individual assassin who is out to terrorize the population, right through all kinds of other levels.

The Revolution in Military Affairs means the capacity for small groups and other nations to actually threaten, out of all proportion to their size and their budgets, the way of life of other people. That capacity is there because the weapons are more sophisticated, more powerful and more difficult to detect and defend against.

The Revolution in Business Affairs is another area that becomes relevant because there are ways and means of communicating, of analyzing, of manufacturing, that play into both of these. We are looking at new kinds of business structures and relationships, not the least of which is globalization. And it's globalization that puts us on the frontlines of wherever we may be in the world with our business, with our military and with a part of our national strategy.

Now, this is a very interesting policy soup, and to think that we can explain it simply, or simplistically, is an error. It was H. L. Mencken who said, "For every complex problem there is a solution that is simple, neat and wrong."

I believe that if there was ever a motto for many Canadian policies, it's that. For the complex problems we want simple solutions. It really doesn't matter if it's wrong or not, just as long as it's simple.

There's a realization at the top of the need for an educational revolution in terms of military thinking. It's not the formal education that is lacking, although there are some people who would argue that, but it's a matter of the opportunity for people to have the time to think through the major issues. I can tell you from personal experience, both during and since my time in the military, that when you've got some complicated problems, you need the time to sit down and just think quietly.

It's very difficult because all the while people are racing around, shouting, and phones are ringing and people are demanding answers, being quite unreasonable about what answer they're going to get and when. That's precisely how you end up with the simple, easy and wrong answer to the complex problem.

If you prepare military people to think in advance about some of the complicated problems in the world, to articulate their thinking to politicians and to do this without sinking into bureaucratic minutiae, all that will contribute to that effective revolution at the top. I don't doubt we have the capability to effect that revolution in Canada. I think we're making strides in that direction. It's going to require the allocation of more educational resources within the military and more time for senior officers to do this. But the fruits of that labour will be to the larger benefit of the nation, and it will be seen very quickly, in a relatively few number of years.

CHARLES "SANDY" COTTON
Lieutenant-Colonel (Retired)
2000

Charles "Sandy" Cotton served with the Royal 22nd Regiment and is currently a director of the Institute for Faith and Ethics in Society, Queen's Theological College, where he lectures on community development and leadership. He was head of the leadership and management department at Royal Military College and a consultant to the Somalia inquiry. In September 2001 Dr. Cotton was ordained a permanent deacon in the Anglican Church of Canada.

Up until September 7, 1962, I was going to work in the textile factory where my father worked. I was a working-class kid, the oldest of five children in Quebec, and I really had no opportunity to go to university, certainly no family funding, and we had no military connections in our background. Someone suggested to me that I should consider ROTP and I applied. I got a telegram from the Department of National Defence which said, "We will pay you to go to university." And it transformed my life. To this day, and this sounds a little bit sentimental, I carry that shredded telegram in my wallet. I still have it because it literally changed my life. I think that's one of the underappreciated things about the military in this society. It's an extraordinary opportunity path for people to grow, to learn and to make contributions.

I knew nothing about the military. I thought if you joined the military, you joined the army. And if you joined the army, you joined the infantry. So my degree was essentially an undergraduate in hockey, football and any bird course I could find, complemented by summer training as an infantry officer. When I graduated, to my great surprise, I was sent to the Royal 22nd Regiment in Quebec City. And it again changed my life. It opened pathways to bilingualism, to an understanding of a different culture, to experiences that even now, as I think about them, I can't forget, like changing the guard at the citadel on July 1, 1967; marching on to Bobbie Gimby's "Ca-na-da"; being an officer of the guard when de Gaulle landed and the "Vive le Québec libre!" stuff. It was wonderful.

Neither my wife nor I spoke very much French at all, and yet we were accepted into the regimental family. In the traditional, combatant side of the military, people work very hard to maintain that sense of family and community and inclusiveness. The degree to which there can be a small, intimate community in this society, in which the mess is the centre of social life, has eroded. Families now distinguish between what they give to the employer, to the institution, and the time they reserve for themselves. My understanding is that most of the officers' messes across the country, for example, do a brisk business during the week at lunchtime, but most of the members do not see it as the focal point of their social or their community life.

Military Culture

Certainly there's a large part of the military culture, which is grounded in the 19th century, in which there was a relative balance in terms of the people who were officers, the landed gentry, the aristocracy and the lower classes who enlisted — all managed by a band of sergeants major and non-commissioned officers. The officers were in many respects to the manor born. They acted as if they deserved a different lifestyle, that they were ordained to command and the soldiers went along with it. It made sense in the way they looked at the world. What has disintegrated, not just through the Charter of Rights, not just through differences in lifestyles, or actually a homogenization of lifestyles, is the degree to which the majority of participants in military systems have those mindsets. The Gurkhas probably still do. In fact, most militaries around the world where the officers are recruited from the elite and the soldiers, if you like, are recruited from the peasantry, seem to work. Both sides understand who should be on top, who's upstairs and who's downstairs.

When we were first at the citadel we would have a small group of officers who would have these extraordinary social evenings where the regimental band would play, where numerous soldiers would get to dress up in servant outfits and they worked really hard to give us this experience which was right out of the 19th century. Extraordinary.

Commitment and cohesion are at the centre of all military systems. The military is a fundamentally conservative institution. Its social structures are profoundly conservative. I have a theory about that, particularly in the army context, and that is when combat begins, the only thing that will allow people to stick together, to cohere and to go forward, is some sense of relationship with each other. And so cohesion has to be implanted into it.

But officers generally are quite conservative beings, and so are NCOs. The military is resistant to change on the cultural level, but not necessarily on the technological level. Technology they welcome with open arms, particularly in Canada, where they're the poor boys in the technology field and they're seeing all these other soldiers with better equipment, more toys. But on the social dimension they're profoundly conservative, resistant to change. They tend to get a mindset that locks into certain ways of doing things. Flogging happened to be one of the motivational tools used to maintain discipline. After a while folks, I guess, assumed it was the only way it could be maintained.

All major cultural changes in military systems are imposed by the outside society. When flogging was banned a great many people, distinguished combat leaders, couldn't imagine troops being cohesive and disciplined and focused and committed without it. There were articles in Victorian army journals. "The British Army will never stand and fight again," and some military leaders resigned in protest. Of course, they seem to have stood and fought and died very well in World War I without flogging, although there were residuals "pour encouraget les autres," the executions, the morale-building executions, if you like.

Now, when I think about Canada, the Canadian officers today have the best-paid, best-educated, healthiest, most intelligent troops in the world. And the challenge is to find the new recipe for cohesion and commitment. The old ones don't work, particularly when a private is more intelligent, may well have a degree and knows more about computers than the commanding general.

Sociology and the Military — The Cotton Report
In some respects I've always been marginal. A working-class kid who went to Bishop's University. An English graduate who went to the Royal 22nd Regiment. An infantry officer who, for whatever reason, in his mid-20s, after seven or eight years of service, became interested in studying sociology. I'd never taken it. And in part that was autobiographical, trying to understand the world that I was in and the world that I was changing and that was changing around me.

I was lucky enough to have two years at Carleton as an infantry captain. This was in the time of Vietnam, of "the pigs," so I was profoundly marginal there, although I was accepted. After my degree I got involved in personnel policy research because in the 1970s the military was experiencing, largely driven by the demographic shifts, baby boom, etc., a recruiting crisis. So I began to study the values of society, the numbers in society, and did that for three years.

And then, "Would I be interested in doing a doctorate in sociology at Carleton?" So I studied the army value systems and the tensions within the military. It was a very, very complex project, partly because it had to please both the university and the commander of Mobile Command, who was the inside sponsor. I think Mobile Command believed that my findings would clearly show that unification was, in plain English, unworkable, an aberration. I think they were surprised by what I found. The findings were later put together as the so-called "Cotton Report" on deep divisions and tensions inside the military system.

I was interested in differences in value systems, different mindsets, different orientations, but I was also interested in the theoretical, the relationship between mindset and a willingness to enter combat. I posed this question, and this was to a 10 percent sample of the army, from generals down to privates: "If the Canadian Forces required you to enter combat, what would be your likely response?" The most surprising finding, and this was the finding that developed a lot of publicity across the country, was that 25 percent of the serving junior soldiers, corporal and below, answered that they would refuse to go. I dismissed it in my analysis as a statistical artifact of sort of general, negative morale and distrust of the officers. I didn't pay much attention to it. A lot of other people did because the possibility that 25 percent of Canada's professional ground troops would refuse to enter combat struck folks as a little bit frightening.

At that time the basic conceptual constructs came out of the United States, as social scientists attempted to understand what had happened in Vietnam. There was the development of what was called the Institutional Occupational Model of the military, and the thesis put out was that the military was changing and not only that, it was changing in bad ways, from a complete social institution, in which people were bonded together and had a sense of duty and calling 24 hours a day and "service to my country" beyond everything else, to a more limited, corporate occupational model, a McDonald's type of model.

The military always seeks to fight the last war. My sense is that many officers, senior officers, the strategic leaders, are in a state of nostalgia. They grieve for a world they believe they have lost, much in the way that churches do and universities, even, a world which was simple and where people knew their place. I don't know why.

I found at the heart of the army, in its senior leadership — and I would include there the regimental sergeants major and the officers, certainly majors and above, people who had radically different value profiles, radically different statistical patterns than others — that there was a profound sense of anger in the interviews I did with them. Anger, passive aggressive frustration with the way the military was changing, the Charter of Rights, the social engineering, the loss of control. I called these people, for lack of a better term, "beleaguered warriors."

Not only was civilian society unsupportive of the military as a vocation, but they perceived that the majority of participants in uniform were also unsupportive, and in some respects saw themselves as preservers of a sacred way of being and doing and thinking. It was perhaps strongest, and this is one of the complexities, in Petawawa.

When I surveyed the Airborne Regiment in Petawawa, the beleaguered warrior syndrome was certainly very well developed and, both at the level of my own cognitions and in my writing, I raised issues about the potential for the dark side of this outlook, this mindset. I now realize that I was seeing something which had a malignancy that could evolve into something profoundly embarrassing, profoundly contradictory and dissonant with Canadian military virtues. In some respects the report was predictive of the seeds of Somalia.

At that time I was head of the leadership and management department at the Royal Military College, and I began to write that the military should not turn inwards in this nostalgic collective recollection of the past, but should preserve — it's a baby-and-bath-water thing — its functional focus on cohesion and commitment, but also work with and align with the deeper Canadian values. I wrote a piece in *Canadian Defence Quarterly* which advocated a Canadian military ethos based not on "either-or thinking," in the sense of you either are military or you are civilian, but based on the assumption that you are both. The scale that I developed has been used around the world to measure military value systems. I called it the MES, Military Ethos Scale.

The debate still goes on, and I chuckle to myself at some of these black-and-white, either-or perspectives based on the military ethos and say, "I don't think they fully understood what I was getting at." To draw a line and to say the military is radically different and cannot be subject to the broader norms, values, culture, laws of the land or traditions of the land is a profession taking the stance, "We want to play by our rules. We want to control what happens." I don't think that works in Canada.

In Samuel Huntington's *The Soldier and the State* he describes the ordered world of West Point and the disorderly chaos of the little town around it. It's very lyrical, very poetic, and he says they cannot connect. One serves the other but they can never be linked together. It will still go on and beleaguered warriors will place their stake in the ground and say, "We are different."

In some of the responses in the *Canadian Defence Quarterly* about my arguments, almost word for word, old beleaguered warriors wrote articles with titles like, "Where Have All the Tigers Gone?"; "Leadership Is the Centre"; "Managers and Business Administration Will Never"; etc.

That's the black-and-white thinking, and the world we're in right now is a world of paradox and integration of polarities. As my life has involved teaching at business school and also teaching in a theological college, I work with senior clergy, who are beleaguered warriors in their own way. And they say, "People have to understand that we are different. We can never be concerned with things like money." I'd rather have a profession which is willing to explore and struggle with managing the paradoxes and the polarities. Quite clearly we want fiscal accountability in military systems and we want, also, passionate emotion that drives people in dangerous situations to be able to risk themselves. But it isn't one or the other. Choosing one produced Somalia. The tribal cronyism of Somalia was a logical outcome of claiming that leadership is the only thing that matters.

The culture of any organization is essentially the consistent and patterned ways of acting, thinking, feeling and looking at the world. It's quite durable, and much of it is invisible. The hardest things to change are the things you can't see, the software in people's heads. Having studied and written and talked about the military culture in Canada for 30-plus years, I would have to say that there is an intellectual stagnation, in some cases an anti-intellectualism, within the officer corps, and certainly many Somalia-related reviews have pointed to that. It is very, very rare for an officer with an advanced graduate degree, particularly at the doctoral level in Canada, to rise above the rank of lieutenant-colonel. Contrary to the United States, for example.

Resisting Change
I have my own ideas about why, at the turn of the 21st century, we find this resistance to change, this intellectual stagnation. I think it goes back to unification.

Unification was a new, untried, alien, aberrant form of social organization for the military — imposed, deeply resisted by the warrior caste. Some analysts would argue that the ethical guts of the officer corps left with the resignations. So we have had this situation for almost the past three decades where the combat institutional structure, the tribes, if you like, the regiments, the naval officer groups, etc., were living in a house they didn't feel worked for them. So much of their effort has been actually reactive, to get the kind of organization that they like and want, and it took them 25 years but they got back the uniforms, they got back the separate headquarters. Their heart was never in making the green unified military work, and I think, in some respects, creative, intellectually complex, professional discourse was developmentally arrested over the past three decades in Canada. As a result, some parts of the military are vulnerable.

Civilianization became in some respects a neurotic focus for the military for much of the 1970s and the 1980s. Defence, in fact, has a uniformed and non-uniformed labour force, but all militaries around the world have that. The civilians provide long-term expertise; the military provides the combat side.

The difference in Canada is in the attempt to integrate and develop this very complex structure, civilians and military people rubbed up against each other. They didn't live in two separate worlds, two different buildings, civilians over there and the "good" people over here, which led, I think, to a perception on the part of the military, in Ottawa especially, that there are far too many civilians, when in fact the numbers didn't show that at all. The civilian percentage of the defence labour force in Canada was quite a bit lower than in other Western industrial nations. It's just that they were in their face all the time. When I was teaching at RMC I once posed, in a sociology of the military profession fourth-year course, this as a final exam question: "Civilianization is the military's word for social changes it doesn't like. Discuss." Some senior officers were quite upset with that question.

There are paradoxical elements to this, though. Many of the civilians in the Department of National Defence, and I can say, certainly, the critical minority of the civilians, are ex-military. One of the gains in Ottawa in the 1970s and the 1980s, and I presume it still goes on, was, as one neared retirement, being able to civilianize one's position. I don't think anyone's really looked very closely at the reality, but that doesn't stop the rhetorical flow at all. In fact, it probably fuels it.

The operational world of the military, which is the true world, and, if you like, the infrastructure, which is always organized and composed of fighting units, are chronically distrustful of headquarters. But there's always been this banding and bonding and sense of collegiality among the officer corps.

When I joined the military in 1962 I was given this little pay-scale card that I could carry in my wallet. The chief of staff of the army's pay was included there. What evolved was that the leadership in the immediate post-unification era was quite politicized. In some respects that has continued on with the senior officers.

I don't fully understand how the choices were made and what the policy rationales were, but colonels and above were defined as comparable to the executive class of the civil service and were actually given a new commission and new terms of service and loyalty to the government of the day. They were also managed, compensated, motivated on a pay-for-performance model with bonuses, etc., which was very common in the executive world, the secular world, the school of business world, and that led to a break in the bonds of trust within the officer corps.

In the final analysis there are very fragile threads of understanding and connection between the human beings who constitute our military organization. Most of the junior officers — that would include majors and below — that I have spoken to in the past 15 years are cynical about their leaders.

Leadership and Trust

If you look at Somalia and then look at the situation in Croatia, particularly the exposure of troops to health-threatening, life-threatening substances and environments, sandbags, etc., there were radical differences between the two, in terms of their internal consequences for the military. The radically profane behaviour associated with Somalia could be defined, and essentially was, as a few bad apples, a rogue system clearly operating outside the boundaries. These, in retrospect, were troubled, bad individuals who never should have gone there in the first place, and it was not threatening to the system or to the upper regions of the chain of command. At least, this was the framing that happened.

Croatia, on the other hand, was a radically different thing. These were good people, dedicated people, competent people. They went and they did, and when they came home some of them had some symptoms, and there had been some leadership identification of potential problems. When the senior military leadership began to see that and reacted as if it was problematic and unsoldierly, then it was profoundly threatening, in my view, to cohesion, trust, up and down the rank levels.

It's not easy to be an operational-level military person in Canada. Systemic burnout occurs as units are rotated, leaders are rotated, and families suffer. It's incredible dedication that these people have, and they go and they make it work and they're respected around the world. When they raise what they believe to be legitimate concerns, such as the long-time sergeant who said, "I refuse to take that untested anthrax inoculation," and the military reacts as if these were problem children, as if it doesn't believe and trust and support dedicated people, it is a great threat to the integrity and credibility of the leadership system.

I wrote a paper on the social, corporate and broader Canadian responsibilities vis-à-vis soldiers who risk themselves and, parenthetically, their families. You can't simply expect them to do it without acting as if you were willing to support them doing it. That's at the heart of the very complex social contract related to military service in a free society. The concepts of unlimited liability are at the very centre of the conservative perspective on military service, and represent to me a framing of military service as unique and special.

Unlimited liability has figured quite strongly in the past half-century as a central concept in the way people, particularly within the military, think about military service. Essentially the implication is that people who are in the military are liable to be put at risk in any circumstances at any time and suffer consequences up to and including the loss of their life. That is a fact. Whether that should be used as a cornerstone of a full-blown claim that the military needs special treatment in our society is something that one could contest, or at least explore. There are many other professions and occupations in this society where there are high risks associated with the role of performance: the police, farmers, miners, people who go to sea, people who fly helicopters.

At the same time, though, underlying everything is, for me, the shared understandings about what it is to be military and what the reciprocal relationship and obligations are between the military and the society it serves. I'm not so sure that Canadians fully appreciate the complexities and the demands of the unlimited liability type of service of Canadians in the past 40 years.

I'd like to make a connection between this perennial topic of leadership and managers. One of the best distinctions I know between the two says,

"Managers do things right. Leaders do the right thing." And I want to make a connection between that and a discussion that I had with a group of senior officers in Ottawa. Someone observed (because I had raised issues of leadership for them), "One of the problems is, these people talk about leadership, but they act like managers. They act like managers and they're unwilling to actually look at themselves too closely."

In those situations where someone has served with dedication, with competence, been wounded, been hurt, suffered family consequences, and then had a minor defence bureaucrat, in uniform or out of uniform, simply say, "You don't qualify for this," or "The relationship's over," my question would be, "Where are all the leaders?" Where are the leaders saying this isn't the way that we forge bonds of trust. This isn't the way that we create a small group of people who are willing to put themselves at risk. The politicians, by and large, and the media — and this is one of the complexities of our time — only find out about these things when the Scott Taylors and the Michel Drapeaus of the world bring them up. Or when, in desperation, someone with their kind of commitment and dedication, who has paid prices, been a true believer and has something that is really important, a legitimate concern, is told to be quiet: "You don't count." I would suspect that many of the soldiers who have gone to the press and gone to Parliament have gone with angry tears in their eyes, with a sadness and an anger, trying to articulate, "I risked it all for you and this is what I get."

I would hold the senior leadership accountable because their primary responsibility in this society is to put together a committed and effective social system oriented toward the application of violence.

The military ethos question for me has always been a matter of minds and hearts. How do people look at the world, how do they feel about it and what are the motives, the interior motives? Much of the reformist activities after Somalia have been, in my view, mildly bureaucratic exercises in appearing to do things, things which must appear to be done, and it's extraordinarily complex. To change culture, to change mindsets, particularly in a conservative, very traditional organization, is not a matter of three hours of compulsory gender-sensitivity training and it's not a matter of taking a six-hour discussion or seminar on models of professionalism.

During the 1980s I gave numerous lectures at professional institutes, socialization institutions, the National Defence College. Toward the end of the 1980s I just gave up because I found that people really weren't interested in tackling complex issues, issues which cannot be explored in a 45-minute talk and 15 minutes of questions, issues which are profound. They are generic to the place of the military in postmodern society. Military service in advanced liberal democracies is a problematic construct. How it's organized, how it's rewarded, how it's supported, who gets to lead it. It is a core issue but an age-old issue: *Cis custodios ipsos custodios.* "Who guards the guards?" The Romans struggled with that.

The Results of Cutting Back

I think the senior leadership of the military has been essentially fighting a rear-guard action for more than three decades. And it developed a kind of a bunker mentality, a perception of threat with a need to defend themselves. I certainly wouldn't call them proactive, imagining the configurations in military operations that they need, and the configurations in equipment that they need. The truth of the matter is that for the most part the defence professionals are given a spending envelope and it's their choice how to spend it. For the most part, at least in the past decade, they have not thought creatively or proactively or strategically about how they might spend those dollars. As a result some poor choices have been made, like the choices to reduce numbers, leading to the operational core of the military becoming, in my view, anorexic, barely able to meet commitments.

They've made some choices to outsource the support systems, cut back in the medical and the personnel support systems, gone out for competitive bidding for software that was developed for corporations, which it turns out doesn't work very well in operational settings. As the demands are increased on the operational core of the military, and as the units get deployed to East Timor, to Croatia, etc., the support capacity is shrivelled. That sends a powerful message to the people doing the work.

In the age of corporate restructuring, this is one of the things that's showing up. In the short run it's reasonably simple and doesn't invoke any dramatic costs or consequences to cut on administrative support and personnel support. The problems don't show up for two, three, four or five years, and then they really show up.

The whole issue of the degree of medical support that is given to operational troops, which has produced numerous embarrassing scenarios for the military, is a result of choices that were made by senior leadership to cut certain things. And there seems to be a resistance in the military to integrate new understandings of biomedical research, the environmental impact of working in certain environments, into notions of institutional liability. So broadly speaking it's reactive leadership. It's not proactive leadership. This is something that has not been fully explored by the media or by commentators that I know of.

The military and the army leadership have had a can-do attitude for much of the past decade, so that when the politicians asked for troops to go here or go there, the army would supply them to stay in the game and to maintain favour. But chronic, relentless deployment of a scarce resource gradually leads to exhaustion and soft costs. The operational leadership, I'm talking about the NCOs and the unit leaders, rotated constantly to new deployments. What are the costs on the families? What are the costs on the individuals involved? How can someone in the early, formative years of their profession pay much attention to the broader complex issues when in fact they just deploy, come home and rest, deploy, come home and rest? One of the roles of leadership, and in some respects it's an essential role, is to protect and nurture capacity, not just for today but for tomorrow.

The role of leadership is to clarify boundaries and to learn to say no. As I said earlier, leaders do the right thing. And there's been a curious reluctance on the part of senior leadership in the military to do the right thing when it comes to protecting, nurturing and supporting the assets, the human capacity, and to say, "No! We can't do it."

In the Korean War many Americans were captured. Many of them turned against their fellow prisoners and co-operated with the enemy. A Turkish battalion was captured virtually intact, and the Chinese approached the leadership and said, "Here's what we'd like you to do," and they said, "No." So they got rid of that person and the next person down the chain said, "No." And they got down to corporals, and the corporals stood, each person in a row. Finally the Chinese gave up. Every single member of that Turkish battalion walked out at the end of the Korean War healthy, whereas the Americans had numerous psychosomatic casualties, death through illness and things. So one of the roles of leadership is to know when the time has come to say, "No. We can't do that."

Generally I would say that the linkages between the military and society are weak and weakening. As the force shrinks in size, the military participation ratio, which is the percentage of age-eligible people who participate at some point in their adult life in military service, shrinks. The professional socialization institutions tend to be insular. As the force shrinks in size, the Royal Military College expands.

I've written that there should be much closer interplay and interaction between Queen's University and the Royal Military College. The new, post-Somalia courses for professional socialization, advanced post-graduate work for the military, are in Toronto. But that's a group of military people getting together to explore military issues.

I would suspect the majority of military people continue to live on bases rather than in the civilian community that they serve. The linkages between senior military leaders and other elites in our society are weak. Whether that has to do with a mildly defensive attitude on the part of the military, I don't know, but they are weak. And in the long run, for me, that must be the area of development.

No one rationally would argue that military service, as military operation, needs to be organized in certain ways and march to functional criteria. Whether the military needs to be an isolated lifestyle and subculture is another issue altogether. I have advocated mid-career sabbaticals, secondments of the military officers to civilian environments. Had I continued in my career, to spend 25 years only in the military, only interacting with other military people, I probably would have the same mindset that I found in my research. But I had experiences of going to civilian universities and being challenged. I've taught in the Queen's School of Business, done management and executive workshops. I work with corporations, and they struggle with many of the same issues that the military struggles with, how to maintain commitment, how to develop capacity. I realize they take risks, and they're incredibly demanding.

One of the paradoxes of our time is that the military sees itself as the most demanding occupation in the world. In fact, people in many mining companies, software companies travel all over the world, often in high-risk situations, so the military doesn't have a monopoly on commitment and noble aspirations.

What we can't afford is the isolation of the military. It breaks down channels of dialogue; it leads to Canadians deriving their images of what the military is from media reports, from sensationalist stories, from all the bad news, or worse, from depiction of military service in the United States context. One of the cultural roots of the Somalia behaviour, particularly the rogue behaviour of members of the Airborne Regiment was, in fact the overidentification with American models, not British models, of military service. It's no accident that it was a Confederate flag that flew in the barracks of the rogue commando.

So how should we do this? We won't do it by working hard to maintain a smaller and smaller, ever-shrinking, long-term professional military, or, as some military professionals do, by wishing away the reserves. We do it, I think, by expanding short-term service and making it attractive to young people for skill acquisition, for a chance to see the world. This is what the Americans have done. The Americans have linked first enlistment to a guaranteed support for a college education, and it has a profound impact. We don't do that at all.

Another issue that people are not discussing in Canada, although it links to some of the post-Somalia reforms, is that the ethnic minorities and the immigrant minorities don't participate in the Canadian military. Why can't Canadians have a Sikh battalion? Why can't there be a 1st Chinese Rangers of Canada? I think it's wonderful, but it takes imagination to imagine that.

More generally, the vast majority of young immigrants coming to this country come into Vancouver, Toronto and Montreal, and they don't develop much of a feel for what Canada is and what Canadian values are. The military might be one of the ways. We don't think of the military the way the Swiss do. The Swiss explicitly design their military and their military service to be a profound force of social cohesion in the country. It is part of being Swiss. And even Swiss citizens who live and work in Canada go back each year to do their military service.

So the aging senior professional leadership of the Canadian military thinks about protecting a past that was, rather than building a future that could be. I believe very strongly that Canadians affirm and support in all kinds of ways the Canadian values that are expressed in peace-keeping operations. And they can't get enough of that. What they don't affirm is an isolated bureaucracy which seems to have a never-ending flow of embarrassing scenarios, and a leadership which doesn't seem to care about the real people who are doing real things in dirty places in the world.

Adjusting to the Future

In Canada the Revolution in Military Affairs will be introduced piece-meal. Take the area of electronics, computers and information technology. Uniform competencies to integrate those 21st-century information technologies into the way military operations are organized in Canada are just not there. The military seems reluctant. Here's an example. Fifteen years ago I was asked to consult on the personnel requirements for the new frigates. The command system of the new frigates is 21st-century technology. And it turned out that one of the roles needed was a very high-end computer whiz, and the market was extremely small.

So they faced the prospect of having a civilian onboard. They didn't want that. Can't have civilians onboard ships. Also, the only parallel civilian job was a computer whiz in a thermonuclear plant, and they earn about $100,000 a year. You couldn't have a non-commissioned officer who was making more than the ship's captain. You just couldn't imagine it.

The military remains wedded to certain forms of a rank system, certain functional structures. I think that the case can be made for a multiplex combat role. We have armoured, artillery and infantry troops in Canada and they are managed along different career lines. It takes a tremendous amount of organizational effort to manage them, recruit them and train them. But if you actually look at the reality of deployments in the past 20 years, they're deployed interchangeably as lightly armed ground troops combining high-tech weaponry.

I asked a question of a senior retired army general at a major Ottawa colloquium. I said, "Can you imagine a day when we can have infantry-armed-artillery people, who are specialized in different areas, but are actually all multiskilled persons?" He said, "No. An infantryman always needs to have artillery in his hip pocket." Which is really to say, "I'm not ready to go there." The logical model for the Canadian Forces is the United States Marine Corps model. The Marine Corps has multispecialties, multiskills. Everybody's a member of the Marine Corps, but there isn't this radical tribal mentality. We've been resistant to going there. There's a lack of imagination, a lack of elasticity, of flexibility

The thinking about management, leadership and command has been sloppy and sophomoric. Command is a special aspect of military life, and the characteristics needed of commanders is a very central issue. Leadership is the foggiest and fuzziest of all of the three. It's the one where you get the highest level of rhetoric and the lowest level of supporting data.

I teach leadership in different settings in the university and I do leadership workshops. The major thrust of thinking around leadership is now what is called post-heroic leadership. The old model of the leader knowing everything, having all the answers and being able to simply command people to do things doesn't work in the modern world, the world in which you need multiple competencies brought together. Often the challenges being faced are not clear yet. The military still works on the heroic model of the great man. If we can only find the right, great leaders with vision, with character, with virtue and profound experience, they will make things all right.

My suggestion would be that the military devote its time and energy and resources to really attempting to clarify and measure competencies of command, command effectiveness, and stay away from leadership because of the conceptual fog that is there. It may feel good to aging defence bureaucrats in uniform to talk about leadership, but it's an extremely foggy concept. And they routinely mix and match and confuse the two. A person in command is designated through the National Defence Act as having certain accountabilities. When they are in command they can do it, when they aren't, they can't. That's why we have changes of commands. A commander may or may not be a leader. But if every commander believes that he or she has the genetic coding and the social approval as one of history's great leaders, then you've got a recipe for organizational chaos and rogue action, where self-styled tribal leaders feel they are above the law and above accountability within the defence system and, more broadly speaking, within civil society in Canada.

Leadership, and I've taught it and explored it and written about it for 20 years, turns out to be one of the most ephemeral of ideas. In a recent, probably the best, review of leadership, the author noted that there had been 220 definitions of leadership in the past 40 years. Well, obviously that poses a problem, particularly with a military mind that likes to have it black and white. Choose one. The stance the military takes now seems to be, "We will take young people of potential who have demonstrated leadership potential. We will put them in complex training and development situations in which they'll be given royal jelly or some magic amalgam that will produce the capacity to lead." Lead who? Lead what?

One of the most influential books right now in leadership is called *Leadership Without Easy Answers*, exploring the world of modern leadership where no one knows the answer and the leader's role is to help people work together to find the question and then identify the answer. The military continues to work primarily on a model of command in which the commander, with staff support, will know the answer.

What is the answer in Canada to a simple thing like, "Should the Canadian air force spend virtually all of its money on fighters rather than transports?" It pleases the air force and the combat pilots to have fighters. On the other hand, it makes it awfully difficult for troop deployments and foreign assistance, relief, disaster assistance when you have so very few Hercules or transports. But those are choices made by the profession. They're not made by Parliament; they're not made by the minister of national defence. The draft of the budget and how the money will be used and what things will be paid for and not paid for are produced largely by the uniformed elite, and it's their choices which shape Canadian defence.

Finding Answers

I've been advocating for an ethics of transparency for almost 20 years. For example, if actions were known to members of one family and close colleagues, to the media and to the government and to the Canadian public, would they be defensible? The military has been very slow, and particularly the combat side of the military, to understand that the eyes and ears of the media reach out 24 hours all around the world, and that military operations now are usually accompanied by CNN film crews. It's this defensiveness that I find so difficult to understand, the avoidance of problems, the avoidance of embarrassment. It's seen as an organizational crisis if we can't give the impression that we know everything and control everything.

Just like my doctoral research, with this finding that 25 percent of Canadian ground troops would answer the dumb question, saying that they would refuse to enter combat, provoked a great national uproar and led to some senators waking up and striking a committee to renew the Forces. Somalia, I think, in the long run and in the light of history, will be seen as a good thing for military service in Canada. It did bring the military under the public eye. It exposed cronyism; it exposed some of the careerist motivations. And out of that darkness comes light. Whether there'll be a real change of heart is another issue altogether.

My understanding of Parliament and the broader society is that Parliament is simply the governance system of the operations of our society, or, if you like, of certain federal things, certainly defence. The senior military leaders, regardless of how they would describe themselves, are equivalent to the people in the hospitals around the Queen's campus, the CEO of the hospital system. And they are accountable to Parliament for certain things. So the governance systems need to specify the ends of operations. The paid staff work at and clarify the means. This is a fundamental thing. There's been a blurring in Canada through benign neglect. There's been a high degree of rotation in the ministers over the past 40 years. The senior leadership, and it may well be from the traumatic impacts of unification, has been at best ambivalent, probably skeptical and cautious, about their civilian masters. So there have been breakdowns in dialogue.

Consider this: in the 1950s and 1960s the great majority of parliamentarians had been in the military. They understood its culture, they understood how it worked. They were empathetic and sympathetic to it. Not the case today. And I think the great danger in Canada is that we continue this topsy-turvy kind of drifting. It's much like the blind reading to the deaf. The media doesn't fully understand the military unless it's a story. Parliament, by and large, doesn't understand that much and certainly doesn't specify or clarify the boundaries. And the senior military people spend an enormous amount of their consciousness trying to defend the past that they've lost. In the 1980s when I would lecture on officership in the 21st century at the staff college, I posed the challenge that the officer corps was coming to the point where it was going to have to confront the radical issue of the difference between what it loved and what it needed. And unfortunately the officer corps has tended to advocate what it loved rather than what it needed.

We don't need dress uniforms. The Israeli military, arguably the most effective, cohesive small military in the world, has no dress uniforms. They go with what works. It's a shame that we don't have operational equipment but we have dress uniforms. Those were strategic choices made by senior military leadership, not by civilians, not by Parliament.

Parliament, again as the governance standing in for the Canadian people, articulating the values, the preferences, through all the political process has to say, "Here are the boundaries. Here are the boundaries of military service." Hundreds of millions of dollars in Canada have been spent by the military in the past 15 years fighting against the Charter of Rights and Freedoms. The defence lawyers, the resistance, incredible! The Charter of Rights is something that Canadians are pretty proud of. It complicates our lives. Now, it may be that in certain specified circumstances we have to almost suspend the Charter for military necessity. And that's what Parliament has to do, and the courts, to settle it. But not if they're viewed with suspicion.

I'd like to tell you a little story. I think this is really germane. One of the best and brightest commerce students I've ever taught just graduated two years ago. Visible minority, East Indian, and an infantry private in the local reserve regiment here. He'd wear his uniform on certain days to class, and he was so proud. He said, "It's part of being Canadian. I'm so happy." He was ecstatic when he became a corporal. And in the summertime he was actually being a high-end management consultant. He had an outgoing, optimistic way so he tried to engage people in dialogue about ways to improve, and he wrote a paper for me on ways to improve the reserves, which no one in the chain of command was interested in. I subsequently got it up to the senior levels.

He felt it was a great shame that the Charter of Rights was not on the wall in the armoury because he was proud of Canada and he was proud to serve his nation. So he posed the question, "Why isn't the Charter of Rights and Freedoms posted in the armoury?" "We don't want that goddamn thing around here!" And he persisted and he persisted and finally he went to a member of Parliament. He's no longer in the reserve, and he's going to be a very significant Canadian down the road, but at his last parade Peter Milliken presented the unit with a framed copy of the Charter and it hangs there now. To me, that encapsulated everything that I've been exploring for 30 years. Young, bright, visible minority, not an officer, a private, wanting to improve, and every step of the way being told by the officers, "We're paid to think, you're paid to do." One day he'll run for Parliament and maybe he'll be in a position to say to some reactive military people, "Here's what you do. You're either proud of the Charter of Rights or you're not. If you're not, then what are you serving this country for?"

ANGUS BROWN
Colonel (Retired)
2001

A ngus Brown is a career armoured officer who switched to
personnel administration in 1991. From 1995 to 1997 he
was director of arms control verification at NDHQ and has
remained a consultant to the Department of Foreign Affairs
and International Trade on the subject. He retired from the
Canadian Forces in 1997 and in 1999 joined the Croatia Board
of Inquiry. As director of personnel career administration at
NDHQ in the early 1990s, he oversaw the difficult downsizing
of the Forces as part of the Forces Reduction Program, includ-
ing the revision of policy and procedures to comply with social
legislation issues.

Targets
The difficulty, of course, was that we were planning this reduction and
we didn't really have good targets to aim at. We were more or less left to
our own devices. Because of the situation, we thought by drawing down
in Canadian Forces Europe, we would be able to reduce the infantry. Just
as we got launched into one of our first iterations of the reduction

program, we suddenly found that there was a tremendous requirement for infantry to go to Croatia and into Bosnia.

One of the major situations that developed was the extended use of the reserves, which was something that was absolutely mandatory because over the years we had always relied on the reserves to up the strength of units in the regular force. Now, of course, we were drawing down those units at the same time, and the reserve units were being disbanded or reduced.

We were left to our own devices to decide who was going to be cut, when and by how many. We would target, for instance, certain groups of ranks or experienced levels that we thought we could probably do without. We would run them with the very rudimentary computer models that we had in those days, and then we would be asked to give implications. Sometimes we would be told to change it and sometimes we would be told not to change it, but I never felt that there was a very cohesive top-down direction of what we had to do in the way of reduction of the Forces. They wanted to go from X thousand to Y thousand, period.

We didn't deal much at National Defence Headquarters with the levels of the organizations or formations that were much below the national level. If we thought that there were probably going to be a surplus of infantrymen because of bringing back 4 Brigade units, then we suggested that people might like to draw down the number of infantrymen. We also dealt with whether we should have more space for people to be promoted. Consequently we would target senior NCOs, sergeants, warrant officers in order to provide a flow of people up the ranks and to allow new blood to rise.

We were trying to look at where the surpluses were in our personnel inventory, nationally, right across the Canadian Forces. But generally speaking we didn't have a whole lot of direction and in many cases some of the changes that we proposed were done with a little bit more guesswork than we would like to have admitted.

In the white paper of 1987 we were going to be very aggressively expanding the Forces, buying new equipment, nuclear submarines and all the rest of it. Of course, in 1989 all that fell when the Berlin Wall fell, and the Russian/Soviet empire crumbled and the various republics all went their own way.

The upshot was that we were in turmoil because the Canadian Forces were reducing. People were crying for a peace dividend and politicians were talking about reducing. Money was cut from the defence budget, which of course translated into resources, people and operating and maintenance budgets. That meant that the Forces had to reduce and we went from some 90,000 or so down to about 75,000. This translated into a few thousand people each year. This led to a lot of instability among the troops and when we introduced the Forces Reduction Program, many people saw this almost as a breaking of a contract.

People in the military had been used to a womb-to-tomb approach to their life. It wasn't a job for life particularly, but it was one of those places where one joined and you were taken care of. To have layoffs, much like the private sector, was a tremendous blow, a tremendous shock psychologically to a lot of people in the military.

There was also a real question about where exactly these cuts would be made. We didn't really have a good new white paper. We didn't really have a strategic security policy. We didn't have specific direction which told us that we would be requiring, for example, a lot more logistics or communications people, as opposed to sharp end, combat arms people. We were doing a lot of our reducing by guess and by God and that led to a certain turmoil because we weren't always accurate.

The can-do attitude among the military is probably its greatest asset and its greatest detriment. You can't run a military force without people having a "I will complete the mission at all odds" kind of approach to life. On the other hand, you can't have that standing in the way of actually monitoring, running — efficiently running — the force. The difficulty is that we tended to expect too much. I always use the phrase that in some cases we tended to run the Canadian Forces on the goodwill of the people.

In my opinion the Canadian Forces as an organization was tasked with and took on too much in light of its capabilities at the time.

For instance, in 1992 we were heavy into reducing the Forces, and we were dealing with combat arms people at that time, artillery, infantry, armour. At the same time we had the government deploying a second battalion to UNPROFOR in the former Yugoslavia. I wondered how that could be rationalized by our senior masters, who on the one hand were saying, "We're cutting down the force," and on the other saying, "By the way, we're taking on more operational deployments."

In the 1990s we tended to look at the Canadian Forces more as a business-operation to be run according to good business methods. So I think they were caught in the dilemma of trying to do the things that they felt they should do as military officers, and at the same time were caught with this horrible business-model approach to running the Armed Forces, which is ridiculous. You can't do it.

Solving Problems
We can do the planning in two different ways.

Right now we tend to do it on the capability-based model, and I think that's wrong because we look at what we have on the ground and we say, "We are capable of doing so much." We should be looking at it based on a commitment model, saying, "What do we want to do? What must we do as the Canadian Forces to further Canadian national security policy?" and then tailor the Forces that way.

If you use the first it's easy because you're always dealing within a finite envelope of resources. For a businessman, or for a person using a business model, you have X million dollars or whatever it is. So much for P, O and M — personnel, operations and maintenance — budgets and away you go. The difficulty, of course, is that you can never do just those things because the world is a very unpredictable place.

If we were to take a look at the commitment model and we were to structure the Forces based on that, the government would say, "We are going to commit forces based on our national security policy in the following areas: one, two, three," be it Europe and defence of Canada, or whatever it might be. Then the Canadian Forces planner would simply turn around and say, "Right, in order to do those tasks, I need the following, and here's the resource bill." If the government can't give that amount of resources, then it's a simple matter of the government saying to the planner, "OK. You can't have all those resources. Therefore we're taking away these resources and we're taking away the following commitments." If you follow the commitment-based model of organizing your armed forces, any prudent planner would build in contingency plans which would cater to the unexpected.

I do believe, however, that most politicians don't understand what they're doing when they commit the Armed Forces, and this is one of our major difficulties. Many people in the Armed Forces were extremely annoyed and disappointed when they heard Mr. Chrétien's famous quip, "We're like boy scouts; we're always there." There's a tremendous difference between deploying military forces and deploying boy scouts and politicians don't really understand that. They see the military as a tool of government, as it should be, but on the other hand there's a terrible possibility of catastrophic consequences if the politicians decide to use the military for things for which it is neither designed nor resourced.

Commitment, Capability and Croatia

I don't think that any of the senior military people can be without blame. It's easy to look back in hindsight and say, "We should have done this versus something else." The army was stretched and knew it was stretched. The people that I talked to, certainly at army headquarters in Montreal at the time, were sounding the alarms quite clearly. The research that I did on the Croatia deployments indicated that there had been some very, very close staff checks done by military staff. They knew that it was going to be extremely difficult for them to fulfill all the tasks. After the first or second or even the third rotations, they were going to run into problems with people and equipment and resources.

This, as I said, was coming at the same time as we were downsizing the Forces, not only in people, but we were not buying the extra equipment that we thought we would have needed under the 1987 white paper. We were talking about redistributing equipment that came out of Europe and putting it into units and formations here in Canada. While the army always sees itself as an expeditionary force, perhaps more so than the navy or even the air force, I do believe that the army hierarchy was fully aware of the difficulties they were running into. Whether or not they were making representations to a higher level, I don't know, but it was my impression that army headquarters were certainly sounding the alarms very early on in the planning for UNPROFOR.

195

The staff checks that were done, for instance, on engineers made it very clear that they could not supply the number of engineers that the United Nations initially asked for, which was somewhere in the order of 350, but 200 to 250 would be the absolute maximum.

On the other hand, don't forget the government was very clear that it was going to deploy. The prime minister and the minister of external affairs both had said that they were going to deploy people into UNPROFOR, period. There was no question about it. It's very difficult, if you're a general or a senior officer, to turn around and say, "Well, I really would rather not go," because there are lots of people behind you who will probably be able to do your job quite easily.

The initial deployment of the first Canadian battalion, CANBAT-1, was approximately 800 to 1,000 people. There were some reductions in later battalion rotations. There was a second battalion, CANBAT-2, that was sent, of approximately 900 people, in late 1992. By this time there had been a couple of rotations of CANBAT-1 as well. So I couldn't tell you how many people actually went through the theatre, but there would probably be somewhere in the order of 1,000 in each of those rotations, taking into account support elements and base troops.

The casualty levels were unexpected. There's no question about it. There were a number of casualties from both misdirected hostile fire and accidents. We had only, up to this time, real experience in places like Cyprus and with the United Nations in the Middle East. Each of those areas had some intense periods. The 1974 Turkish invasion of Cyprus, for instance, resulted in some Canadian casualties and we had an ongoing drain of people who ran over mines and that sort of thing in the Middle East. We had never really gotten involved in an area where the belligerents didn't want to have us there and actively targeted some of our own people. So the casualties were a bit of a surprise; they were certainly not given any kind of publicity to the general public, although we, at National Defence Headquarters and especially in army headquarters, were very aware of people coming back injured, wounded and sometimes dead.

My impression was that the change of peace support operations, from a benign type of United Nations interposition force to a more active or more robust peace support operation that we found in the Balkans, took awhile to get back. It took awhile to sink in. I don't think it ever really sunk in, although certainly we were aware of the fact that people were coming back wounded. We thought this might be more accidental than anything else.

Then, of course, you'd talk to a few people who had been in theatre, and they had been subjected to mortar attacks or had been subjected to direct, aimed hostile fire. It became clear that, really, this was a quite different kettle of fish. I don't believe that this permeated throughout National Defence Headquarters quickly. It took a long while. In fact, the testimony that was given by the successive battalion commanders in the Croatia Board of Inquiry, Dykow, Calvin and Lessard, revealed that all had gone over on reconnaissance, and all made drastic changes to their training program upon return to Canada because they saw it was quite a different operation than they had been used to in previous UN deployments.

I have no proof and I found nothing in my research that says that there was an act of conspiracy, if you will, to keep it bottled up. I don't believe there was. I think what might have happened was that there was a lack of passage of information, partially because everyone was trying to reassess exactly where they were in this whole situation of changing peacekeeping operations. Sometimes things weren't passed back as quickly or as accurately as they could have been.

In many cases when you deploy to a UN operation, intelligence is seen as a hostile act. I think what happened was that because intelligence had not been done as well as it would have been done in a full, all-out war situation, the function tended to atrophy a bit. Beginning at the battalion level, intelligence officers were not really doing an intelligence function as much as they were information officers, and intelligence tended to have been downplayed in more benign peacekeeping operations. Once the battalions got into places like Croatia, they found that they had geared themselves to the same sort of intelligence tempo and were behind the eight ball because they should have been in much more of a wartime tempo in their intelligence gathering.

In my papers for the Croatia Board of Inquiry I alluded to the fact that in some cases intelligence situation reports came back saying no real change in activity was expected or seen, when in fact they had just recorded an increase in shelling activity in their sectors. Part of the problem was that there was no second-level or "beyond intelligence" assessment function. There was no capability. We were deploying battalion-level battle groups all by themselves. We had no second sober thought, if you will, at a higher level of information, as would have happened in actual wartime. You would have had the battalion intelligence information being passed back to the brigade, the brigade going back to the division and so on, all of which would have made certain assessments, taken account of other intelligence sources and then passed down and revised intelligence assessments to the tactical level. This didn't happen because we didn't have those levels of the battalion group.

Once again, don't forget that this was a changing era in 1991 and 1992 when we went into Croatia. We didn't deploy formations that big in other places, such as Cyprus, and we didn't need those kinds of intelligence levels. We had always done the suitcase deployments with a battalion battle group. That was it. And we had lost a certain amount of expertise. Although we had practised it at home and in Europe at the brigade level and above, we had never done it at the UN level. So it wasn't a matter of making a conscious effort not to send those sorts of things; they just were never there.

By the same token, we always had a contingent commander who was a rank more senior to the battalion commander, but he was normally only for administrative and disciplinary purposes, and he had no real staff. In fact, we often double-hatted a Canadian officer of a higher rank who happened to be at the force headquarters or a sector headquarters. His Canadian contingent job was very much secondary, with no staff, to his UN officer job.

For instance, I mentioned in my research for the Croatia Board of Inquiry that General MacKenzie had been the designated Canadian contingent commander while he was at the same time commander of sector Sarajevo. If we thought that he was going to spend a lot of time doing a lot of Canadian higher-level, higher-formation kind of work for the Canadian battle group — wrong. He could certainly give them tactical direction as the sector commander, but he didn't have the staff to do anything purely Canadian for them, and while he was busy doing other things, he could only really do minor administrative or disciplinary things. I'm sure even during the hectic period at Sarajevo and the airport opening he probably couldn't even do that.

I think the UN probably underestimated or, let me put it another way, they probably estimated correctly, but were reluctant to provide the resources. Initial estimates for troops to go into the Balkans were somewhere in the order of 40,000. The UN Security Council, I believe, actually authorized 13,000 troops. As a matter of contrast, when KFOR and SFOR had to go into Kosovo years later, they went in with somewhere in the order of 40,000 to 50,000 troops, heavily armed, lots of armour, artillery, mechanized infantry, the whole bit, as opposed to 13,000 lightly equipped, infantry-type guys who were going to sit in outposts.

It's difficult to say what was going through the minds of the people at the UN. I suspect that they were probably thinking that, once the UN was deployed, world opinion would be on the side of the people in the blue helmets. Then the belligerents would understand that people in the world community were serious and they would pay attention. When it became obvious that cease-fires weren't worth the paper they were written on, and that indeed some of the belligerents saw the UN as much an enemy as some of the other factions there, I think there were a number of changes to the mission that took place.

We saw the mandate start to expand. At one point one officer indicated that he'd counted them: there were over 100 different UN resolutions dealing with the forces, UNPROFOR-1 and UNPROFOR-2. So mission-creep was inevitable. We saw that in some cases the mission was initially to supervise repatriation of prisoners and civilians and provide humanitarian assistance to convoys, but then those were extended and mission-creep just went on and on and on, so that the mandate became quite difficult to pin down. It became very unclear.

That led to all kinds of things in the Canadian context. If there's a change in the mandate, it has to be authorized in Ottawa by, presumably, Foreign Affairs, which is the lead department. Then, of course, DND has to send out its authorization as well. We often had the anomalous situation of a mandate that had changed slightly and troops on the ground could either not be deployed, or had to get some sort of authorization to do something all the way from Ottawa. It was tremendously difficult for the troops there.

Reasons for Stress

The whole question of stress is one that's very real, and there are many, many reasons for it. There was stress because of the change of the mandates at various times. There was stress because of the fact that they were in a much more robust type of environment, where they were actually receiving fire. There was also the whole question of units being dispersed and parts of units being dispersed. In one case we had a battalion in the northern part of the sector which had a company deployed 550 kilometres away. That's like saying to a battalion commander in Ottawa, "Send one of your companies down to Toronto and, by the way, I want you to support it with all its normal, routine, daily logistics. You have to command it as well. You have to be responsible for it all." So you put extra stress on people. The truck drivers have to drive farther to do their normal jobs, people have to work harder to communicate, people have to do more and more difficult things when they're trying to command an organization like this. All of these factors were compounded, one on top of the other.

I believe as well that there were some guys in Croatia who weren't sure whether they were going to have a job or not when they came home because we were into this whole Forces Reduction Program. The whole thing was probably a personal turmoil in many minds. Stresses don't have to be from the same source. You can have many different stresses which will probably prey on the individuals' minds and make their jobs a lot more difficult. For that matter there were probably any number of people who should have had stress leave, who were serving no farther than NDHQ because they were also subject to changing mandates and confusing direction and goodness knows what.

Combat Capability

It's generally accepted by most observers and people who have looked at it that the Gulf War probably indicated to the Canadian army that it had been surpassed by its allies technologically. They were going to have a difficult time keeping up. The American army had made incredible strides forward technologically. Its equipment was top-notch; its communications were rapidly moving into the digital age. I think it would have been more and more difficult for us to operate, even as part of an American or a British division. That was the general assessment among people in Canada at the time. And it probably struck one of the first warning bells for the Canadian army.

I don't think there's any doubt that our combat capability is well below where we were even 15 or 20 years ago. We were able to operate in northwest Europe in a high-intensity environment. We were able to operate as part of an American division, a German division, a British division. Belgians worked for us, and all our allies had a certain interoperability. We weren't the best-equipped troops in NATO, but we were well trained. We could do a tremendous variety of things and we had a very good reputation as being able to be people that NATO could rely on and who could actually get things done. Today we talk a lot about general combat capability, but I don't personally believe that we have it. I don't see how you can have the same sort of general combat capability with half the number of people and fewer pieces of equipment than we had before.

Some people will say we have a very high combat capability in specific areas, and I don't doubt that for a minute. The army has brand-new, very effective surveillance equipment and vehicles, the Coyote system for one. That's probably one of the best in any army today. But the fact of the matter is that armies do a lot more than just surveillance and reconnaissance. The fact of the matter is that there is not a general combat capability. It is a very specific combat capability. It's difficult for me to believe that we have a much better combat capability in the Canadian Forces today when we have aircraft that are on the verge of a major overhaul, the F-18s. We have a tank that is definitely trailing-edge technology and we have a very, very, small number of very good frigates.

A lot of people in 1989 and beyond thought that they were going to get a tremendous peace dividend, and we could dispense with a very large, heavy, cumbersome, combat-capable, call them what you will, armed forces. The fact of the matter is that we've had a lot more instability since 1989 than we had up to 1989 since the inception of NATO. We are being called upon to do more things and we certainly took on a lot more complex peacekeeping jobs in the 1990s. That trend will probably continue because you are talking about a multipolar world now as opposed to just a relatively stable, bipolar world.

Soft Power, Equipment and Training
I don't think you can decry completely our human-values agenda. It's probably very noble and very good. The fact of the matter is, though, that since way back foreign policy and national security policy really

cannot be accomplished solely by foreign aid or by pressure in various diplomatic and international fora. It may come down to the point where you actually have to use armed forces, if not to actually do something, then to threaten to do something, or to work in concert with your allies or like-minded security partners to do what has to be done. I think that Chapter VII operations under the UN charter are typical examples of why you need armed forces. The difficulty is that, because you can never forecast what you're going to be doing, and from time to time these are going to change, sometimes drastically, you had better have general combat-capable armed forces to do it. If that's one of the tools the government wants to have, why would you have a set of knives with one of them blunt?

The lack of proper budgeting resources to replace our capital equipment has always been a major source of concern. I certainly remember, at my rank level, in NDHQ and other places, worrying about the whole question of troop safety. Sea Kings were on everybody's lips and got a lot of publicity, but there were many other things — vehicles, equipment, guns that were old, ammunition that wasn't being replaced on a regular basis. All these things deteriorate over time. Being in a military operation, being in a military force is a dangerous business. It's a bit like heavy construction. You're dealing with big, cumbersome, deadly equipment if it's not taken care of and if it's not handled properly. You're constantly on the lookout for safety of the equipment, the maintenance of the equipment, the training of the people and so on. There was always a concern expressed that we would not have high enough training levels that would allow us to use live ammunition safely.

There was a very definite concern about training, particularly among the army officers, although some of those concerns were shared by other services as well. In the army, particularly when you were in 4 Brigade in Germany, you were always on major exercises. You were always taking trips to gun camps to fire the equipment with live ammunition. You were always on exercise doing some level of training, right up to divisional-level exercises. This was a normal routine, an annual cycle.

In Canada there was suspension of live-firing exercises at battalion and brigade level, effective about 1989. I was the base commander at Suffield and we ran live-firing exercises for one brigade out of Calgary in 1988. In 1989, because of lack of resources and because of troops being committed elsewhere, 5 Brigade did not come down, although it was planning to come to Alberta to do a live-firing exercise. I understand that there has not been large, brigade-level, collective training done in the army for some years. This isn't endemic only to the army, although it probably manifests itself most there.

There's no question in my mind that if you don't practise, you can't do it. This is difficult stuff. We are not talking about simple operations of everybody lining up and walking forward. We're talking about tremendously complex co-ordination here. We're talking about making sure that quite disparate parts of formations can do the right things at the right time in the right quantity: things such as live firing, dropping artillery rounds at a certain place, and more importantly, stopping artillery rounds at a certain place when friendly troops come into the area. The simple co-ordination of moving company groups around in a mechanized environment is something that must be practised.

I was talking to a number of majors the other day, some of whom are still serving, and of the four or five of those majors who were sitting in the room with me, only one had actually seen a mechanized infantry company with a tank troop raid on the ground. Now, these were combat arms majors, so I don't believe that you can say, if these majors are at that point, that we have any general combat capability.

Taking Responsibility
The research that I did for the Croatia Board of Inquiry indicated that there had been constant back-and-forth contact between Foreign Affairs and DND as well as some contact or communication with the PMO and other parts of government. It's difficult to know exactly how much because most of the material is classified as Cabinet confidential, and I wasn't privy to it in my research.

But the impression that I formed was that the people who were responsible for passing information back and forth between departments did so. Now, it's one thing to pass information back and forth between departments; it's quite another thing to be in a position to make an executive decision. I think all the government departments were working under some very clear indicators that the prime minister of the day had said, "We will deploy." Simple as that. Both he and the foreign affairs minister at the time had said that Canadians would get involved, and then it was simply a matter of both Foreign Affairs and particularly DND stating the level at which they could do the job. By the way, there must have been, in my humble opinion, some subtle encouragement. When, for instance, the prime minister says, "I'd really like to do this," I think it would be very interesting to find the general or the senior bureaucrat who would say, "Oh no, we can't." I don't think that those kinds of folks exist.

The problem manifests itself where we are deploying company groups and they are being expressed as certain numbers of people. To East Timor we were deploying 300 or 400 people and I believe on a recent African deployment we sent one company, which was expressed as so many hundred people. You don't deploy military forces as so many hundred or X number of people. You deploy formed units because they're formed to be enabled to have the capability to work. You can't start hiving them off.

I referred earlier to the Croatian battalion that had to deploy one of its companies 550 kilometres away, the distance, really, between Ottawa and Toronto. That company could only exist, could only operate for a very short period of time because it was away from its umbilical cord. It was away from all its command tentacles, if you will. It was like cutting off part of the octopus and saying, "You live somewhere else." You can't do that with military units. You can only do it with small parts of military units for a very short period of time on an independent mission. So I think this whole question of Foreign Affairs saying, "We're going to contribute so many hundred people," is an indicator to me that people don't properly understand how to employ military units.

The military contract has many facets. The question of the contract as seen by the military participant, the officer or non-commissioned officer, is really quite interesting. There are many areas where I think that people tend to follow this life because they do so out of a patriotic sense of adventure, a genuine love of country and wanting to do something. They fit well into military organizations, so they go and do it. I believe, however, that when a soldier or sailor or airman is asked to go and put themselves in harm's way for the good of the country, they have a right to expect that the politicians or the executors of that decision have taken every reasonable and conscientious step that they can to make sure that the risk is in the best interest of the country and is necessary.

It's very difficult to explain to soldiers, and I've had to do it on a couple of occasions, when they ask, "Why are we here? What are we doing here?" You've got to be able to tell them that we're here because we want to bring peace to this part of the world because of this, that and the next thing. They're not stupid; they want to know. "Why is Canada sending soldiers to this particular operation?" If that's not made clear, and if it can't be answered in 25 words or less quite directly to the soldier, sailor or airman, then the chances are, in my view, that it hasn't been thought out very well by the people who make those decisions.

I don't believe that anybody would renege on going anywhere. Canadian soldiers, sailors and airmen have shown many, many times in history that they're quite prepared to put their lives on the line and do a very good job as long as they understand why they're there. The problem is that it's hard to motivate people, it's impossible to ask people to put themselves in harm's way, possibly make the ultimate sacrifice, if they are not sure why they're in this part of the world and they're asking "What, by the way, was the Canadian interest again?" It's got to be clear and people have to think that through.

There have been quite a number of times when the Canadian Forces generally have fallen down in taking care of their people, and there are a number of reasons for that. We are living with a much different concept than people joining the army from womb to tomb. It doesn't happen anymore. A lot more people are living away from their units in peacetime. We encourage people not to live on bases. For economic reasons, because we didn't have casualties, we abandoned and disbanded our casualty section in NDHQ. And then guess what? We started to have casualties and we had to reinvent the wheel, make it all happen again.

We, the Canadian military, have not been blameless and I don't believe for a minute that we should pretend otherwise. I think that General Baril, to his credit, recognized this and set in motion some reforms, some steps to make things proper. Also, I think that we must be very cognizant of the fact that on the outside, in Civilian Street, people tend to have better benefits now than they ever did before. What might have looked 40 years ago as very good military benefits with us taking care of our people, now are either no better than, and perhaps even lag behind, the benefits that people in civilian industry have.

The military tends not to be held in tremendously high esteem. I believe that too often DND is looked at now as just another government department, just another bureaucracy. I think that, humans being humans, I would expect most of them to give the boss what he wants. Now, there is a line beyond which most honourable people would not go, and I don't for a minute think that any of them have gone beyond that line. I think, though, there's a fairly large gap between the politicians and the military.

A national defence policy should flow from a national security policy, but we've never had a proper national security policy. So a number of times in the past we've made our defence policy based upon the last budget that was produced. We don't tend to be looked at as a unique operation.

I believe that we may have to go through another war to get it right. That's a terrible thing to say, but it may be that in peacetime democracies are incapable of doing this kind of thing. There are government mechanisms that other countries have that perhaps do it a bit better, the committee system in the U.S., for example. Will they work in Canada? Probably not, under our present parliamentary system.

HOWARD MICHITSCH
Major (Retired)
2000

Howard Michitsch is a contributor and commentator on defence and military affairs for a variety of publications and broadcasters. He retired from the Canadian Forces as director of land personnel at NDHQ where he was responsible for the development of personnel policies, including efforts at gender integration of combat units. He served on two tours of Bosnia, first as commanding officer of UN military observers and then with the Canadian Multi-National Brigade, implementing the Dayton peace accord under NATO direction.

I've always been interested in the military and I started when I was very young. I joined the cadets when I was 12 and then the reserves. In 1976, once I finished school, I joined the regular force as an infantry officer. I figured if I'm going to be in the army, the infantry was where it was at. That's the most difficult, the most challenging task. The "No Life Like It" campaign didn't really influence us that much. We used to say there were "No Life Jackets."

We used to joke when we finished our training and were young second lieutenants that we got to jump out of airplanes, rappel out of helicopters, lead a platoon of 35 men, all these challenging things, and they paid us too. At that time we'd almost have done it for free.

We had the opportunity upon graduation from the infantry school to choose our regiments and ask for a particular battalion. I chose the Princess Patricia's Canadian Light Infantry. I'd had a lot of respect for all the PPCLI soldiers and officers that I'd run into, so I asked to go to Calgary to the 1st Battalion and they sent me to the 3rd Battalion in Victoria. Because of the warmer climate and being on the island, they nicknamed us the Champagne Battalion.

I served in the Champagne Battalion for four years. I taught at the officer candidate school in Chilliwack and then went to the 1st Battalion in Calgary. I ended up there for about seven years, then commanded a recruiting centre in Toronto, went to Bosnia for a year, came back to Ottawa, lasted about 18 months in headquarters and decided that there were two good days in my life, the day I joined the military and the day I said goodbye.

There's a certain amount of physical leadership required, no matter what you do. You have to be out there. You have to be dealing with the soldiers and they have to see you. If they don't see you, they won't react to you. You can't be with them all the time, you have other duties, but you have to at least be seen out in the front and be seen to take the same risks and endure the same privations that they are. If you're seen to be living in a nice house that's been commandeered and you have heat and you don't go outside in the rain, you're not going to have much respect and the soldiers won't follow your orders.

The field commanders that I've had the privilege to serve under, General MacKenzie, General Milner, General Vernon and others, were excellent. But things really get distorted when you come to Ottawa. With the civilian bureaucratization of the military, senior officers tend to take on the temperament of a senior bureaucrat, rather than a general officer commanding. In fact, the term "general officer commanding" was deleted years ago. That's why some of the better field commanders don't go beyond major-general. They retire because they don't want to fit into the political hierarchy that is National Defence Headquarters.

I did a tour in Cyprus in 1980 as a line platoon commander and as the intelligence officer for the unit. I went back to the same place in 1991 as the operations officer and headquarters company commander. I was responsible for the reconnaissance platoon and communications, the signals platoon and co-ordinating all the sector's activities. It hadn't changed a bit. When I came back I did two back-to-back tours in Bosnia from 1995 to 1996. I was replacing a good friend, a fellow by the name of Major Stan Willow and Stan wrote me a letter from Bosnia. The first line was, "Dear Howard, this ain't Cyprus."

Yugoslavia — The United Nations and NATO
The Canadian military, when it first went into the former Yugoslavia, was told by the United Nations that we didn't need our armoured vehicles and we didn't need our heavy weapons. But we'd had the same experience in Cyprus in 1974, where we didn't have any heavy anti-tank weapons,or armoured personnel carriers during the Turkish invasion of the island, and we were unprepared. I think that lesson was hoisted aboard by the army, so we went into Yugoslavia with armoured personnel carriers and anti-tank missile systems. These were armoured personnel carriers that were at the end of their operational life and now they're being taken out of service. At that point, though, there were no tanks brought into Yugoslavia, not by the Canadian Forces in any case.

But the Canadian Forces were up against tanks and armour. If you see a lot of tanks moving, it is very frightening for the average person and also, I might say, for the infantryman who has to take on these behemoths. There were definitely tanks that both sides were using and the belligerents definitely had heavy armour, along with armoured personnel carriers.

I was there in 1995 for the Croatian army invasion of the Krajina, which had historically been a Serbian area. A lot of the Serbian armour had been drawn away and was involved in another battle, so the area was held somewhat lightly. By using fast reconnaissance aircraft and various other intelligence means, the Croatian army executed Operation Storm and blew through the Krajina very rapidly. They moved their armour away from the defensive areas and there was no stopping them.

The idea was to provide safety and support to civilians and to monitor the cease-fire, but the Canadians basically stayed in their posts, as did the Jordanians, and the Croatian army went around them or neutralized them. The Canadian army wasn't that well prepared to take on an armoured onslaught. Each battalion had eight TOW missile systems, but that wasn't sufficient for defence against that kind of an armoured onslaught. That was not the role we were given. It was more like an observer role. Had the role been to defend against this possible attack, then we would have been able to deploy. The Jordanian army were manning outposts, but they were not equipped or prepared for that kind of armoured warfare. Given the nature of the army and given the nature of the terrain, they really weren't prepared for a well-executed, combined arms assault.

I was in Bosnia when the United Nations left and NATO came in with attack helicopters, jet aircraft and aircraft carriers out in the Adriatic. The British brought tanks, the Germans brought tanks, the Americans brought the 1st Armoured Division, an extremely powerful organization. No other army has anything near as powerful. They came in, and we were like John Wayne in the bar, saying, "All right, everybody put down your guns."

Because we had more firepower and the ability to use it, and we were sanctioned to use force if necessary, everybody quieted down in a real hurry. One part of the peace agreement called for cantonment of various weapons. "We want all your tanks over in a particular place so they can be monitored and can't be moved around." At one point they said, "No, we're not going to do that," and the commander turned around and said, "Well, you can either move them to where I want them or we'll destroy them in situs," so they moved the armour and various other anti-aircraft weapons systems to the cantonment sites.

The best peacekeeping tool is a tank. Nobody wants to challenge you. If you're too lightly armed, they'll simply ignore you and go around you.

The mandate between UNPROFOR and IFOR was substantially different. We were given the ability to use force and because it was a NATO structure, a rapid-reaction corps commanded by a British general, we all knew what we were talking about. Everybody spoke the same military language.

With the United Nations forces, all armies are not created equal, no matter what you say. I remember having an argument with someone from Bangladesh over what a bunker was. That would seem to be pretty simple, but that's the kind of difficulty that happens in the United Nations force, caught in that kind of environment.

The Role of the Military/Canadian Realities

Our government doesn't like to advertise the fact that we actually have to pull triggers and sometimes kill people, but that is the role of the military. We are to be the government's last resort when it comes to force and we are armed that way. No other organization in the country has the weaponry and the power that the military has and that's what it's for.

However, the government has to give the direction, and ever since Lester Pearson invented peacekeeping, we picked up that role, and it's a very politically palatable role. If you're actually fighting people and your sons and daughters are coming home in body bags, people begin to question why we are there. "What is the point?" Whereas on the world stage we can point and say, "We've been on every single peacekeeping mission that the United Nations has ever embarked upon." At the same time we don't know why. Why should we be involved in some of these issues? Because it's easier to put the Canadian soldiers in a position where they won't really have to cause damage or be used as soldiers in the true sense of being a warrior, so that the government can easily make this palatable to the people of Canada, and we can be on the world stage.

At the end of the cold war we had our role in Germany and in Europe. We knew we were going to deploy; we had sufficient weapons, ammunition, planning. We were part of a very powerful organization. We practised defending Europe on the East German–Czechoslovakian border, and we practised moving very quickly into defensive posture. That readiness level cost more than $1 billion a year, to keep a powerful Canadian brigade in Germany, along with its ancillary units and the air force as well. Once there was no real requirement for us to maintain heavy combat forces, the government of the day found it economical to start losing these kinds of capabilities. We used to have four brigades, now we're down to three, and there are some serious problems with the training.

When you know you're on a very tight rotation schedule, then any CO will focus on what he really needs for peacekeeping or peacemaking. But while doing that we are ignoring that the raison d'être of the military is to fight and win wars on any kind of a battlefield.

I'm astounded that some of the younger officers have never done an assault river crossing. We did those until it became second nature. I used to say, "If I do another one of those, I'm going to be sick." But that's a skill that seems to be dissipating. We don't really get a chance to do it on the ground. Semiannual concentrations, where all the brigades come together, can't be done. There's not enough money to train them together, so we can't learn to fight together as a Canadian division. We're losing those skills that made us a top-flight army. If you think of NATO as the NHL, we punched above our weight. We played with the big leagues, but now we're in danger of slipping down below the NATO standard and slipping out of the NHL, down to the OHL.

We need to maintain a force and it's very easy to see why. In 1950 when the Korean War started, we were unprepared. We had to go fight in another war, five years after the last one. We lost everything in five years. And we were in Korea for three years. The most destabilizing nation in Southeast Asia is North Korea. Is there some possibility we might have to go and do it again? When they can fire missiles at China and missiles at Japan, the second largest economy in the world, can we allow that kind of destabilization, or can we just opt out and tell our allies that we can't play anymore?

I think we used to be far better trained than any army in the world. We really focused on training our people. We believed in cross-training inside an infantry battalion where a soldier would be qualified as a rifleman, and then maybe as a machine gunner, as a driver, as an anti-tank missile gunner, as a pioneer, that is, an infantry engineer. I was cross-trained as an infantry engineer and as an intelligence officer. Given the restrictions on the funds now for training, we're becoming far less flexible. This isn't the fault of the commanders. If you only have so much money, you have to focus on what's just in front of you. When I was a company commander we probably spent four to five months a year training in the field, often in Suffield, Alberta, where we could fire everything live as if it were a war. Now we don't do that very often. The British pretty much have the base all summer. They use it to keep their soldiers' skills up, but we can't use it!

The problem is the government hasn't done a strategic assessment. The fact that the government views the world differently than the military does drives the budgeting and drives their defence policy. That affects the annual training cycle.

If the raison d'être of the army is to fight and win wars, the most expensive thing you can have, according to Winston Churchill, is an army that loses. If the army loses, you not only lose the money that you invested, but you also lose lives and what you were trying to protect in the first place. It's lose, lose, lose across the board.

So if we keep underfunding an army that will potentially fall or lose, then we haven't established what we want our army for. If it's for peacekeeping, then we have to come out and tell people we are not in the war business anymore. But if Canada really wants an army that can defend her interests, then we need an army that can fight, kill and win.

Ottawa — The Integration of Women

I was posted to Ottawa after Bosnia, to the Directorate of Land Personnel. I was really looking forward to taking some of my experiences and working on how we could take care of our soldiers better. Initially I did work on housing, but I soon got the task of dealing with gender issues within the army. Because of the human rights decision in 1989, we had to completely integrate women into all areas of the military, specifically the combat trades.

Well, they were virtually nonexistent in combat units. So we embarked upon, first, a study to find out why, and then a plan to try and recruit more women for the military combat units. If it was simply to assimilate them, that's relatively easy. You accept our ethos; you accept our way of doing business. But that's not what was decreed by the government. Once we start talking "integrate women," that assumes that women bring something valuable to the table of the military ethos of being a warrior. We had to integrate women and delete those policies that were seen to be perhaps discriminatory toward women.

The difficulty was, we kept trying to maintain a standard. We wanted to have one physical fitness standard, one standard of carrying equipment, one strength standard. Too often they genderized the standards. If a man had to do 40 sit-ups, a woman only has to do 30. Well, if you're playing in the NHL, you can't do that. You have to take your absolute best people and put them on the team.

But we were ordered by the government to integrate women. The military was told that we were being discriminatory, so, looking at the original post-action report from 1989 when we put through the first 100 or so women, we found that out of all of those women, only one passed. The primary reason that women failed was physical. They simply don't have the body mass, the sprinting strength and the endurance that a man has. It's simply that way.

The U.S. Navy's done a lot of studies on this. The U.S. Marine Corps has done a lot of studies on this. The United States is very, very much against women being in the fighting trades for a lot of these reasons. That's not to say that the job of an infantryman is the same as some-one who's an anti-aircraft missile-guidance system gunner, where they sit in the vehicle and look at a screen and push a button. But for the hard field artillery and hard infantry roles, it takes an awful lot of physical strength.

So we said, "Let's institute a physical fitness test at the recruiting centre." But once we put the basic one in for men, not too many women passed, and now you find at the recruiting centres that there are two basic PT (physical training) tests, one for men, one for women. So if women are at a lower level of physical ability to start with, obviously they're not going to make it all the way through training. Also their attrition rate is far higher than it is for males; the male attrition rate is about 35 percent.

I was responsible for dealing with the issue, and I commissioned the personnel research team to do a wide-ranging study across the country with focus groups, men and women, French- and English-speaking, regular and reserve. What we wanted to do was get a really good, solid snapshot of what was going on, interpersonal relations, how women were being employed and how the men felt about it. One thing that did come out was that men are very uneasy having the women around.

With the harsh anti-harassment training, which is absolutely required, women felt put upon to a certain degree. When I was training I was put through mock interrogations, tied up with a sandbag over my head, because if you ever get captured, that should not be the first time you get your hands tied and put under an interrogator's light.

We all saw on television Captain Pat Rechner taken prisoner by the Serbs and chained to a bridge, and we saw how he maintained his cool. Courageous man, no question. But that wasn't the first time he was put through that. He had been put through that in a mock environment. Then when a woman was put through it, the picture ended up on the front page of *The Sun* and the commander of the army said that there would be no more training until we came up with a new policy on this type of thing. Some of the toughening process that you need to survive has been disallowed because it can be viewed as harassment, but where does tough training end and harassment begin?

I think the women take it far too personally because this type of training is important to prepare you for battle. Men look at it as just part of the deal and part of the toughening process. At one point we would do live-fire training in Wainwright and in Suffield, and we would put animal entrails in the "enemy trenches" and fire artillery and bullets at the area and do a proper attack. When the soldiers arrived at that objective, they saw guts and they saw blood. The first time you see the entrails of a creature, whether it be human or whatever, should not be when you're actually in the theatre of operations.

You need to be psychologically toughened for this and I think some of the psychological toughening is being taken away because of the addition of women. Women don't really like this sort of toughness, this stolidness, stoicism, strength, focus, the ability to work in a hierarchy and follow orders immediately. We found in the study that they want to be inclusive in a discussion before a decision's made. Well, the battlefield is not the place.

This starts off when we're children. Boys play games with team captains, girls have no-lose games, they play house, they play doctor, they play nurse. Now, I'm sure there are sociologists and anthropologists who will argue the point, nature versus nurture, but nobody can really tell me what the balance is.

The aim of the study was not to prove why women shouldn't be in the military. The aim was to discover how to make the army, in particular the combat units, a more accepting environment for women. It had really nothing to do with combat effectiveness and my own personal views. My task was to integrate these women and come up with policies that would facilitate that. You don't necessarily agree with every order you receive. You carry on and do the order.

My own conclusions were that there was harassment going on. That was a given. Most women didn't look at the military as a long-term career, at least not in the combat units. The 18- to 24-year-old is our prime recruiting target and those are also prime child-bearing years. If we get women and put them through expensive training, they become non-deployable once they get pregnant.

A lot of fraternization goes on and it has a devastating effect within a small group. If you have a section of 10 soldiers, two are women and a couple of people are sleeping together, this breaks up the command structure, and if the leader of that group is sleeping with one of the women, then it virtually becomes inoperable. The other men look at it and the baser instincts start to come out. We don't seem to have as many troubles in a unit when the women are not there.

One of the other studies we examined viewed your employment with the military on a spectrum. At one end of the spectrum: "I view myself as a warrior and this as a calling." At the other end of the spectrum: "I'm simply an employee of the Department of National Defence." The more people identify with being an employee of the Department of National Defence, the more they agree that women should be in combat. The more you go across that spectrum to the warrior ethic, the less it's accepted by the men who are actually doing the job. So if we find that a woman wants to buy into the military ethic the way we are and can physically do the job, there is no reason why they should not be able to do it. It's being told to integrate them, not assimilate them, that causes difficulties for the army. At least that was the conclusion that I came to.

I examined studies concerning this going back as far as 1979. I used every resource that was available to me in the Canadian Forces and the Department of Defence. I also dealt with the United States and looked at some of their studies and there was a lot of research from other countries. The reason for the study that I had done was to see where these trends had gone and to get a snapshot of the way it is today. We knew in 1979 that we had this view of either being an employee or being a warrior, and 20 years later it's not changed at all.

A lot of the issues that came out of the study stem from leadership, whether it be at the corporal or master corporal level, right up to the general officer level. In each of those, between the junior NCOs, senior

NCOs, officers, and general and senior officers, there were different requirements for the instruction. So rather than trying to come up with another program called "Gender Integration" or whatever, I named it "Leadership in a Diverse Army," the LDA program. My concern now is that by having this anti-harassment training and the leadership and the diverse army program, we might be adversely affecting that warrior ethic that we've tried to bring back.

We hired some very well-known diversity and gender experts from Canada and the United States, and we held the first-ever generals' and brigade commanders' symposium. Every general officer in the army and every brigade commander, all of the staff officers, full colonel and above, attended this training. General Leach was the commander and he made sure that everybody attended. If the boss goes, everybody goes. It went very well, but to a large degree this was giving information to the senior staff that the sergeant already knows. The general officer hasn't been in that kind of environment for many years, simply because he's risen high in rank.

Quotas

We needed to recruit some women, and we needed critical mass because one woman in a platoon of 36 is virtually guaranteed to fail. Through our own experience we observed that the critical mass was between 25 and 33 percent of a platoon, company, what have you. Our target was that 25 percent of the recruiting quota for the year would be to recruit women. The point was to see how many we'd get at the front end. Subsequently people misinterpreted that as being 25 percent must pass in the final instance.

The army and the command responsible for recruiting put a lot of money into this. We're talking millions of dollars to recruit women. We did job fairs in major centres and other centres. We looked at statistics to find out where most women come from who join the military, and we went to those places and tried to farm them a bit more. There was a lot of study that went into how much money to spend and the type of tools we should use to recruit them. Even then, with this all-out recruiting effort, we couldn't get anywhere near the numbers that we were hoping for. To be a hard combat officer or a hard combat soldier is not a young woman's number-one choice of employment.

I think the target was on the order of 500 and they got about 125 women who joined, of whom maybe 20 or 30 finally passed, a very low pass rate, even with the reduction in training standards and different PT tests along the way.

The military should not make any changes to its standards. It should not make any changes to physical requirements. The one woman that made it through training in 1989 was actually a lumberjack. Five foot ten, 160 pounds. She had the same weight, height and build as I do. And if that's what it takes to be an infantry soldier, well, that's what it takes.

We found that pound for pound men are far more powerful than women. We have got about 40 percent more lower-body strength, about 60 percent more upper-body strength, higher endurance because of bigger hearts. There's more blood in the system of a man the same weight as a woman. All these physical attributes that men have, that make us die sooner, are required. You need this explosive strength to run, to carry very heavy things.

I had an interesting conversation with a female colonel many years ago. She said, "We have a new, lighter rifle now, so this should make it easier for women to be in the infantry." And I said, "No, the weight is not going to change." She said, "But the rifle weighs two or three pounds less." "Yeah, but we only carried 80 rounds of ammunition with the old rifle, in four magazines. With the new rifle, we're going to carry five magazines. Each has got 30 rounds in it, that's 150 rounds. So we've increased our firepower, the weapon is fully automatic and the weight load is exactly the same."

The weight load for a soldier in the Roman legions was the same as we have today. Instead of a short sword, a spear and a shield, a bronze breastplate and a bronze helmet, my helmet is Kevlar, my flak jacket's Kevlar and my weapon is an automatic rifle. A soldier will also carry grenades, grenade launchers and ammunition. That's exactly the same weight load. It hasn't changed in more than two millennia.

I keep hearing about people saying that the military's not the same, but if I take you to Bosnia right now, if I take you to Kosovo, you'll still see soldiers on foot, wearing flak jackets, carrying heavy weapons, moving about the ground patrolling, detaining people, confronting crowds.

There's still a wide requirement for physical ability. Raw physical strength and endurance is still required. You still have to wear a flak jacket and a helmet and carry a rifle.

I don't see how we can say that today it's different than it was yesterday. We still need soldiers to get on the ground, and it's not your ground unless you've got soldiers on it and you put a flag on it. If we don't have the strength to do it, it's not going to be done.

After 18 months I went off on an American course and realized we were going in the wrong direction. Shortly after that I left the military.

Training

It was once said that if you'd been in the army 10 years, you didn't have 10 years' experience, you had one year's experience 10 times. Well, repetition is good, it means you'll do the right things. You are trained to do it. That is what repetition's all about. We had a very good training schedule, always knowing that we could deploy quickly, knowing we could do long road moves, and knowing that every soldier had trained every year and qualified, at least first class or marksman on his weapon, as a normal course of events.

But we're letting ourselves slide down the slope of unpreparedness. To keep soldiers highly trained and honed and their equipment and their skills ready to go at a moment's notice is very expensive. How much does the government want to pay for this? To fire one missile is $25,000 but we have to fire those missiles, and by not having the money to train an anti-tank gunner, we're not keeping them at a high level of readiness. We might have the equipment but the soldiers are not good with it. I think there was one incident in Bosnia where we actually fired the TOW system and they missed three times. That should never have happened. They weren't ready.

We need to maintain the readiness and it takes money. We can speak about the government's view of what the threat is around the world, but the way it trickles down to your average platoon commander or company commander or brigade commander is, how many training days can I do and how many people can I train? When a particular battalion is going to be on the next rotation in six months, most of the brigade resources go to you so you can train. Everybody else is starved. We have people who are not getting the training. I don't think the soldiers are as well prepared as they were 10, 15 years ago, certainly not as well prepared as we were during the cold war. There is absolutely no question.

When I was with the ACE Mobile Force, the Canadian battalion, we were deployed to Europe. We had a 48-hour notice to get our reconnaissance party there, and we were there, complete, within 10 days. Now we're looking at deployment dates of vanguard within 30 days and main body within 90 days. If the government says we have six months to get ready to go on an operation, that's not a problem. Maybe we can do it in six months.

But the government hasn't paid to have units on 10 days' or seven days' or 14 days' standby, and the danger comes when the government tries to use the military without paying for the readiness. If you want to send somebody within 30 days, we really can't do that. But if the government says you must go, because the military works for the government, and so it should, we have to do what we're told, and that's where the difficulty arises.

Leadership

Leadership is a wide-ranging subject, and I think I can safely say that within a combat unit, a battalion or a regiment, that the leadership is generally pretty good. In fact very good. I've been very proud to serve under the COs that I've served under, and I worked with some superb other officers and NCOs. I don't think you see the leadership problem at lieutenant-colonel and below. You see the leadership problem at colonel and above. That's where the issues are. The problem comes at the higher end.

Full colonel's and general officer's pay is calculated in tandem with senior civil service bureaucrats. Some of these general officers got as high as an 18 percent pay raise, but hadn't had a pay raise in many years. Leadership is the CDS standing up in front of a TV camera and saying, "We are not going to take this pay raise until our soldiers get theirs first." That would have been leadership and that's what's missing right now.

Sometimes the people chosen for particular command slots are the wrong people. I wouldn't say that's a widespread problem, but in Somalia there was a breakdown at the commanding officers' level. You have to remember, you're controlling the dogs of war here. That's what soldiers are, and you have to keep a leash on them. They're only to use force when you say so, when you give them a certain set of circumstances where they are allowed to, not when they think they should. That leash must be kept on, and I think, in that particular circumstance some soldiers slipped off the leash, and they did some really nasty things that no soldier should ever do.

The poor guy should have never been put in the job. He'd been out of commanding troops for some years. He was parachuted in, virtually at the last moment, and I think, because the commander wasn't really up to speed and the unit was not subsequently prepared, the threads of discipline weren't established.

The soldiers on the ground paid the price, but we never really found out what happened at the upper level. We never got the final answers, like who was responsible for making certain decisions, why were certain people put in certain positions and what sort of political aspects were involved with this? Most soldiers would have been grateful to have seen it all laid out on the table. I expected far more from the inquiry but we never found out what happened.

The expression "mission, men, myself" always rang true as part of the military ethos. You take care of your mission and you take care of your men. You take care of yourself last.

Prior to 1991, 1992, the generals and the senior officers took care of us. That was the deal. Since then that bond, where I follow your orders and put myself in danger because I'm subject to the unlimited liability contract, has crumbled. People have been cut loose and left on their own, twisting in the wind.

DOUGLAS BLAND

Lieutenant-Colonel (Retired)
2000/2001

A respected author and lecturer, Douglas Bland is a professor and holds the chair in defence management studies at the School of Policy Studies at Queen's University. Dr. Bland is a graduate of the army staff college in Kingston the NATO Defence College at Rome, and holds a doctorate in public administration from Queen's University. Since 1990 he has been a consultant for the federal government's Advanced Management Program and was also a technical advisor to the Government of Canada's Commission of Inquiry into the Deployment of Canadian Forces to Somalia. He wrote The Administration of Defence Policy in Canada 1947–84, *which was published in 1987 and* Chiefs of Defence: Government and the Unified Command of the Canadian Armed Forces *(1995). In 1997–98 Professor Bland also published* Canada's National Defence, Volume 1: Defence Policy *and* Volume 2: Defence Organization *and in 2000 edited* Backbone of the Army: Non-Commissioned Officers in the Future Army.

The relationship between armed forces and society in general is extremely important. When there is a strong link between the armed forces, the people and the government, when they are united, when there is a consensus that they are involved in a just campaign, it's very difficult to beat a liberal democracy.

Where we've had problems, or other democracies have had problems, is when that triangle has broken down, as in Vietnam. When the army and the government and the people were out of consensus and they could not pursue a war. In the present context of conflicts within peacekeeping, there's a lot of consensus in the government, in the population and most of the Canadian Forces that this is a good and worthy thing to do.

That's why we keep doing it, spending money and taking casualties doing it. In the growing conflict with terrorism you will see, at the moment there is a strong consensus. We'll see how that holds up over time. But it's not just the people and the Armed Forces, it's the people, the Armed Forces and the government that's important.

Strategic Thinking
Sir Wilfrid Laurier many years ago remarked that one ought not to worry about the militia because, though they're good for maintaining civil order, Canada will be protected by the Munroe Doctrine. He was referring to the fact that there are very few threats to Canada and if there were threats to Canada, then the United States would take care of them.

Other prime ministers haven't been as blunt as that, but the sentiment is always there in Canadian politics that we are in a very secure place and therefore we can choose what kind of operations we're going to get into. That produces a particular kind of Armed Forces and a particular kind of military and political thinking.

The politicians know or sense that Canada is invulnerable, that the only threat to Canada would come from a worldwide war that would destroy everything and there's no defence against that. So we can depend on our isolation and our support from the United States, which they give to us in their own interests. That, then, allows us to spend very little on defence, or just enough to allow us to take part in certain operations outside the country.

George Stanley wrote that Canadians have held on to the apron strings of colonialism and that we haven't cut them yet. That was true into the 1980s, and perhaps even the 1990s. Our attitudes and advice have come from colonial masters, from senior allies, from the big players around the world, and because we have grown up accustomed to not addressing these issues, we haven't developed a professional force to do that. We're great doers but not great thinkers in strategic ideas.

The Armed Forces for most of our history have been expected by their political leaders to do two things. One, to maintain a degree of aid to civil authorities in Canada, to put down riots, strikes, to stop floods and fight ice storms and so on. And two, to provide a component that can work with our allies and other people outside Canada on those kinds of operations the government thinks are important. Never in our history have we thought of the Canadian Forces as an independent entity that would work outside of what we came to term in the 1950s "alliance-manship." And that persists today.

The government expects the Armed Forces to be around for domestic purposes, but they have rarely called on the Canadian Forces to intervene in international operations, except at the behest of allies, the imperial Crown and so on. Because of that political habit, there's been little demand on the military to develop strategic thinkers and to think from national points of view, as opposed to alliance points of view. But things have changed for Canada in significant ways since the end of the cold war.

I wrote some time ago that we were "home alone" strategically. While previously most of Canada's strategy, commitments, doctrines and military ideas have come from the empire, the United States or from our allies, at the end of the cold war we found that these partners were not going to give us that sort of direction. Therefore, like the kid in the movie, we had to make do for ourselves. That's the difficulty we're dealing with right now. The allies, for the most part, aren't bothering to tell us what to do. NATO doesn't have much of a strategy and the United Nations has no strategy. We're trying to find ways to do things from a Canadian point of view, and that's difficult for us.

You need a demand from society and from government for officers to provide strategic advice. You need a professional body of officers, mostly senior officers, who have a wide experience in strategic issues and concepts, who can then formulate strategic policies for government. In both these regards we've been very weak. Governments aren't much interested, the population's demand for strategic thinking isn't great, and therefore the military haven't been trained or conditioned to think strategically.

Reality and Myth

Canadians have a well-earned respect for the Canadian military in peacekeeping operations and it has grown into a national myth. There is a sense that this is what we do best in the world, our comparative advantage, and in some respects our national mission is to save the world, make it over into our own image and help everyone through peacekeeping operations. But the fact of the matter is that Canada has hardly ever seen a war it didn't want to become involved in.

We fought in the Boer War, we fought the Chinese, we fought the Japanese, we fought the Koreans, we fought the Germans twice, we fought the Italians. We conducted campaigns in Egypt. We invaded Russia. We fought the British and the French and the Americans and each other and the Native people. That's our real history, our real military history. We've earned a reputation as a nation that can be depended upon to provide good soldiers in the interests of international security. That's where our real background is.

However, the conflict between our real history and our myth as peacekeepers sets up a contradiction within the Armed Forces because they are asked to take part in the real world in actual operations, with an ideological sense that we can do it in some kind of peaceful way without hurting anybody, including ourselves.

And that doesn't work.

Contradictions and Government Policy

The contradictions in Canadian foreign and defence policy affect the Armed Forces in various ways. The notion that, "We're invulnerable, and if we aren't, there's nothing we can do about it and therefore there's no reason to spend money on the Armed Forces," reduces defence budgets. Every government does that.

There is another challenge because, in this new ideological view of the Armed Forces, there is the sense that we can employ the Armed Forces without arms. This attitude gets in the way of purchases of real fighting capabilities, like submarines, fighter aircraft, tanks and artillery pieces. So the Armed Forces today are challenged because of reduced funds and a reduced demand from the government for war-fighting capability. Yet they know, and have experienced over the last few years, that the government will put them in war-fighting or near-war-fighting circumstances, and this causes an enormous amount of frustration for the leaders of the Armed Forces and danger for the people on the ground.

The idea of our American defenders is another contradiction in our military and our foreign policy history. Wilfrid Laurier may have believed that the Americans would defend us in their own interests and therefore we didn't need armed forces. And President Roosevelt at Queen's University in 1938 made a solemn promise that Canada would not be invaded by "any other empire," meaning the British Empire. In return, Mackenzie King promised the Americans that no one would be able to attack the United States through Canada, which is an interesting promise in the era of ballistic-missile defence in 2001. But there is this sense that the Americans are of course doing this for their own interests and not for our interests. It spawns the notion that we need a Canadian policy of defence against help. We need a policy that defends us from American help whether we want it or not.

You see that popping up every once in a while in the administrations of John Diefenbaker, Pierre Trudeau and Jean Chrétien. And although the Americans are our defenders, we don't want to acknowledge it and we want to control it somehow. But we rarely have found a way to do that. Because if we do not depend on the Americans to defend us, then we're going to have to spend money to defend ourselves, and we don't want to do that now, do we?

In describing the current conditions of the Armed Forces and Canadian defence and security policy, I've made the point that there is a deliberate policy of the government to disarm the Armed Forces, to allow them to wither away to a state where they cannot be used. This seems an odd thing for a government to do, but governments have been warned repeatedly since the mid-1980s that if they did not properly fund the Armed Forces for the commitments the government had undertaken, then they would eventually end up in a position of having very little capability in the Armed Forces.

No one in government can argue that they haven't been told this because they have been told by chiefs of defence, deputy ministers, people outside the Armed Forces and people inside the Armed Forces. The government knows the consequences of its decision to accept that the Canadian Armed Forces will run down to an almost unusable state. On top of that there's the ideological argument that armed forces with real war-fighting capabilities are not necessary or even useful in the modern world.

So the attitude of the government that we're not going to spend any money and we don't need them anyway has allowed the Armed Forces to run down to the point where one chief of defence staff, Jean Boyle, announced that the Canadian Forces had no war-fighting capabilities whatsoever. The government knew all these things would happen and carried on anyway. Therefore it is a deliberate policy of the government not to have a useful military.

Military Attitudes and Responsibilities

You cannot make a credible argument that all the problems of national defence result from political interference or neglect. A major part of the problem rests with military advisors and military commanders themselves over a period of time.

Many years ago Brooke Claxton, one of our fine defence ministers, from 1947 to 1956, lectured the general officers and told them that they had to make policy that fit with the facts of national life. By that he meant that the Armed Forces would have to offer their advice to build forces within the context of Canadian social, political and economic policy. Many officers forgot that.

They thought that their job was to build forces for commitments and operations in a manner that they thought was useful. We saw the misapprehension by military officers of the facts of national life, that they often have not understood the boundaries of defence expenditures or what capabilities are acceptable to the Canadian community. For instance, proposals in the 1987 defence white paper to buy nuclear submarines flew completely in the face of Canadian realities, and was obviously defeated for that reason. The officers and senior advisors in Canada have to understand that defence policy is social policy. It's political policy and it has to be built and managed within the context of Canadian national life.

Every state has its own particular brand of civil-military relations, that is, the relation between the civil authority, civilians elected to Parliament, and the military. In Canada it is characterized by a distancing between the civil authority and the military. The civil authority, members of Parliament and senators, tend not to understand or make much effort to understand defence business, national security planning, and the exact details of where the money goes, how it's spent, how big an Armed Forces you have and the consequences of their decisions. The military, on the other hand, because it is not often subject to parliamentary oversight, tends to wander away from the political context of Canada and then to sometimes think that it cannot be held to account by members of Parliament.

Much of the angst in the Somalia inquiry, when military officers were placed on the stand and asked detailed questions by the members of the inquiry, arose from the fact that officers weren't used to being asked detailed questions. There was a sense, from certain senior officers, a notion of, "How dare you ask me that?" This comes from a background of not being asked questions. There's an interesting contradiction that runs through this notion. The military and their advisors and supporters often complain that Parliament isn't watching what they're doing, isn't aware, isn't informed, doesn't make decisions. But when a strong minister shows up and starts to make decisions, they howl to the rooftops because the politicians are interfering in military affairs.

Paul Hellyer's move to change the structure of the Armed Forces brought indignation from the military. Donald Macdonald's and Pierre Trudeau's ideas about changing Canada's relationships with NATO brought indignation from the Armed Forces. The Somalia inquiry questions insulted some officers. They want the politicians to pay attention to national defence and their advice, but they don't want to be asked questions about it.

There is, in many Western military communities, this notion that the military is the repository of national values, that it carries the spirit of the nation, the nation's honour and so on. And in many respects that is true, when you think of the military's contribution to national development, to national defence, to self-sacrifice. Tens of thousands of Canadians have been killed in the service of the country within the Armed Forces, and they carry in our minds these high values for Canada.

But at the same time, again because of our real history, where generations of military officers have, as James Eayrs once said, "grown up allied," their entire experience has been working with allies, mostly outside country, with little attention from Canadians and no attention from politicians. They have developed an alliance point of view, not a national point of view. And when the politicians reassert themselves into the defence field, asking questions, making decisions and so on, there is an inevitable clash between what the military think national interests are and what politicians think they are.

Interestingly, you can make the same analogy right now. The minister of defence, Art Eggleton, has said that if the Canadian Forces have to deploy someplace, we'll go with allies. The allies will provide capabilities that we don't have. The allies will provide resources that we don't have. The allies will get us to the theatre. This is the same sort of dreamy world that doesn't work when you get into actual operations.

Canada's Role

Often throughout our history, and certainly through the cold war experience and so on, many Canadians were confused, I think, about our position and our place and our influence in alliances, in the NATO alliance, with the United States and even with the United Nations. They felt that because we were good and faithful companions, ready to go to most operations, that this gave us great influence in councils of the major powers and in the major alliances of the world. They were repeatedly disappointed to find out, as in the Kosovo operation, that we were, if not locked out, set aside from the councils of the great when they decided many of the basic issues of that campaign.

People are discouraged to find out that we don't have any influence: "So why should we join these coalitions in the first place?" But they have to have a different perspective on what influence we're talking about. We will have no influence whatsoever on what happens to Canada and Canadian interests and Canadian values if we are not in these alliances.

We are at the table, not necessarily to influence the decision making of the great powers, but to influence their decisions that might affect us. If we're not there, they're going to make the decisions anyway, and we'll have no say in what happens.

That's been our great experience in the First World War and in the Second World War and in cold war operations. Our members of the diplomatic staff and the military staff were always very keen to become involved in coalition politics, not to influence coalition politics per se, but to guard Canada's interests and position in these kinds of endeavours.

The central characteristic and tradition in Canadian foreign policy is acting through coalitions. If there weren't coalitions in the world, then we would have no say, we would have no place to go, so Canadian diplomats have tried very hard to join just about everything, to help influence what is happening, perhaps in a small way, but to guard Canada's interests. That involves us in all sorts of responsibilities that go along with membership in such coalitions. One of the most important characteristics of the coalitions that we've joined, whether in the First World War, Second World War, in the cold war and even in the UN to some extent, is unity amongst the allies, and that carries costs as well as benefits.

The second thing that's been happening since the 1990s that's interesting is that under the government's human-security agenda, under the American agenda of spreading democracy and commerce around the world, we have gone into the world to do what Lloyd Axworthy said Canadians wanted us to do. He said that we want to be involved in other people's problems. The difficulty with that construct is that when you become involved in other people's problems, you invariably pick sides. You decide that someone is causing the problem and they're the bad guys. And we normally, in the Western mode of thinking, use as criteria for deciding who's good and who's bad our view of democracy, human rights, commerce, freedom and so on.

A lot of countries don't follow those same measures. So we go abroad. We get involved in other people's problems. We pick sides and then we suffer the consequences of retaliation, for instance, as happened in New York, because we are on different sides.

We went into the Balkans, into the former Yugoslavia, perhaps with the best of intentions to get involved in other people's problems to help them sort out what we may have thought was a misunderstanding amongst these people. "We'll just give them time to talk it out and it will all be fine." But we invariably ended up picking sides. And when the Kosovo Albanian/Serbian matter broke out into armed conflict, we picked a side. We picked the Albanians more or less over the Kosovars, over the Serbs, and that brought us into the war and we couldn't, obviously, get away from that.

Now the Forces are deployed into Macedonia. We picked the Macedonians against the Albanians, so we have changed sides. We can expect a response from the Albanians. When you go into the world to spread your ideas, as a missionary for Christianity or for liberal democracy or for whatever, you end up taking sides. That's what gets us involved in these kinds of operations, and it's for that reason why we can't back out of the coalitions, not because we're in the coalitions in the first place and have no say.

The problem is that we seem to have in the last 10 years, under the foreign policy of human security and so on, elected to make those choices, to become involved in the world, to become involved in other people's problems as Lloyd Axworthy has said, to go hither and yon around the world from Africa to East Timor and throughout the Middle East and into the Balkans, but without understanding either the consequences of those actions, or the means that you need.

In other words, there is an imbalance in our strategy between our goals and our means. And this seems to be not well understood in some political circles in Ottawa and in some government parties.

When the government, for instance, said, "Let's flash off to Zaire and help in the situation," there seemed to be some confusion that Canada actually had the resources to undertake the mission that the prime minister set out for the Armed Forces, that is, to lead a multinational force in a faraway place. It is that confusion and it is that mismatch between ends and means that puts us in a position of being embarrassed as a country, or it might put our Armed Forces and our members of our Armed Forces in great danger and risk to life and limb.

Because the chief characteristic of Canadian national defence and security planning is surprise, we are always surprised by the events that occur around the world, whether it's the tragedies in the Balkans or in Somalia or some other place, or airliners crashing into large buildings in attacks by terrorists.

We are always surprised, or the government seems always to be surprised, to find out that Canada has very few hard military assets to allow it to fulfill its international responsibilities, its international desires. And the members of the Armed Forces are often surprised to find out that politicians don't understand this fact of life.

In past times we've had a lot of time to get organized for events. But now, more recently, we are seeing that the continued decline in the capabilities of the Canadian Forces has put us into a situation where the choices we can make to act internationally are becoming fewer and fewer. That is why we are not involved in very many peacekeeping missions anymore. And why we have almost no capability to react to new surprises that have occurred in the defence and security field.

We've been lucky because there haven't been large-scale continuing emergencies. There have been very important situations, as in the breakup of the former Yugoslavia, that can be packaged out and people can take small bits without any threat to Canada or any threat to the operation. But if we enter into a long, continuous operation, we are going to find very quickly that the cupboard is nearly bare, that the state of the Armed Forces' readiness is very low, and their ability to generate more forces is almost zero. And that will put us into a backwater position at any international discussion.

The Bookends
People speak today about the need for the Armed Forces to be rapidly deployable, to be able to go into crisis situations, to have an almost immediate impact on a crisis, either to prevent it or to defeat an opponent. We had that.

In 1956, for instance, the Canadian Armed Forces went to the Middle East on the first major Canadian peacekeeping operation. They deployed two major units, several minor units, all onboard Canadian ships, in Canadian aircraft, with Canadian commanders, with Canadian logistics support, with all the modern communications equipment of the day. That enabled Canada to have an immediate impact on an international security problem.

Not being able to do that today is not a factor of technology. It's not a factor of trying to invent how to do these things. It's not a matter of having officers with enough brainpower to figure out how to do these things. Why we can't have that impact today is a direct result of government's policies over numbers of years that have reduced our capabilities.

We have no transport fleets. We have a minor air force fleet. We have very few units of the size and capabilities we had in 1956. We have next to no logistic sustainable ability. We have a poor communications setup. These failures, not in the military themselves, were displayed when we tried to deploy Canadian stand-alone forces to Zaire a few years ago. There's the bookends of Canadian defence policy. Complete capability to act more or less independently as a major player in peacekeeping operations and conflict prevention in the Middle East in 1956, and next to no capabilities, a failed mission by most standards, by any criteria, in Zaire. The variable in the equation is lack of government commitment to building and maintaining capabilities in the Armed Forces, pure and simple.

Problems

Much of the planning in the Canadian Forces during the 1970s and the 1980s was focused on our NATO operations and the growing difficulties of maintaining capabilities for those commitments in the face of falling defence budgets. These problems became evident to the military and to certain political leaders who paid attention to these things when the Armed Forces conducted operations such as Operation Bold Step, which was a large staff exercise held in the mid-1980s to test all the war plans together. We found out in those tests that we couldn't deploy the necessary forces, and even if we could deploy the CAST Brigade to Norway and forces to Europe and to the Atlantic and in NORAD and North America, we couldn't sustain them. We found that we had more plans for more forces than Canada owned or could support.

During Exercise Bold Step I was working on the NATO staff in National Defence Headquarters in Ottawa. I was one of the staff officers responsible for the maintenance and the co-ordination of our NATO plans. As this exercise unfolded on paper and we made the paper deployment of forces overseas, it became obvious that when they arrived in Norway they were going to need a great deal of ammunition.

When I took the plans to senior leaders to explain how this was to happen, I pointed out that we had a memo of understanding with the Norwegian government that they would provide ammunition for our troops when they arrived in Norway. Only, however, on the condition that we would replace the ammunition within 30 days. The chief of the defence staff at the time, apparently unaware of these details, was furious because we had no ammunition to give to the Norwegians within 30 days, or within 60 or 90 days.

On top of that, the memo of understanding negotiated by officials at the Department of National Defence and the Department of External Affairs with the Norwegians and with NATO said that Norwegians would provide medical care for Canadian casualties, surplus to their own requirement. In other words, if they had empty beds, wounded Canadians could lie in them. However, when we showed the senior leadership that memo and placed beside it a NATO assessment of Norwegian capabilities on the medical side, it pointed out very clearly that the Norwegians were absolutely without medical capabilities for their own forces.

One of the concepts that is often trotted out by military people in their desperation to fill government plans for commitments overseas is the notion of host-nation support. That is, that we can depend upon other nations to provide for the Forces things that we don't have, on the idea that we're small, they're big, therefore they must have a surplus.

Our whole planning process in this period was built on a house of cards, on assumptions that allies would provide for us from their surpluses. They don't have surpluses. The government and the military, or the military in particular, had allowed this set of faulty plans to develop over a long period of time for two reasons.

First, they believed that in time you could make the thing work by negotiating with host-nation support. They'd find some way to support the government's policy. Secondly, the military have always planned in Canada on this rather hopeful assumption that next year things are going to be better. We don't have enough resources this year, but next year the government's going to give us more money.

The message was taken to the political leaders: "We need more money." Some problems can be solved by throwing money at them and this was one of those times. The military and the chief of the defence staff, General Thériault, felt that the government did not take the issue seriously.

General Manson, who took over, then ran another exercise, this time what you'd call a live exercise with real troops and real ships and real airplanes, and attempted to deploy the Canadian Forces, the CAST Brigade, to north Norway in accordance with our commitments to NATO. We found that there was no supply, there was no ammunition, there was no medical support. We found that the NATO plans were faulty and the allied plans were faulty in many respects and that we couldn't keep up that commitment. Then he carried that message to government.

In the 1987 white paper some adjustments were made. The Canadian Forces withdrew from most of the north Norway commitment and attempted to concentrate all its forces in the central European theatre. But, in 1989, just as those reorganizations that would have cost a great deal of money were taking place, the government decided to pull the rug out from under the defence plan by cutting the defence budget.

When we look at various operational plans and commitments that have gone astray, have not been fulfilled as you might expect them to be or are obvious failures of military operations, as in Somalia, it is very easy to turn to the military and blame them for these situations. In some cases, as in Somalia, the blame is evidently there. Military leaders were responsible for much of what happened.

But when you look at the inability of the Canadian Forces in the 1970s and 1980s to fulfill commitments to NATO, or to maintain a capability to act as peacekeepers in places like Zaire, or to sustain and reinforce operations in the former Yugoslavia, that is not a military problem.

Military officers, chiefs of the defence staff and other advisors have told governments time and again that they would find themselves in this situation if they did not provide resources to meet the commitments the governments have been making.

Choices
The government has two choices. They can scale back commitments and expectations of the Armed Forces, or they can properly fund them. It seems governments are incapable of making those kinds of choices. They can't make the choice to scale back commitments, in other words, to stop taking part in international operations, or find more money for the Armed Forces because that just doesn't seem to play well domestically.

There are other legitimate demands on the government's budget and the government will spend the money there. But at the same time some Canadians have high expectations of Canada being an international player and they would frown greatly if government said, "Well, actually, we're not playing in the international arena anymore."

I think there are a couple of reasons why we go through operations in NATO, operations in the UN, operations in the netherworld of present-day security operations with failures, problems, and seem not to have any change. People look at the operations in Somalia and Rwanda and Zaire and see the same mistakes being repeated again and again.

One way to explain it is that military forces in most nations, change radically for two main reasons. One, they are obviously defeated. There is a crisis so obvious to the nation that someone has to do something. Secondly, they change because a civilian minister of defence walks into the ministry with ideas of his own to change things. This happened in the United Kingdom time and again, and it has happened occasionally in Canada. It is almost always outside factors that cause the military to change radically, to face new situations.

In Canada, because we have been conditioned to wait for allies to tell us what to do, that's been a slow process and a very ambiguous process in the last number of years. Another thing is that our failures have not been so obvious and dramatic, even including Somalia, as to call for a radical transformation of defence policy. And third, there haven't been many political leaders who have wanted to get at the crux of our strategic national-interest planning basis, so we've been fixing bits and pieces as we go along.

Losing Track

One of the types of capabilities that fall away during peacetime, or groups of capabilities, are logistics capabilities, and one of those is medical support. In peacetime you don't need large military hospitals, field hospitals, ambulances and so on. You cut back those things in the interests of maintaining your core capabilities. And you write paper plans with allies that they will provide for medical support.

But what is going to happen as soon as the first shot is fired in a conflict is that the political community in Canada is going to reassert itself and become interested in national defence issues. And it's going to start asking questions about where is Private Schnooks who was apparently injured? Then we would say, "We don't know; he's in the allied medical system someplace." Because in Europe, we've had no casualty-clearing capability. We had no way to track casualties. We wouldn't have known what happened to our brigade overseas if it became engaged in operations.

The lack of that capability and the lack of staff planning in that capability is reflected today in our operations, when people come back from Bosnia. When they're in Bosnia, when they're in Africa, whenever they're in operations, we lose sight of them, we lose track of them. We don't know how many casualties we have. We don't know where they are, we don't know how they're injured and we don't know how to treat them when they come back. These are modern consequences of past decisions, the tyranny of past decisions.

The Canadian historian Steve Harris has written that, by habit, Canadians lend troops to allies. It's a telling remark because when you look at our operations in NATO, and especially our operations for the United Nations over the last 30 years or so, what we have done is make a contribution to a UN operation, send the troops, deploy them and then leave their support, their employment, their strategy, their tactics and their livelihood, in many respects, to an international organization. We lend them and forget them. That has had terrible consequences for the troops when what we came to think of as run-of-the-mill operations, like the Cyprus deployments, changed into dangerous deployments, as in Bosnia, Kosovo, Somalia and Zaire. When the allied support wasn't there, you couldn't lend them and forget about them. You had to do something.

Waking Up

All of these mythical notions, that Canadians live in a fireproof house and don't have to spend much on national defence because our presence is enough, came crashing down when we ended up in a very different kind of world, a very difficult kind of world. One of the interesting things about the Somalia affair, in perhaps a macabre way, is that it brought together in a very short period all the contradictions in Canadian defence policy over many years. All of a sudden we were on a mission without a strong ally that was directing it. We were lending troops to an operation where there was no host nation. We were home alone, we had to think for ourselves, we had to come up with our own strategic thinking for this kind of operation. It wasn't traditional peacekeeping and it wasn't military operations as we understood them.

Canadians had to face the surprise that when you go on peacekeeping operations the people you're peacekeeping might not like you, and that you're not out there to save the world, at least from their point of view. On peacekeeping operations, whether it's Chapter VI or Chapter VII, a nuance that's lost on most Canadians, you may have to shoot somebody, and Canadian Forces officers may have to spend lives in order to achieve government policy.

What the Canadian people need, and essentially have if they would use them, are laws that govern the conduct of military operations, that define what is a lawful or unlawful command. They have that in the National Defence Act. What they also need is an officer corps reasonably separated from the partisan political process in Ottawa, and I say reasonably because the chief of the defence staff, as the connecting individual between society and the Armed Forces must be in some ways connected. They need an armed force that offers clear, technical and clinical advice to the political leaders of the country and to each other. They need to be, as the Prussians used to say, "Frank unto the Kaiser."

But above all, we need to have a vigilant Parliament. We need to have political leadership that is informed, concerned and aware of what is happening in the Armed Forces. After all, the Armed Forces spend billions of dollars. They have the Canadian national reputation at hand and their employees are all armed. The welfare of these people and their very lives depend upon the decisions taken by members of Parliament. Real policies, real concern, real political action is what's going to serve Canada best.

AFTERWORD

M any of the conversations in *No Life Jackets*, the first volume of *Talking Heads Talking Arms*, were conducted at the time of the 1994 white paper on defence. But Canadians weren't interested in the military, or so we were told by the broadcasters we approached with the idea for a documentary on defence issues. So we put the project away for a time.

The media scramble over the Somalia affair eventually did focus the public's attention on the military — for the all the wrong reasons. The debate might have benefited from the context we were proposing, and we have now followed through with our plans. The result is the documentary series *A Question of Honour*.

By the time the more recent interviews were under way, a pattern in the deployment of the Canadian Forces overseas was becoming evident. The Gulf War, Bosnia/Croatia, Somalia, the Zaire rescue mission and the Kosovo operation provided an obvious framework for the programs. Clearly the operational tempo of the Canadian Forces was escalating and becoming increasingly dangerous. The military institution in Canada was floundering due to scandal, misdirection and budget cuts. But few took notice. The warnings from those interviewed in 1994 look ominously prescient from our vantage point, eight years later.

It is not often that one has the opportunity to get all of the considered thoughts and recollected experiences of those interviewed for a project out into the public's view. I am grateful that, with these volumes, we are able to give full expression to the opinions of almost everyone who contributed time and encouragement to this project.

Rob Roy
Producer, *A Question of Honour*
July 2002

GLOSSARY

4 Brigade

Shorthand for a formation that changed its name several times over the years of its existence. It was first 27 Canadian Infantry Brigade, sent to Europe in the early 1950s. It was renamed 1 CIBG (Canadian Infantry Brigade Group) in 1953 as a result of army reorganization and replaced in rotation by 2 CIBG in the mid-1950s and in 1957 by 4 CIBG, the strongest unit deployed. It was considered to be a light division by the British, but lacked full logistic support and strategic mobility. The brigade acquired armoured personnel carriers in the mid-1960s and became 4 Canadian Mechanized Brigade Group. It dropped "Group" after the Gulf War and became 4 CMB.

Canada 21 Council

Janice Gross Stein was project director of this mostly liberal group, which published its findings in an article in *Canadian Foreign Policy* (Spring 1994 edition) titled "Canada 21: A Moment and a Model." The new Liberal government provided the impetus for the formation of the Canada 21 Council. The council's conclusions to a large degree dismissed historical security concerns and responses in favour of identifying new non-military threats to sovereignty and security and advocated a light peacekeeping force as a model for Canada's military.

CAST Brigade Group

The Canadian Air-Sea Transportable Brigade Group. The brigade group was a commitment made to NATO at the time that Canada was planning to cut back on its European force, but according to many the commitment was always meant to be political tokenism. The Canadian troops that were to be withdrawn from Europe and returned to Canada were to be a main contribution to this brigade which, in the event of a Soviet invasion of Norway, would be sent to the northern part of the country to "beat off the Russian hordes." In 1968 the CAST Brigade Group committed troops from 2 Combat Group in Petawawa and later 5 Groupement de Combat in Valcartier. There was some question as to how the troops would get to Norway. It has been reported that at one time there was some suggestion to send them by Newfoundland ferries, but the idea was rejected. What seems to have happened is that everyone forgot that this was supposed to be tokenism. In 1984 when the military put the plan under scrutiny on paper in Operation Bold Step, nothing was available: no ships, no ammunition and apparently not even a plan to get troops to the docks in Montreal. In 1986 a live-action exercise, Bold Lion, was carried out using Canadian soldiers stationed in Canada. The exercise met with some success, but it ultimately proved that the whole idea wasn't feasible. Some people have suggested that many senior military officers were hoping, in the lead-up to the 1987 white paper, that if the commitment to the CAST Brigade was shown to be unrealistic and was dropped, they could then reinforce and rebuild 4 Brigade.

CDS   Chief of the defence staff.

CFAO   Canadian Forces Administrative Orders. Orders in which policies on every aspect of the Canadian military are explicitly laid out.

Corvette   A small escort vessel (length approximately 62.5 m) based on a mid-1930s design for an ocean-going whale catcher. The name can be traced to small French warships of the 18th century. A total of 121 corvettes, many of the "Flower" class, were built in Canada during World War II. The crew varied in size, from 83 in the early version to 109 in later designs.

Croatia Board of Inquiry   Inquiry called in August 1999 to investigate whether members of the Canadian Forces serving in the Canadian contingent of UNPROFOR and assigned to the area commonly known as Sector South during the period 1993 to 1995 were exposed to environmental contaminants in quantities sufficient to pose a health hazard during the course of their duties. The operational name given to this mission by the Canadian military was Operation Harmony. The inquiry, presided over by Colonel Joe Sharpe, examined a wide range of subjects that influence the health and welfare of Canadian soldiers. Among other things, the board concluded in its report in 2000 that there was no scientific proof that the soil in Sector South contained contaminants in sufficient quantities to cause the serious health problems suffered by some members of the Canadian Forces who served there over the three-year period. However, the board was unable to rule out environmental contaminants entirely as a possible cause of at least some of the symptoms reported by veterans of Operation Harmony.

DND

Department of National Defence.

F-18

CF-18 jet fighter plane.

Frigate

An escort vessel larger than the corvette (length more than 91 m) introduced into the RCN early in World War II. Many were built in Canada, especially of the "River" class, for use by the RCN and other navies. After the war 21 were rebuilt as "Prestonian" class frigates and were used mainly as training vessels during the early years of the cold war. Between 1991 and 1996, 12 "Halifax" class patrol frigates, substantially larger than their wartime forebears, were built and added to the navy's fleet.

Green Line

The dividing line indicating the buffer zone separating the Greeks and the Turks in Cyprus, so called, reportedly, because when defining the boundaries on the map, the British officer in charge drew the line with a green ballpoint pen.

IFOR/SFOR

Implementation Force/Stabilization Force. In Bosnia, successors to UNPROFOR, the UN Protection Force. On December 14, 1995, the General Agreement for Peace was signed in Paris, after negotiations resulted in the Dayton peace accord. Under UN Security Council Resolution 1031, NATO was given the mandate to implement the military aspects of the agreement. IFOR (Operation

Joint Endeavors) began on December 20, 1995, and consisted of approximately 65,000 troops, with a mandate for one year. After the successful Bosnia elections in September of 1996, NATO defence ministers concluded that a reduced military presence was needed to provide stability and strengthen the peace. NATO organized SFOR (Operation Joint Guard, Operation Joint Forge) under UNSCR 1088, which was activated on December 20, 1996, at the conclusion of IFOR. SFOR initially numbered 32,000 troops. Post-2000 that has been reduced to below 20,000. Thirty-three nations, including Russia, have taken part in these NATO missions.

JTF 2

Joint Task Force 2. JTF 2 was established in 1993 to take over the anti-terrorist responsibilities from the RCMP. Believed to number approximately 350, these soldiers train with the elite U.S. and British units: the Rangers, Delta Force and the SAS. These commandos are an open secret and as one journalist has said, "Canada's JTF 2 are experts at remaining out of sight, out of mind and out of the headlines." Until early March 2002 the government and DND refused to comment on any of the top-secret operations or activities of the elite Canadian unit. On March 5 DND confirmed that members of JTF 2 were heavily engaged with hold-out al-Qaeda fighters in Operation Anaconda in eastern Afghanistan near the Pakistan border.

KFOR

The International Security Force, Kosovo, was established by the UN Security Council on June 12, 1999, two days after President Ahtisaari of Finland and Victor Chernomyrdin, former prime minister of Russia, negotiated an end to the fighting with

Slobodan Milosevic. At full strength the multi-national force was estimated to be 50,000.

NATO	North Atlantic Treaty Organization.
NCO	Non-commissioned officer.
NDHQ	National Defence Headquarters (located in Ottawa).
NORAD	North American Aerospace Defence Command is a binational United States and Canadian organization charged with the missions of aerospace warning and aerospace control for North America. Aerospace warning includes the monitoring of man-made objects in space, and the detection, validation and warning of attack against North America, whether by aircraft, missiles or space vehicles, utilizing mutual support arrangements with other commands. Aerospace control includes providing surveillance and control of Canadian and United States airspace. (Definition from the NORAD Web site: http://www.spacecom.af.mil/norad/.)
PPCLI	Princess Patricia's Canadian Light Infantry.
PT tests	Physical training tests.
R22 R	Royal 22nd Regiment. A French Canadian infantry regiment based in Quebec City.
RMA	Revolution in Military Affairs.
RMC	Royal Military College, Kingston, Ontario.
SHAPE Technical Centre	Supreme Headquarters Allied Powers EuropeTechincal Centre. A Nato scientific,

technical and defence research establishment in The Hague.

SAS

Special Air Service. The British Army's elite special forces unit, considered to be one of the best military organizations in the world.

UCK

Ushtria Clirimtare e Kosoves. The Albanian name for what became known as the KLA, the Kosovo Liberation Army. It first appeared in Macedonia in 1992.

UNITAF

Unified Task Force. A multinational force numbering approximately 37,000 troops, organized and led by the U.S. In December 1992 it was authorized by the Security Council to use "all necessary means" to establish a secure environment for humanitarian relief operations in Somalia. This was a Chapter VII operation.

UNOSOM I

United Nations Operation in Somalia. A Chapter VI operation for humanitarian relief which was established in April 1992 and to which the Canadian government committed the Airborne Regiment in October 1992.

UNOSOM II

United Nations Operation in Somalia, 1993–1995. In May 1993 the mandate of UNOSOM II was to take appropriate action, including enforcement measures, to establish a secure environment throughout Somalia, and to complete the task begun by UNITAF for the restoration of peace, stability and law and order. In October 1993, 18 American soldiers lost their lives in the violence that erupted in Mogadishu. The next year the mission was extended a number of times until finally UNOSOM II's mandate was ended on March 31, 1995. Initially a multinational force of 28,000, by the end troops stood at just under 8,000 and comprised contingents from Pakistan, Egypt and Bangladesh.

UNTSO
United Nations Truce Supervision Organization, Middle East. This was the first peacekeeping operation by the United Nations. It was established in 1948 and is still in existence.

Van Doos
Nickname of the Royal 22nd Regiment.

APPENDIX 1
People Mentioned in the Conversations

PRIVATE KYLE BROWN

Brown was on duty guarding Shidane Arone on March 16, 1993. While he was guarding the prisoner, Master Corporal Clayton Matchee, who was off duty, tortured the Somali teenager and ordered Brown to get a camera. The trooper took the requested pictures and went off duty, leaving Matchee with Arone. The next day when it was learned that the prisoner had died, he turned himself in and handed over the camera. Matchee is alleged to have attempted suicide and was found unfit to stand trial. Brown took the brunt of the prosecution and was sentenced to five years in military prison. He was dishonourably discharged upon completion of the sentence.

KARL VON CLAUSEWITZ, 1780–1831

Prussian general and writer on military strategy. He fought in the wars against Napoleon, including Waterloo, and was appointed director of the German War School in 1818. His masterpiece *On War* was published after his death. The doctrines expounded in it, including that of total war (that all citizens, territory and property of the enemy nation should be attacked in every way possible) had an enormous effect on military strategy and tactics around the world.

GENERAL H. D. G. "HARRY" CRERAR

As an artillery officer, he served with the Canadian Corps in the First World War. In World War II he briefly commanded 1 Canadian Corps in Italy and then became commander of the 1st Canadian Army, succeeding General McNaughton, through the 1944–1945 campaign in northwest Europe.

JAMES EAYRS
Born in London, England, in 1926, he is a professor at the University of Toronto and an acclaimed military historian and commentator on foreign policy. His major work is *In Defence of Canada*, published in five volumes between 1965 and 1983.

HEINZ GUDERIAN
Born in 1888, Guderian became the leading theorist in armoured warfare in Germany during World War II. He was a great military tactician and in 1943 he became the inspector general of Panzer troops, and a year later Hitler named him his chief of staff, a post he filled until March 1945, when he argued with his boss one too many times and was dismissed. He was not tried by the Nuremburg Tribunal as it was decided that he had neither direct responsibility nor clear knowledge of war crimes. He died in 1954.

SIR JOHN WINTHROP HACKETT, 1910–1997
British soldier and academic. After studying at Oxford he was commissioned in the Hussars (1931). In World War II he served with distinction, notably with the 4th Parachute Brigade at Arnhem in 1944. He held several post-war commands, culminating in commander-in-chief of the British Army of the Rhine, and of the Northern Army Group in 1966. He later became principal of King's College, University of London (1968–1975). He wrote:

> What a society gets in its armed services is exactly what it asks for, no more, no less.
> What it asks for tends to be a reflection of what it is. When a country looks at its fighting forces, it is looking in a mirror; the mirror is a true one, and the face that it sees will be its own.

C. D. HOWE
Born in Waltham, Massachusetts, in 1886, Clarence Decatur Howe came to Canada in 1908 to teach civil engineering at Dalhousie University in Halifax. In the mid-1930s he became Canada's first minister of transport and at the beginning of World War II he directed the Ministry of Munitions and Supply. He is generally credited with Canada's post-war

industrial boom and held so many positions in government prior to the Liberal defeat in 1956 that he has often been referred to as the "minister of everything."

SAMUEL HUNTINGTON

Professor of international relations at Harvard University. Author of *The Soldier and the State: The Theory of the Politics of the Civil-Military Relationship*. This book has been described as a "classic, conservative articulation of radical professionalism," in which Professor Huntington suggests that in order to keep the peace, military leaders have to take for granted and anticipate the "irrationality, weakness and evil in human nature."

GENERAL A. L. G. "ANDY" MCNAUGHTON

Charismatic commander of the 1st Canadian Army in World War II. He was succeed by Harry Crerar, and in 1944 became the minister of national defence. To many, General McNaughton was the closest thing to a national hero that Canada had during the war.

HENRY LOUIS MENCKEN, 1880–1956

American editor, author and critic. One of his best known works, *The American Language*, was published in 1921. Here are several more of his observations.

> "Faith may be defined briefly as an illogical belief in the occurrence of the impossible."
> "Liberals have many tails and chase them all."
> "Democracy is the art of running the circus from the monkey cage."
> "A politician is an animal which can sit on a fence and yet keep both ears to the ground."

PETER MILLIKEN

Liberal member of Parliament for Kingston and the Islands. He became Speaker of the House of Commons in January 2001.

GENERAL GORDON REAY

Reay was born in 1943 in Royston, England, and grew up in Montreal. He began his military career as a cadet in the RMC in 1961. He was appointed commander of Canadian Land Forces in 1991, a post which he held until September 1995 when he retired. In 1999 he joined the Mine Action Team of the Department of Foreign Affairs and International Trade and was the special advisor to Canada's ambassador in Croatia. He was killed in a car accident during a working visit to Zagreb in December of 2000.

GENERAL GUY SIMONDS
A protégé of Field Marshal Montgomery, who later described him as "the best general the Allies produced during the war, " he led the 1st Canadian Infantry Division in Sicily in 1943, after which he assumed the command of 2 Canadian Corps, which was operating in northern Europe. According to some historians, his finest hour came during the Battle of the Scheldt in the Netherlands when he assumed temporary command of the 1st Canadian Army which led to the liberation of the Belgian port of Antwerp.

GEORGE STANLEY, 1907–2002
Stanley was born in Calgary and attended Oxford as a Rhodes Scholar in 1929. In 1936 he became a professor of history at Mount Allison University in Sackville, N.B., taking time off to serve in the military during the war as a historian with Canadian Army Headquarters in London. He was head of the history department of RMC for 20 years, during which time he suggested the basic design for the Canadian flag, which was adopted in 1965. He returned to Mount Allison in 1969 and served as New Brunswick's lieutenant governor from 1982 until 1987. He has published many books, including *The Birth of Western Canada, A History of the Riel Rebellion* and *Canada's Soldiers.*

APPENDIX 2

Chapters VI and VII of the Charter of the United Nations

CHAPTER VI
PACIFIC SETTLEMENT OF DISPUTES

Article 33
1. The parties to any dispute, the continuance of which is likely to endanger the maintenance of international peace and security, shall, first of all, seek a solution by negotiation, inquiry, mediation, conciliation, arbitration, judicial settlement, resort to regional agencies or arrangements or other peaceful means of their own choice.
2. The Security Council shall, when it deems necessary, call upon the parties to settle their dispute by such means.

Article 34
The Security Council may investigate any dispute, or any situation which might lead to international friction or give rise to a dispute, in order to determine whether the continuance of the dispute or situation is likely to endanger the maintenance of international peace and security.

Article 35
1. Any member of the United Nations may bring any dispute, or any situation of the nature referred to in Article 34, to the attention of the Security Council or of the General Assembly.
2. A state which is not a member of the United Nations may bring to the attention of the Security Council or of the General Assembly

any dispute to which it is a party if it accepts in advance, for the purposes of the dispute, the obligations of pacific settlement provided in the present Charter.

3. The proceedings of the General Assembly in respect of matters brought to its attention under this Article will be subject to the provisions of Articles 11 and 12.

Article 36

1. The Security Council may, at any stage of a dispute of the nature referred to in Article 33 or of a situation of like nature, recommend appropriate procedures or methods of adjustment.
2. The Security Council should take into consideration any procedures for the settlement of the dispute which have already been adopted by the parties.
3. In making recommendations under this Article the Security Council should also take into consideration that legal disputes should as a general rule be referred by the parties to the International Court of Justice in accordance with the provisions of the Statute of the Court.

Article 37

1. Should the parties to a dispute of the nature referred to in Article 33 fail to settle it by the means indicated in that Article, they shall refer it to the Security Council.
2. If the Security Council deems that the continuance of the dispute is in fact likely to endanger the maintenance of international peace and security, it shall decide whether to take action under Article 36 or to recommend such terms of settlement as it may consider appropriate.

Article 38

Without prejudice to the provisions of Articles 33 to 37, the Security Council may, if all the parties to any dispute so request, make recommendations to the parties with a view to a pacific settlement of the dispute.

CHAPTER VII
ACTION WITH RESPECT TO THREATS TO THE PEACE, BREACHES OF THE PEACE AND ACTS OF AGGRESSION

Article 39

The Security Council shall determine the existence of any threat to the peace, breach of the peace or act of aggression and shall make recommendations, or decide what measures shall be taken in accordance with Articles 41 and 42, to maintain or restore international peace and security.

Article 40

In order to prevent an aggravation of the situation, the Security Council may, before making the recommendations or deciding upon the measures provided for in Article 39, call upon the parties concerned to comply with such provisional measures as it deems necessary or desirable. Such provisional measures shall be without prejudice to the rights, claims or position of the parties concerned. The Security Council shall duly take account of failure to comply with such provisional measures.

Article 41

The Security Council may decide what measures not involving the use of armed force are to be employed to give effect to its decisions, and it may call upon the members of the United Nations to apply such measures. These may include complete or partial interruption of economic relations and of rail, sea, air, postal, telegraphic, radio and other means of communication, and the severance of diplomatic relations.

Article 42

Should the Security Council consider that measures provided for in Article 41 would be inadequate or have proved to be inadequate, it may take such action by air, sea or land forces as may be necessary to maintain or restore international peace and security. Such action may include demonstrations, blockade and other operations by air, sea or land forces of members of the United Nations.

Article 43

1. All Members of the United Nations, in order to contribute to the maintenance of international peace and security, undertake to make

available to the Security Council, on its call and in accordance with a special agreement or agreements, armed forces, assistance and facilities, including rights of passage, necessary for the purpose of maintaining international peace and security.

2. Such agreement or agreements shall govern the numbers and types of forces, their degree of readiness and general location and the nature of the facilities and assistance to be provided.

3. The agreement or agreements shall be negotiated as soon as possible on the initiative of the Security Council. They shall be concluded between the Security Council and members or between the Security Council and groups of members and shall be subject to ratification by the signatory states in accordance with their respective constitutional processes.

Article 44

When the Security Council has decided to use force it shall, before calling upon a member not represented on it to provide armed forces in fulfillment of the obligations assumed under Article 43, invite that member, if the member so desires, to participate in the decisions of the Security Council concerning the employment of contingents of that member's armed forces.

Article 45

In order to enable the United Nations to take urgent military measures, members shall hold immediately available national air-force contingents for combined international enforcement action. The strength and degree of readiness of these contingents and plans for their combined action shall be determined within the limits laid down in the special agreement or agreements referred to in Article 43, by the Security Council with the assistance of the Military Staff Committee.

Article 46

Plans for the application of armed force shall be made by the Security Council with the assistance of the Military Staff Committee.

Article 47

1. There shall be established a Military Staff Committee to advise and assist the Security Council on all questions relating to the Security Council's military requirements for the maintenance of

international peace and security, the employment and command of forces placed at its disposal, the regulation of armaments and possible disarmament.

2. The Military Staff Committee shall consist of the chiefs of staff of the permanent members of the Security Council or their representatives. Any member of the United Nations not permanently represented on the committee shall be invited by the committee to be associated with it when the efficient discharge of the committee's responsibilities requires the participation of that member in its work.

3. The Military Staff Committee shall be responsible under the Security Council for the strategic direction of any armed forces placed at the disposal of the Security Council. Questions relating to the command of such forces shall be worked out subsequently.

4. The Military Staff Committee, with the authorization of the Security Council and after consultation with appropriate regional agencies, may establish regional subcommittees.

Article 48

1. The action required to carry out the decisions of the Security Council for the maintenance of international peace and security shall be taken by all the members of the United Nations or by some of them, as the Security Council may determine.

2. Such decisions shall be carried out by the members of the United Nations directly and through their action in the appropriate international agencies of which they remember.

Article 49

The members of the United Nations shall join in affording mutual assistance in carrying out the measures decided upon by the Security Council.

Article 50

If preventive or enforcement measures against any state are taken by the Security Council, any other state, whether a member of the United Nations or not, which finds itself confronted with special economic problems arising from the carrying out of those measures shall have the right to consult the Security Council with regard to a solution of those problems.

Article 51

Nothing in the present Charter shall impair the inherent right of individual or collective self-defence if an armed attack occurs against a member of the United Nations until the Security Council has taken measures necessary to maintain international peace and security. Measures taken by members in the exercise of this right of self-defence shall be immediately reported to the Security Council and shall not in any way affect the authority and responsibility of the Security Council under the present Charter to take at any time such action as it deems necessary in order to maintain or restore international peace and security.

APPENDIX 3
Research Guide and Further Reading

Prepared by Martin Shadwick, senior research fellow, Centre for International and Security Studies, York University and Robert Roy, producer/researcher for *A Question of Honour.*

Journals (Canadian)

Behind the Headlines
Canada World View
Canadian Foreign Policy
Canadian Historical Review
Canadian Journal of Political Science
Canadian Military Journal
Canadian Public Administration
Canadian Public Policy
International Journal
Peacekeeping & International Relations
Policy Options

Journals (International)

American Review of Canadian Studies
Contemporary Security Policy
Current History

Foreign Affairs
Foreign Policy
International Security
Jane's Defence Weekly
Jane's International Defence Review
Journal of Ethics and International Affairs
Journal of International Affairs
Journal of Peace Research
Journal of Strategic Studies
NATO Review
ORBIS
Review of International Studies
The Washington Quarterly
World Policy Journal
World Politics

Also useful are the *SIPRI Year Book* and the International Institute for Strategic Studies publications, including *Strategic Survey* and *The Adelphi Papers.*

Web Sites

Government Departments and Agencies:
Canadian Security Intelligence Service (CSIS)
http://www.csis-scrs.gc.ca
Department of National Defence (DND)
http://www.dnd.ca
Department of Foreign Affairs and International Trade (DFAIT)
http://www.dfait-maeci.gc.ca
Office of the Auditor General of Canada (OAG)
http://www.oag-bvg.gc.ca
Office of Critical Infrastructure Protection and Emergency Preparedness (OCIPEP)
http://www.epc-pcc.gc.ca

Government Libraries/Research Centres/Publications:
Canadian Centre for Foreign Policy Development (CCFPD)
http://www.cfp-pec.gc.ca
Canadian Forces College (War, Peace and Security Server)

http://wps.cfc.dnd.ca
Canadian Military Journal (CMJ)
http://www/journal.dnd.ca

Parliamentary Committees:
Standing Committee on Foreign Affairs and International Trade
Standing Committee on National Defence and Veterans Affairs
Standing Senate Committee on Defence and Security
Standing Senate Committee on Foreign Affairs
http://www.parl.gc.ca

Non-Governmental Organizations:
Canadian Institute of International Affairs (CIIA)
http://www.ciia.org
Canadian Institute of Strategic Studies (CISS)
http://www.ciss.ca
Conference of Defence Associations Institute (CDAI)
http://www.cda-cdai.ca
Council for Canadian Security in the 21st Century (CCS 21)
http://www.stratnet.ucalgary.ca
Institute for Research on Public Policy (IRPP)
http://www.irpp.org
Lester B. Pearson Canadian International Peacekeeping Centre
http://www.Cdnpeacekeeping.ns.ca
Project Ploughshares
http://www.ploughshares.ca
Royal Canadian Military Institute (RCMI)
http://www.rcmi.org

International Organizations:
North American Aerospace Defence Command (NORAD)
http://www.spacecom.af.mil/norad
North Atlantic Treaty Organization (NATO)
http://www.nato.int
United Nations (UN)
http://www.un.org

NO LIFE JACKETS

Books of Note

Defence and Military Affairs:
Bland, Douglas L. *Canada's National Defence:* Vol. 1 *Defence Policy* and Vol. 2 *Defence Organization.* Kingston: School of Policy Studies, Queen's University, 1997 and 1998.

Bland, Douglas L. *Chiefs of Defence: Government and the Unified Command of the Armed Forces of Canada.* Toronto: Canadian Institute of Strategic Studies, 1995.

Davis, James R. *The Sharp End: A Canadian Soldier's Story.* Vancouver: Douglas & McIntyre, 1997.

DeWitt, David, and David Leyton-Brown, eds. *Canada's International Security Policy.* Scarborough: Prentice-Hall Canada, 1995.

English, John A. *Lament for an Army: The Decline of Canadian Military Professionalism.* Toronto: Canadian Institute of International Affairs, 1998.

Granatstein, Jack L. *Canada's Army: Waging War and Keeping the Peace.* Toronto: University of Toronto Press, 2002.

Gray, Colin S. *Canadians in a Dangerous World.* Toronto: Atlantic Council, 1994.

Horn, Bernt, ed. *Forging a Nation: Perspectives on the Canadian Military Experience.* St. Catharines: Vanwell, 2002.

Hunt, B. D., and R. G. Haycock, eds. *Canada's Defence: Perspectives on Policy in the Twentieth Century.* Toronto: Copp Clark Pitman, 1993.

Jockel, Joseph T. *The Canadian Forces: Hard Choices, Soft Power.* Toronto: Canadian Institute of Strategic Studies, 1999.

MacKenzie, Lewis. *Peacekeeper: The Road to Sarajevo.* Vancouver: Douglas & McIntyre, 1993.

Maloney, Sean M. *Canada and UN Peacekeeping: Cold War by Other Means, 1945–1970.* St. Catharines: Vanwell, 2002.

262

Maloney, Sean M. *War Without Battles: Canada's NATO Brigade in Germany 1951–1993*. Toronto: McGraw-Hill Ryerson, 1997.

Middlemass, Danford, and Joel Sokolsky. *Canadian Defence: Decisions and Determinants*. Toronto: Harcourt Brace Jovanovich, 1989.

Milner, Marc, ed. *Canadian Military History: Selected Readings*. Toronto: Copp Clark Pitman, 1993.

Morton, Desmond. *A Military History of Canada: From Champlain to Kosovo*. Fourth edition. Toronto: McClelland & Stewart, 1999.

Pugliese, David. *Canada's Secret Commandos: The Unauthorized Story of JOINT TASK FORCE TWO*. Ottawa: Esprit de Corps, 2001.

Rempel, Roy. *The Chatterbox: An Insider's Account of the Irrelevance of Parliament in the Making of Canadian Foreign and Defence Policy*. Toronto: Dundurn, 2002.

Taylor, Scott, and Brian Nolan, *Tarnished Brass: Crime and Corruption in the Canadian Military*. Toronto: Lester, 1996.

Taylor, Scott, and Brian Nolan. *Tested Metal: Canada's Peacekeepers at War*. Ottawa: Esprit de Corps, 1998.

Foreign and Defence Policy:

Cooper, Andrew. *Canadian Foreign Policy: Old Habits and New Directions*. Scarborough: Prentice-Hall Canada, 1997.

Hampson, Fen Osler, Norman Hillmer and Maureen Appel Molot, eds. *Canada Among Nations 2001: The Axworthy Legacy*. Don Mills: Oxford University Press, 2001.

Hillmer, Norman, and J. L. Granatstein. *Empire to Umpire: Canada and the World to the 1990's*. Toronto: Copp Clark Longman, 1994.

Keating, Tom. *Canada and World Order: The Multilateralist Tradition in Canadian Foreign Policy*. Second edition. Toronto: Oxford University Press, 2001.

Nossal, Kim Richard. *The Politics of Canadian Foreign Policy*. Third edition. Scarborough: Prentice-Hall Canada, 1997.

Rempel, Roy. *Counterweights: Canada's German Policy*. Kingston: McGill-Queen's University Press, 1996.

International Security Policy:
Gray, Colin S. *Modern Strategy*. London: Oxford University Press, 1999.

Hampson, Fen Osler, et al. *Madness in the Multitude: Human Security and World Disorder*. Toronto: Oxford University Press, 2002.

Irwin, Rosalind, ed. *Ethics and Security in Canadian Foreign Policy*. Vancouver: University of British Columbia Press, 2001.

Tucker, Michael J., Raymond Blake and P. E. Bryden, eds. *Canada and the New World Order: Facing the New Millennium*. Toronto: Irwin, 2000.

The Gulf:
Deere, David, ed. *Desert Cats: The Canadian Fighter Squadron in the Gulf War*. Stoney Creek: Fortress, 1991.

Somalia:
Bercuson, David. *Significant Incident: Canada's Army, the Airborne and the Murder in Somalia*. Toronto: McClelland & Stewart, 1997.

Desbarats, Peter. *Somalia Cover-up: A Commissioner's Journal*. Toronto: McClelland & Stewart, 1997.

Loomis, Dan G. *The Somalia Affair: Reflections on Peacemaking and Peacekeeping*. Ottawa: DGL Publications, 1996.

Rwanda:
Off, Carol. *The Lion, the Fox and the Eagle: A Story of Generals and Justice in Rwanda and Yugoslavia*. Toronto: Random House, 2000.

The Balkans — Bosnia/Croatia and Kosovo
Cohen, Lenard. *Serpent in the Bosom: The Rise and Fall of Slobodan Milosevic*. Vancouver: University of British Columbia Press, 2000.

Maloney, Sean M. *Chances for Peace: Canadian Soldiers in the Balkans 1992–1995*. St. Catharines: Vanwell, 2002.

Maloney, Sean M. *Operation KINETIC: The Canadians and Kosovo 1999–2000* (forthcoming).

Taylor, Scott. *INAT: Images of Serbia and the Kosovo Conflict*. Ottawa: Esprit de Corps, 2000.

INDEX